Manual of Christian Doctrine

Manual of Christian Doctrine

by

L. BERKHOF
President-Emeritus, Calvin Theological Seminary

AUTHOR OF

Systematic Theology,
The History of Christian Doctrines,
Manual of Christian Doctrine,
Summary of Christian Doctrine,
Riches of Divine Grace, etc.

WM. B. EERDMANS PUBLISHING COMPANY
Grand Rapids Michigan

MANUAL OF CHRISTIAN DOCTRINE

Library of Congress Number 40-16250

Set up and printed, November, 1933

Seventh printing, February, 1960

PRINTED IN THE UNITED STATES OF AMERICA

PREFACE

After the publication of my Systematic Theology, the publisher requested me to prepare for publication a more compendious work on Christian doctrine, which might be fit for high school and college classes, and might also be used profitably by our older catechumens. Mindful of the great importance of the proper indoctrination of the young people of the Church, I did not have the courage to refuse, but undertook to prepare a brief manual. The work seemed particularly important to me in view of the widespread doctrinal indifference of the present day, of the resulting superficiality and confusion in the minds of many professing Christians of the insidious errors that are zealously propagated even from the pulpits, and of the alarming increase of all kinds of sects that are springing up like mushrooms on every side. If there ever was a time when the Church ought to guard her precious heritage, the deposit of the truth that was entrusted to her care, that time is now. I have tried to give a rather comprehensive and yet concise statement of our Reformed conception of the truth, and sincerely hope that its clarity may not have suffered through its brevity. At the end of every chapter I have given a list of questions which will help the student to test his knowledge of what it contains. In my references for further study I have been rather sparing, since

I did not desire to overload the student in any way Moreover, I have limited myself almost exclusively to Reformed authors. I hope it will not seem presumptuous that I have invariably referred first of all to my own work on Systematic Theology, since this Manual is based on the larger work throughout and can best be understood in the light of its more detailed discussion of Christian doctrine. May the King of the Church make this Manual a blessed influence in the instruction of our covenant youth.

L. BERKHOF.

Grand Rapids, Mich.
May 10, 1933.

TABLE OF CONTENTS

INTRODUCTION

THE DOCTRINE OF THE PERSON AND WORK OF CHRIST

THE PERSON OF CHRIST

THE WORK OF CHRIST

THE DOCTRINE OF THE APPLICATION OF THE WORK OF REDEMPTION

GENERAL ESCHATOLOGY

INTRODUCTION

INTRODUCTION

RELIGION

A. **Religion a universal phenomenon.** Man has been described as "incurably religious." This is but another way of saying that religion is a universal phenomenon. Missionaries testify to its presence in some form or other, among all the nations and tribes of the earth. It is one of the most remarkable phenomena of the life of man, touching the deepest springs of his spiritual existence, controlling his thoughts, stirring his emotions, and guiding his actions. While it is generally hailed as one of the greatest blessings of mankind, some denounce it as one of the most pernicious factors in the life of the world. But even its greatest enemies cannot deny its paramount significance and its tremendous influence in the lives of individuals and nations. It naturally forces itself upon the attention of all serious-minded people. Even the philosopher Hume, though a radical sceptic and opponent of the supernatural, once said: "Look out for a people entirely void of religion, and if you find them at all, be assured that they are but a few degrees removed from the brutes."

B. **The essential nature of religion.** Just what is religion? In our day many seek an answer to this question by studying the religions of the world and the various manifestations of religion in human life. By a comparative study they would discover the real nature of religion, and insist on discovering a definition sufficiently broad to cover all the forms in which the religious life manifests itself among the nations of the world. But this is not the proper method to follow. While it may give us an insight into the present manifestations of the religious life of the world, it does not enable us to determine what is the real nature of religion. The Bible only enables us to get a proper conception of the ideal.

Religion is concerned with man's relation to God, and man has no right to determine the nature of this relation. It is God's prerogative to specify how man should be related to Him, and He does this in His divine Word. The word "religion" is in all probability derived from the Latin word *relegere,* meaning to *re-read, to repeat, to observe carefully,* and frequently served to designate a constant and diligent observance of all that pertained to the worship of the gods. Religion is described in the Old Testament as "the fear of the Lord." This "fear" is not the same as that "dread" which is so characteristic of heathen religions, though the element to dread is not always absent. It may be described as *the feeling of reverent regard for God, tempered with awe, and the fear of disobedience or (occasionally) of the punishment for disobedience.* As such it represented the response of the pious Israelite to the Old Testament revelation of the law.

In the New Testament the gospel message is prominently in the foreground, and man's response to the divine revelation assumes a somewhat different form, namely, the form of "faith." While there are other terms for religion in the New Testament, such as *godliness,* I Tim. 2:10, and *godly fear,* Heb. 5:7, the word "faith" generally serves to describe the religious attitude of man. By this faith we accept the testimony of God in His Word as true, and entrust ourselves to Him, as He has revealed Himself in Jesus Christ, for our salvation. In the New Testament the element of trust is very much in the foreground. To the glorious message of redemption there is an answering faith on the part of man, consisting in a childlike trust in Jesus Christ, and becoming at the same time a fountain of love to God and His service.

In the light of Scripture we learn to understand that the word "religion" denotes a relation in which man stands to God. The characteristic element in religion has been found in *piety, fear, faith, a feeling of dependence,* and so on. But these are all affections which are also felt with reference to man. The really characteristic thing in this, *that in religion man is conscious of the absolute majesty and infinite power of God, and of his own utter insignificance and absolute helplessness.* This does not mean, however, that religion is merely a matter of the emotions, nor that it is a necessity simply imposed upon him. Man's relation to God in religion is a *conscious* and *voluntary one,* and instead of enslaving him leads him into the enjoyment of the highest liberty. Religion may be defined as *a conscious and voluntary spiritual relation to God, which expresses itself in life as a whole and particularly in certain acts of worship.* God Himself determines the adoration, worship, and service that is acceptable to Him. All will-worship, contrary to the Word of God, is absolutely forbidden.

C. **The seat of religion.** Opinions differ very much respecting the seat of religion in the human soul. Some lose sight entirely of the central significance of religion in the life of man, and conceive of it as located in and functioning through just one of the faculties of the soul. Others stress the fact that the whole psychical nature of man is involved in the religious life.

1. One-Sided Views of the Seat of Religion. Some find the seat of religion in the intellect. They look upon religion as a kind of knowledge, a sort of incomplete philosophy, and thus virtually make the measure of man's knowledge of God the measure of his piety. Others locate religion in the feelings. According to them religion has little or nothing to do with knowledge, but is merely a feeling of dependence on some superior Being. Man does not really know God, but becomes immediately aware of Him deep down in his soul. Still others claim that religion has its seat in the will. Man is aware of the imperative voice of conscience within him, dictating his course of action. In religion he simply recognizes the duties prescribed by conscience as divine commands. On this view religion merely becomes practical morality. These views do not do justice to the fundamental and central place of religion in human life. They are contrary to Scripture and even to modern psychology, since they ignore the fundamental unity of the human soul and proceed on the assumption that one faculty of the soul may act apart from the rest. It is always the whole man that functions in religion.

2. The Scriptural View of the Seat of Religion. The only correct and Scriptural view is that religion is seated in the heart. In Scripture psychology the heart is the center and focus of the whole moral

life of man, the personal organ of the soul. Out of it are all the issues of life, thoughts, volitions, and emotions. Religion is rooted in the image of God, and that image is central, revealing itself in the whole man with all his talents and powers. Consequently, man's relation to God is also central, and involves the whole man. Man must love God with all his heart, and with all his soul, and with all his mind. He must consecrate himself to Him entirely, body and soul, with all his gifts and talents, and in all relations of life. Since religion has its seat in the heart, it embraces the entire man with all his thoughts and feelings and volitions. It is the heart that man must give to the Lord, Deut. 30:6; Prov. 23:26. In religion the heart controls the intellect, Rom. 10:13, 14; Heb. 11:6, the feelings, Ps. 28:7; 30:12, and the will, Rom. 2:10, 13; Jas. 1:27; I John 1:5-7. The whole man is made subservient to God in every sphere of life. This is the only view that does justice to religion, and recognizes its supreme importance in the life of man.

D. **The Origin of Religion.** The question of the origin of religion has engaged the attention of many scholars during the previous century, and still looms large in present-day treatises on religion. Under the influence of the theory of evolution some proceed on the assumption that man developed from a non-religious into a religious being, and make determined efforts to show how the transition came about. They who seek the solution of this problem in the light of God's revelation, however, come to an entirely different conclusion. They find that man was created as a religious being.

1. Naturalistic Views of the Origin of Religion. Some regarded religion as the product of *the cunning of priests or the craft of rulers,* who played on the credulity and fears of the ignorant masses, in order to gain and maintain control over them. Others designated *fetish-worship* (i. e., the worship of inanimate objects which were considered sacred, such as a stone, a stick, a bone, a claw, etc.) as the seed out of which the higher forms of religion developed. Still others suggested that *a worship of spirits, perhaps the spirits of departed ancestors,* was the most fundamental form of religion, out of which all the other forms gradually developed. A rather popular idea is to the effect that *nature-worship* gradually gave birth to religion. Man felt himself weak and helpless in the presence of the great and imposing phenomena of nature, and was thus led to worship these phenomena themselves or the hidden powers of which they were but the external manifestations. In more recent years the idea is gaining favour with some that religion in some way evolved out of a general belief in *magic.* These theories fail to explain the origin of religion, however. They start with an assumption that is contradicted by the facts, namely, that man was originally non-religious. Such a non-religious man has never yet been discovered, and for that very reason it has been impossible to see religion in the making. Moreover, they proceed on the purely naturalistic assumption that the lowest form of religion is necessarily the oldest, and that religion is the result of a purely naturalistic evolution. They lose sight of the fact that there may have been deterioration in the

religious life of the race. And, finally, they frequently assume the very thing which they must explain. The deceptive priests, the worship of fetishes and of spirits, the feeling of dependence on a higher power, and the idea that there is some invisible power behind the forces of nature, — these are the very things that need explanation. They are already manifestations of religion.

2. The Scriptural View of the Origin of Religion. God's special revelation can enlighten us as to the origin of religion. It acquaints us with the fact that religion finds its explanation only in God. If we would explain the origin of religion we must proceed on the assumption that God exists, for real religion without a God is unthinkable. If religion is not founded on reality, it is a deceptive illusion, which may have some practical value for the present but will disappoint in the end. Moreover, since man cannot of himself discover God and know Him, it was necessary that God should reveal Himself. Without such a self-revelation on the part of God it would be utterly impossible for man to enter into religious relationship to Him. God did reveal Himself, and in His self-revelation determined the worship and service that is well-pleasing to Him. But even this self-revelation of God would not have availed to the establishment of a religious relation, if God had not endowed man with a capacity to understand it and to respond to it. Religion is founded in the very nature of man, and was not imposed on him from without. It is a mistake to think that man first existed without religion and

was then endowed with it as something added to his being. Created in the image of God, man has a natural capacity for receiving and appreciating the self-revelation of God. In virtue of his natural endowments man seeks communion with God, though by nature he now seeks it in the wrong way. It is only under the influence of God's special revelation and of the illumination of the Holy Spirit that the sinner can, at least in principle, render to God the service that is his due.

Questions for Review:

How do many in our day seek to discover the essential nature of religion? Which is the only way in which we can learn to know this? What is the derivation of the word "religion"? What terms describe the religious attitude in the Old and in the New Testament? How would you define religion? What mistaken notions are there as to the seat of religion in man? What is the center of the religious life according to Scripture? What different explanations have been given of the origin of religion? Which is the only satisfactory explanation?

References for Further Study:

Berkhof, *Reformed Dogmatics, Introductory Volume* pp. 104-122; McPherson, *Christian Dogmatics*, pp. 9-18; Wisse, *Religie en Christendom*, pp. 7-57; Visscher, *De Oorsprong der Religie;* Edwards, *The Philosophy of Religion*, pp. 29-178.

REVELATION

The idea of religion naturally leads on to that of revelation. While many attempts have been made to explain religion apart from revelation, the conviction is now growing that all religion originates in revelation. And this is the only correct view of the matter. If God had not revealed Himself, man would not be in position to know Him at all, and all religion would be impossible.

A. **Revelation in General.** Before entering upon a discussion of the different kinds of revelation which God has given unto man, it is necessary to make a few remarks on revelation in general.

1. The Idea of Revelation. God is the incomprehensible One. Man cannot know Him as He is in the hidden depths of His divine being. Only the Spirit of God can search the deep things of God, I Cor. 1:10. It is impossible for man to have a perfect knowledge of God, for in order to possess this he would have to be greater than God. Job's question is a pointed denial of man's ability to comprehend the Infinite One: "Canst thou by searching find out God? Canst thou find out the Almighty unto perfection?" Job 11:7. At the same time it is possible for men to know God in a measure which is perfectly adequate for his personal needs. But he can acquire even this knowledge only because it has pleased God to reveal Himself. This means, according to the presentation of Scripture, that God has removed the veil which covered Him and has exposed Himself to view. In other words, He

has in some way communicated knowledge of Himself to man, and has thereby opened the way for man to know Him, to worship Him, and to live in communion with Him.

2. Distinctions Applied to the Idea of Revelation. In course of time two kinds of divine revelation were distinguished, namely, *natural* and *supernatural,* and *general* and *special* revelation. Generally speaking these two distinctions move along parallel lines; at the same time they differ in certain particulars which deserve notice.

a. *Natural and supernatural revelation.* This distinction is based on the mode of God's revelation. In origin all revelation is supernatural, because it originates in God. There is a difference, however, in the way in which God reveals Himself. Natural revelation is that revelation which is communicated through the phenomena of nature, including the very constitution of man. It is not a revelation given in words but embodied in facts which speak volumes. Figuratively, nature can be called a great book in which God has written with letters large and small, and from which man may learn of his goodness and wisdom, "his everlasting power and divinity," Rom. 1:20. Supernatural revelation, on the other hand, is a revelation in which God intervenes in the natural course of events, and in which He, even when He uses natural means, such as dreams and oral communications, employs them in a supernatural way. It is a revelation that is both verbal and factual, in which the words explain the facts and the facts illustrate the words.

b. *General and special revelation.* The second distinction hinges on the nature and object of God's revelation. General revelation is rooted in creation and in the general relations of God to man, is addressed to man considered simply *as the creature and image-bearer of God,* and aims at the realization of the end for which man was created and which can be attained only where man knows God and enjoys communion with Him. Special revelation, on the other hand, is rooted in the redemptive work of God, is addressed to man *as a sinner* and adapted to the moral and spiritual needs of fallen man, and aims at leading the sinner back to God through the specific knowledge of God's redemptive love revealed in Christ Jesus. It is not like general revelation a light that lighteth every man, but a light that illumines the pathway of those who are made receptive for the truth by the special operation of the Holy Spirit.

3. Denial of God's Revelation. The fact of the divine revelation was frequently denied in one form or another. Both general and special revelation, but the former less than the latter, were the object of this denial.

a. *Denial of general revelation.* The atheist, who denies the very existence of God, naturally disputes all revelation. So does the agnostic, who does not believe that man can know God and who therefore speaks of Him as the great Unknowable One. Pantheists occasionally pretend to believe that God reveals Himself. Yet the idea of revelation does not fit in their system at all. They do not recognize the existence of a personal God, who can consciously and voluntarily reveal Himself; and even if they did, they would not know of any object outside of God to which He could make Himself known. With them God and man are one.

b. *Denial of special revelation.* Eighteenth century Deism, while acknowledging God's general revelation, denied the necessity, the possibility, and the reality of any *special supernatural* revelation. It regarded the general revelation of God as sufficient even for fallen man, and considered the assumption that it was not sufficient as a reflection on the wisdom or power of God. It would seem to imply that God was wanting either in the necessary wisdom or in the requisite power to create a world that would meet all the requirements of a divine revelation under all conditions. Under the influence of pantheistic Idealism present-day liberal theology also denies God's special revelation. It reduces the Bible to a part of His general revelation and simply wipes out the distinction between the natural and the supernatural.

B. **General Revelation.** While both the general and the special revelation of God now exist alongside of each other, the former was prior to the latter in point of time, and is therefore considered first.

1. The Idea of God's General Revelation. General revelation does not come to man in the form of direct verbal communications. It consists in an embodiment of the divine thought in the phenomena of nature, in the general constitution of the human

mind, and in the facts of experience or history. God speaks to man in His entire creation, in the forces and powers of nature, in the constitution of the human mind, in the voice of conscience, and in the providential government of the world in general and of the lives of individuals in particular. The poet sings: "The heavens declare the glory of God; and the firmament showeth His handiwork. Day unto day uttereth speech, and night unto night showeth knowledge," Ps. 19:1, 2. And Paul says: "For the invisible things of Him since the creation of the world are clearly seen, being perceived through the things that are made, even His everlasting power and divinity," Rom. 1:20. This general revelation never has been exclusively natural, but always contained an admixture of the supernatural. Even before the fall God revealed Himself to man supernaturally in the covenant of works. And in the course of the history of revelation God frequently revealed Himself in a supernatural way outside of the sphere of special revelation, Gen. 20:3 ff.; 40:5 ff; 41:1 ff.; Judg. 7:13; Dan. 2:1 ff.

2. The Present Actual Insufficiency of General Revelation. While Pelagians, Deists, and Rationalists concur in regarding the general revelation of God as quite sufficient for the present needs of man, Roman Catholics and Protestants are agreed as to its insufficiency. There are several reasons why it must be regarded as inadequate:

a. *Sin altered both this revelation and man's receptivity for it.* As a result of the fall of man the blight of sin rests on creation in general. The element of corruption entered God's beautiful handiwork and obscured, though it did not altogether obliterate, the handwriting of God. Nature, it is true, still shows the earmarks of its divine origin, but is now full of imperfections and a prey to destructive forces. It has ceased to be the perspicuous revelation of God which it once was. Moreover, man was blinded by sin, so that he cannot read the divine script in nature, and became subject to the power of error and perversion, so that he opposes the truth by unrighteousness and even exchanges it for a lie. John 1:5; Rom. 1:18, 25; Eph. 4:18; Col. 1:13; I John 2:9, 11.

b. *General revelation does not convey any thoroughly reliable knowledge of God and spiritual things.* In virtue of the facts stated in the preceding paragraph, the knowledge of God and of spiritual and eternal things conveyed by general revelation is too uncertain to form a trustworthy basis on which to build for eternity; and man cannot afford to pin his hopes for the future on uncertainties. The history of science and philosophy clearly shows that general revelation is no safe and certain guide. One system of truth after another was constructed, only to be overthrown by a following generation. "Our little systems have their day; they have their day and cease to be."

c. *General revelation does not even afford an adequate basis for religion in general.* The history of religions shows, and this is recognized ever increasingly, that there are no religions that are based exclusively on natural revelation. It is becoming more and more evident that a purely natural religion does not and cannot exist. Gentile nations and tribes all appeal to some more special revelation, supposedly given by the gods, as the basis of their religion.

d. *It is altogether insufficient as a foundation for the Christian religion.* By general revelation we may receive some knowledge of the goodness, the wisdom, and the power of God, but we do not learn to know Christ, who is the only way of salvation, Matt. 11:27; John 14:6; 17:3; Acts 4:12. It knows nothing of saving grace, of pardon and redemption, and therefore cannot lead sinners out of the slavery of sin into the glorious liberty of the children of God. It is not part of the redemptive process set in motion by God for the salvation of man. This is the supreme reason for its insufficiency. God desired to save sinners unto the glory of His name, and therefore had to enrich mankind with a more special revelation, a revelation of redeeming grace in Jesus Christ.

3. The Value and Significance of General Revelation. The fact that, after the fall of man, general revelation was superseded by a special revelation may easily lead to an under-valuation of the former. We should not forget, however, that God's original revelation remains of great importance.

a. *In connection with the gentile world.* God's general revelation, including the supernatural elements that were handed down from generation to generation and often distorted beyond recognition, furnishes after all the firm and lasting foundation for the gentile religions. It is in virtue of this that even the gentiles feel themselves to be the offspring of God, Acts 17:28, that they seek after God, if haply they might feel after Him and find Him, Acts 17:27, that they see in nature God's everlasting power and divinity, Rom. 1:19, 20, and that they do by nature the things of the law, Rom. 2:14. While they live in the darkness of ignorance and sin, pervert the truth by turning it into a lie, and serve gods which are no gods, but lies and vanity; yet they also share in the illumination of the Logos and in the general operation of the Holy Spirit, Gen. 6:3; Job 32:8; John 1:9; Rom. 2:14, 15; Acts 14:16, 17; 17:22-30. As a result their religions, while described as false in Scripture, also contain elements of truth which afford points of contact for the message of the Christian missionary.

b. *In connection with the Christian religion.* When God gave his special revelation, He did not simply place this alongside of His original revelation, but incorporated in it the truths embodied in His general revelation, corrected their perversion, and interpreted them for mankind. Consequently, the Christian now reads God's general revelation with the eye of faith and in the light of His Word, and for that very reason is able to see God's hand in nature and His footsteps in history. He sees God in everything round about him, and is thus led to a proper appreciation of the world.

But if special revelation engenders a true appreciation of general revelation, it is equally true that general revelation promotes a proper understanding of special revelation. Scripture can be fully understood only against the background of God's revelation in nature. The latter frequently sheds a welcome light on the former. Moreover, general revelation also offers Christians and non-Christians a common basis on which they can meet and argue. The light of the Logos that lighteth every man is also a bond that unites them. Finally, it is also due to God's general revelation that special revelation does not appear, as it were, suspended in the air, but touches the life of the world at every point. It maintains the connection between nature and grace, between the world and the kingdom of God, between the natural and the moral order, between creation and re-creation.

C. **Special Revelation.** Alongside of the general revelation in nature and history we have a special revelation, which is now embodied in Scripture. The Bible is *par excellence* the book of special revelation, a revelation in which words and facts go hand in hand, the former interpreting the latter, and the latter giving concrete embodiment to the former.

1. THE NECESSITY OF SPECIAL REVELATION. Through the entrance of sin into the world God's general revelation was obscured and corrupted, so that the handwriting of God in nature and in the very constitution of man is not as legible now as it was in the morning of creation. Moreover, man became subject to the power of darkness and ignorance, of

error and unbelief, and in his blindness and perverseness now fails to read aright even the remaining vestiges of the original revelation. He even takes delight in exchanging the truth of God for a lie. General revelation no more conveys to man absolutely reliable knowledge of God and spiritual things, is not properly understood by man, and does not avail to restore him to a condition of friendship with God. Therefore special divine operations were necessary, serving a fourfold purpose: (*a*) to correct and interpret the truths which are now gathered from general revelation; (*b*) to illumine man so that he can once more read the handwriting of God in nature; (*c*) to furnish man with a revelation of God's redemptive love; and (*d*) to change his entire spiritual condition by redeeming him from the power of sin and leading him back to a life in communion with God.

2. The Means of Special Revelation. The means of God's special revelation can in general be reduced to three kinds:

   a. *Theophanies or manifestations of God.* According to Scripture God is not only a God afar off, but also a God at hand. Symbolically, He dwelt between the cherubim in the days of the Old Testament, Ps. 80:1; 99:1. His presence was seen in fire and clouds of smoke, Gen. 15:17; Ex. 3:2; 19:9, 16 f.; 33:9; Ps. 78:14; 99:7, in stormy winds, Job 38:1; 40:6; Ps. 18:10-16, and in the gentle zephyr, I Kings 19:12. These were all tokens of His presence, in which He revealed something of His glory. Among the Old Testament appearances that of the "Angel of the Lord" occupies a special place. This Angel was evidently not a created angel. On the one hand He is distinguished from God, Ex. 23:20-23; Isa. 63: 8, 9, but on the other hand He is also identified with God, Gen. 16:13; 31:11, 13; 32:28. The prevailing opinion is that He was the second person in the Trinity, cf. Mal. 3:1. Theophany reached its highest point in the incarnation of Christ, in whom the fulness of the godhead dwelt bodily, Col. 1:19; 2:9. In Him the Church becomes the temple of the Holy Spirit, I Cor. 3: 16; 6:19; Eph. 2:21. An even fuller realization of God's dwelling with man will follow, when the new Jerusalem descends out of heaven from God, and the tabernacle of God is pitched among men.

b. *Direct communications.* God communicated His thoughts and His will to man in various ways. Sometimes He spoke to the organs of His revelation with an audible voice, Gen. 2:16; 3:8-19; 4: 6-15; 9:1, 8, 12; 32:26; Ex. 19:9; Deut. 5:4, 5; I Sam. 3:4. In other cases He resorted to such means as the lot and the Urim and Thummim, I Sam. 10:20, 21; I Chron. 24:5-31; Neh. 11:1; Num. 27:21; Deut. 33:8. The dream was a very common means of revelation, Num. 12:6; Deut. 13:1-6; I Sam. 28:6; Joel 2:28, and was also used in revelations to non-Israelites, Gen. 20:3-6; 31:24; 40:5; 41:1-7; Judg. 7:13. A closely related but higher form of revelation was the vision, which was very common in the case of the prophets, Isa. 6; 21:6f.; Ezek. 1—3; 8—11; Dan. 1:17; 2:19; 7—10; Amos 7—9. The prophets received these visions while they were awake and sometimes in the presence of others, Ezek. 8:1ff. More generally, however, God revealed Himself to the prophets by means of an inner illumination through the spirit of revelation. In the New Testament Christ appears as the highest, the true, and, in a sense, the only prophet. He communicates His Spirit, which is also the spirit of revelation and illumination to all those that believe, Mark 13:11; Luke 12:12; John 14:17; 15:26; 16:13; 20:22; Acts 6:10; 8:29. In Him all those that are His have the anointing of the Holy One and are taught of the Lord, I John 2:20.

c. *Miracles.* According to Scripture God also reveals Himself in miracles. It is especially from this point of view that the miracles of Scripture should be studied. While they excite a feeling of wonder, they are not, like the so-called miracles of heathen sorcerers, primarily portents which fill man with amazement. They are above all manifestations of a special power of God, tokens of His special presence, and frequently serve to symbolize spiritual truths. As manifestations of the ever-coming kingdom of God, they are made subservient to the great work of redemption. Hence they frequently serve to punish the wicked and to help or deliver the people of God. They confirm the words of prophecy and point to the new order that is being established by God. The miracles of Scripture, too, culminate in the incarnation, which is the greatest and most central miracle of all. In Christ, who is the absolute miracle, ali things are restored and creation is brought back to its pristine beauty, Acts 3:21.

3. The Contents of Special Revelation. There are three points that deserve special mention in connection with the contents of God's special revelation.

a. *It is a revelation of redemption.* Special revelation does not simply serve the purpose of conveying to man some general knowledge of God. It discloses to man specific knowledge of the plan of God for the salvation of sinners, of the reconciliation of God and sinners in Jesus Christ, of the way of salvation opened up by His redemptive work, of the transforming and sanctifying influence of the Holy Spirit, and of the divine requirements for those who share in the life of the Spirit. It is a revelation which renews man, which illumines his mind, inclines his will to good, fills him with holy affections, and prepares him for his heavenly home.

b. *It is both word- and fact-revelation.* This revelation of God does not consist exclusively in word and doctrine, and does not merely address itself to the intellect. God reveals Himself not only in the law and the prophets, the gospels and the epistles, but also in the history of Israel, in the ceremonial worship of the Old Testament, in theophanies and miracles, and in the redemptive facts of the life of Jesus. Moreover, special revelation not only conveys to man knowledge of the way of salvation, but also transforms the lives of sinners by changing them into saints.

c. *It is a historical revelation.* The content of special revelation was gradually unfolded in the course of many centuries, and is therefore of a historical and gradually developing character. The great truths of redemption appear but dimly at first, but gradually increase in clearness, and finally stand out in all their grandeur in the New Testament revelation. There is a constant coming of God to man in theophany, prophecy, and miracle, and this coming reaches its highest point in the incarnation of the Son of God and in the indwelling of the Holy Spirit in the Church.

Questions for Review:

What is divine revelation? How do natural and supernatural revelation differ? What is the difference between general and special revelation? Where do we meet with the denial of general revelation? Who deny the reality of special revelation? What is the nature of God's general revelation? Why is it insufficient for the present needs of the human race? What value does it have for the gentile world? What significance has it for Christianity? Why was God's special revelation necessary? What means are employed in special revelation? What is the general character of the special revelation given by God?

References for Further Study:

Berkhof, *Reformed Dogmatics, Introductory Volume*, pp. 123-146; McPherson, *Christian Dogmatics*, pp. 18-24; Warfield, *Revelation and Inspiration*, pp. 3-50; Orr, *Revelation and Inspiration*, pp. 1-154; Shedd, *Dogmatic Theology*, I, pp. 61-84.

SCRIPTURE

From the discussion of special revelation we pass on to that of Scripture. The transition is natural and easy, since Scripture is the book of God's special revelation. Three points call for consideration here, namely, the relation of Scripture to special revelation, the inspiration of Scripture, and the perfections of Scripture.

A. **The Relation Between Special Revelation and Scripture.** In general it may be said that God's special revelation assumed a permanent form in Scripture, and was thus preserved for posterity. God intended that his revelation should be His perennial speech to all the successive generations of men, and therefore had to guard it against loss, corruption, and falsification. He did this by providing an infallible record of it, and by watching over this with providential care. It cannot be said that special revelation and Scripture are in every respect identical. The term "special revelation" is not always used in the same sense. It may denote a series of divine self-communications, but it may also serve as a designation of Scripture.

1. The Sense in Which Special Revelation and Scripture Differ. If the term "special revelation" is used to designate the direct self-communications of God, then it cannot be regarded as simply another name for the Bible. This is perfectly evident from the fact that Scripture contains a great deal that was not communicated in a supernatural way, but was learnt by experience or gathered by historical

study and from the additional fact that prophets and apostles often received the divine communications given unto them long before they committed these to writing, Jer. 25:13; 30:1; 36:2; John 20:30; 21:25. Using the term "special revelation" in this specific sense, we cannot say that the Bible is God's Word, but only that God's Word is contained in the Bible. It should be noted, however, that this does not justify the distinction between the Word of God as divine and its record as human. Neither does it warrant the *unqualified* statement that the Bible *is not* but *contains* the Word of God. The terms "Word of God" and "special revelation" are also used in a sense in which they are identical with "Scripture."

2. THE SENSE IN WHICH SPECIAL REVELATION AND SCRIPTURE ARE IDENTICAL. The term "special revelation" may also be applied to that whole complex of redemptive truths and facts, with its proper historical setting, that is found in Scripture and has the divine guarantee of its truth in the fact that the whole Bible is infallibly inspired by the Holy Spirit. In that sense the whole Bible from Genesis to Revelation, and it only, is for us God's special revelation. If the term is understood in this sense, then it is proper to maintain that the Bible *not only contains* but *is* the Word of God. Scripture derives its significance exactly from the fact that it is the book of revelation. It is not merely a narrative of what happened years ago, but the perennial speech of God to man. Revelation lives on in Scripture and brings even now, just as it did when it was given, light, life, and holiness.

B. **The Inspiration of Scripture.** The Bible is and will continue to be the Word of God for all the successive generations of man only in virtue of its divine inspiration. The whole of Scripture is given by inspiration of God. This makes it the infallible rule of faith and practice for mankind. Since this inspiration is often denied and even more frequently misrepresented, it calls for particular attention.

1. SCRIPTURE PROOF FOR INSPIRATION. The doctrine of inspiration, just as every other doctrine, is derived from Scripture. The Bible itself testifies abundantly to its inspiration, and favors the strictest view of inspiration, as even rationalists are willing to admit. Writers of the Old Testament are repeatedly commanded to write what the Lord commands them, Ex. 17:14; 34:27; Num. 33:2; Isa. 8:1; 30:8; Jer. 25:13; 30:2; Ezek. 24:1 f.; Dan. 12:4; Heb. 2:2. The prophets were conscious of bringing a divine message, and therefore introduced it by some such formula as "Thus saith the Lord"; "The word of the Lord came unto me"; "Thus the Lord Jehovah showed me"; etc. These formulæ frequently refer to the spoken word, but are also used in connection with the written word, Jer. 36: 27, 32; Ezek., chapters 26, 27, 31, 32, 39. Isaiah probably even speaks of his own written prophecy as "the book of Jehovah," Isa. 34:16. The writers of the New Testament frequently quote passages from the Old Testament as words of God or of the Holy Spirit, Matt. 15:4; Heb. 1:5 ff.; 3:7; 4:3; 5:6; 7:21, etc. Paul speaks of his own words as Spirit-taught words, I Cor. 2:13, and claims that

Christ is speaking in him, II Cor. 13:3. His message to the Thessalonians is the word of God, I Thess. 2:13. Finally, he says in the classical passage on inspiration: "Every Scripture (referring to the sacred writings of the Old Testament of which he speaks in the preceding) inspired of God is also profitable for teaching, for reproof, for correction, for instruction which is in righteousness," II Tim. 3:16. The rendering here given is that of the American Revised Version. That of the Authorized Version deserves preference, however: "All Scripture is given by inspiration of God, and is profitable for doctrine, for reproof, for correction, for instruction in righteousness." It is favored even by the rendering given by Moffatt.

2. THE NATURE OF INSPIRATION. In discussing the nature of inspiration attention should be called first of all to two erroneous views.

a. *Mechanical Inspiration.* The process of inspiration has often been conceived in a rather mechanical way. It was represented as if God simply dictated what the human authors of the books of the Bible had to incorporate in their writings. The latter were mere penmen of the Holy Spirit, recording His thoughts in words of His choosing. Their mental life was in repose, and did not in any way contribute to the contents or form of their writings. Thus even the style of Scripture is the style of the Holy Spirit. Further investigations have shown, however, that this position is quite untenable. It clearly appears from Scripture itself that the writers were not mere passive instruments in the production of their books, but were real authors. In some cases they evidently gave the fruits of historical investigations, for they refer to these investigations, Luke 1:1-4, and sometimes even mention their sources, as in the books of Samuel, Kings, and Chronicles. In other cases they record their own personal experiences, as in the psalms and frequently also in the prophetic books, in Acts, and in the epistles. Moreover, each one of them writes in his own individual style. The style of Isaiah is not like that of Ezekiel, nor the style of Paul like that of John.

b. *Dynamical Inspiration.* In opposition to the mechanical conception of inspiration, many in the eighteenth and nineteenth century advocated what they called dynamical inspiration. This theory renounces the idea that there was any direct operation of the Holy Spirit on the production of the books of the Bible, an operation that finds its purpose precisely in the production of those books; and substitutes for it the idea of a general inspiration of the writers. This inspiration was a permanent characteristic of the writers, and therefore incidentally also influenced their writings. It does not differ essentially but only in degree from the spiritual enlightenment of believers in general. It penetrates all parts of Scripture, but not all in the same measure. The historical books of the Bible do not share it in the same measure as the doctrinal books. And while it renders the Biblical writings generally trustworthy, it allows for the possibility of errors, especially in the historical books. This theory certainly does not do justice to the Biblical data on inspiration. It robs the Bible of its supernatural character, reduces it to the level of general revelation, and destroys its infallibility.

c. *Organic Inspiration.* The theory of inspiration which is now generally accepted in Reformed circles is usually called "organic inspiration," though some designate it as "dynamical inspiration." The term "organic" serves to stress the fact that God did not employ the writers mechanically, but acted on them in an organic way, in harmony with the laws of their own inner being. He used them just as they were, with their character and temperament, their gifts and talents, their education and culture, their vocabulary, diction, and style; illumined their minds, prompted them to write, repressed the influence of sin on their literary activity, and guided them in the choice of their words and in the expression of their thoughts. This view is clearly most in harmony with the representations of Scripture. It represents the writers of Scripture not as mere amanuenses but as real authors who, while sometimes recording direct communications of God, yet on other occasions set down in writing the results of their own historical investigations or register their experiences of sin and forgiveness, of joy and sorrow, of threatening dangers and gracious deliverances. It also accounts for the individuality of the books of the Bible, since each writer naturally had his own style and put on his literary productions his own personal stamp and the stamp of the time in which he lived.

3. THE EXTENT OF INSPIRATION. There are differences of opinion, not only regarding the nature of inspiration, but also with respect to its extent.

a. *Some Claim Inspiration for the Thoughts but not for the Words.* Many deny the inspiration of Scripture altogether. Others, however, are averse to such a complete denial, but feel that the advocates of the doctrine should retrench somewhat and speak of thought- rather than of word-inspiration. The thoughts, they say, were divinely inspired, but the words depended simply on the choice of the human authors. This is not a very plausible view, however. Thoughts cannot be dissociated from words. Says Dr. Orr: "Thought of necessity takes shape and is expressed in words. If there is inspiration at all, it must penetrate words as well as thought, must mould the expression, and make the language employed the living medium of the idea to be conveyed," *Revelation and Inspiration,* p. 209.

b. *Others Maintain that Inspiration Pertains Only to Certain Parts of Scripture.* Under the influence of eighteenth century Rationalism lax views of inspiration found ready acceptance. It became rather common to deny the inspiration of the historical books of the Bible, and to limit it to the doctrinal writings. And even the inspiration claimed for the doctrinal books, though at first still regarded as supernatural in character, was finally conceived as a purely natural process, consisting in a special spiritual enlightenment. It had the effect of making the writers trustworthy witnesses in moral and spiritual matters, but offered no guarantee against all kinds of historical, chronological, and scientific mistakes. There is no agreement in the camp as to the exact extent of inspiration. Some limit it to doctrinal matters others to the New Testament, still others to the words of Jesus, and, finally, there are those who regard only the Sermon on the Mount as inspired In the last analysis every individual makes out for himself which parts of Scripture are and which are not inspired. The moment one accepts this view, he has virtually lost his Bible.

c. *According to Scripture Inspiration Extends to Every Part of the Bible.* Jesus and the apostles speak of the books of the Old Testament as "Scripture" or "the Scriptures," and frequently appeal to them as such, in order to substantiate their teachings. For them an appeal to "Scripture" is clearly equivalent to an appeal to God. It is the end of all controversy. Besides, as we have seen in the preceding, some of the New Testament writers repeatedly quote passages of the Old Testaments as words of God or of the Holy Spirit This is especially the case in the Epistle to the Hebrews. Moreover, Peter places the epistles of Paul on a level with the writings of the Old Testament. And, finally, the New Testament contains quotations from twenty-five Old Testament books all regarded as "Scripture," though some of them are taken from historical books. We cannot divide Scripture into two parts, the one divine and the other human. It is just as impossible to say where in Scripture the human ends and the divine begins or *vice versa,* as it is to tell where in man the body ends and the soul begins. The two interpenetrate, and as a result of this interpenetration the Bible is in its entirety, on the one hand, a human production, and on the other, a divine creation.

d. *Inspiration Extends to the Very Words of Scripture.* The Bible is verbally inspired. It should be noted particularly that this is not the same as saying that it is mechanically inspired, though opponents frequently insist on identifying the two. The doctrine of verbal inspiration does not assume that God dictated the words of the Bible, but that He guided the writers of the Biblical books in the choice of their words and expressions so as to keep them from errors, without in any way disregarding their vocabulary or suppressing their individuality of style and expression. Some prefer to call it plenary inspiration, in order to guard against the danger of identifying it with mechanical inspiration. This doctrine is fully warranted by Scripture. In many instances the Lord told Moses and Joshua exactly what to write, Ex. 3 and 4; 6:2; 7:1; 12:1; Lev. 4:1; 6:1, 24; 7:22, 28; Jos. 1:1; 4:1; 6:2, etc. The prophets speak of Jehovah as putting His words in their mouth, Jer. 1:9, and as directing them to speak His words to the people, Ezek. 3:4,

10, 11. Paul speaks of his words as Spirit-taught words, I Cor. 2:13, and both he and Jesus sometimes base an argument on the use of a single word, Matt. 22:43-45; John 10:35; Gal. 3:16.

C. **The Perfections of Scripture.** The Reformers deemed it necessary to develop the doctrine of Scripture, in order to off-set the errors of the Roman Catholic Church. They stressed particularly the following points:

1. THE DIVINE AUTHORITY OF SCRIPTURE. The Church of Rome as well as the Reformers ascribed divine authority to Scripture; yet they did not both mean exactly the same thing. The Roman hierarchy insisted on it that the Bible has no authority in itself, but owes its existence and therefore also its authority to the Church. Over against this position of Rome, the Reformers emphasized the fact that Scripture has *inherent* authority in virtue of its inspiration by the Holy Spirit. The Bible must be believed for its own sake; it is the inspired Word of God and therefore addresses man with authority. This view of the supreme authority of Scripture was generally accepted by the Churches of the Reformation until the chill winds of Rationalism swept over Europe and reason was enthroned as the arbiter of truth. Under its influence many now place the Bible on a level with other books and deny its divine authority. It is of the utmost importance, however, to maintain this authority. Scripture has first of all *historical* authority, that is, it is a true and absolutely reliable record, and as such entitled to a believing acceptance of all that it contains. But in addition to that it also has *normative* authority as a rule of

life and conduct, and as such demands absolute subjection on the part of man.

2. THE NECESSITY OF SCRIPTURE. While the Roman Catholic Church recognizes the importance and usefulness of Scripture, it does not regard it as absolutely necessary. In its estimation it is more correct to say that Scripture needs the Church than that the Church needs Scripture. Some of the mystical sects, such as the Montanists, the Anabaptists, and the Libertines of Geneva, also denied the necessity of Scripture, and ascribed far more importance to the "inner light," the word of the Holy Spirit spoken in the hearts of God's people. The Reformers joined issue with them on this point. They did not deny that God might have dispensed with the use of the written Word, but defended the position that the Word was necessary in virtue of the divine good pleasure to make the Word the seed of the Church. From that point of view Scripture is and remains necessary to the very end of time.

3. THE PERSPICUITY OF SCRIPTURE. In the estimation of the Church of Rome the Bible is obscure and is badly in need of interpretation even in matters of faith and practice. For that reason an infallible interpretation is needed, and this is supplied by the Church. Over against this position of Rome the Reformers emphasized the perspicuity or clearness of Scripture. By doing this they did not deny that there are mysteries in the Bible which the human mind cannot fathom, did not claim that man can very well dispense with the labours of commentators, and did not even mean to assert that the way of salvation is so clearly revealed in Scripture that every

one can easily understand it, irrespective of his spiritual condition. Their contention was simply that the knowledge necessary unto salvation, though not equally clear on every page of Scripture, is yet communicated to man throughout the Bible in such a simple and comprehensive form that anyone who is earnestly seeking salvation can easily gather this knowledge for himself, and need not depend for it on the Church or the priesthood. The perspicuity of Scripture follows from such passages as Ps. 19:7, 8; 119:105, 130, and the spiritual man is said to be able to judge and understand it, I Cor. 2:15; 10:15; I John 2:20.

4. THE SUFFICIENCY OF SCRIPTURE. Neither the Church of Rome nor the Anabaptists regard the Bible as a sufficient revelation of God. The latter have a low opinion of Scripture and assert the absolute necessity of the inner light and of all kinds of special revelations, while the former regards oral tradition as a necessary complement of the written Word. According to Roman Catholics this tradition embodies truths which the apostles preached but did not commit to writing, and which were handed down in the Catholic Church, without interruption, from generation to generation. These are now contained chiefly in the decrees of the councils, in the writings of the holy fathers, in the deliverances of the Pope, and in the words and usages of the sacred liturgy. In opposition to this position the Reformers maintained the perfection or sufficiency of Scripture. This does not mean that everything that was spoken or written by the prophets, by Christ, and by the apostles is contained in Scripture, but simply that

the written Word is sufficient for the moral and spiritual needs of individuals and of the Church. It involves the denial that there is alongside of Scripture an unwritten Word of God of equal or even superior authority.

Questions for Review:

What is the relation between special revelation and Scripture? What different meanings has the term "special revelation"? Is it correct to say that special revelation and Scripture are identical? What Scripture proof can you give for the inspiration of the Bible? What is mechanical inspiration and what objections are there to it? What is meant by "dynamical inspiration"? Why is it unacceptable as applied to Scripture? How would you describe the theory of organic inspiration? What advantages has it? What would you say to the theory that the thoughts and not the words of Scripture are inspired? What objections are there to the notion of a partial inspiration? How would you prove that inspiration extends to every part of Scripture, and even to the very words? What is the nature of the authority of Scripture? In what sense are the Scriptures necessary, perspicuous and sufficient? What is the position of the Church of Rome on these joints?

References for Further Study:

Berkhof, *Reformed Dogmatics, Introductory Volume*, pp. 147-179; McPherson, *Christian Dogmatics*, pp. 24-29; Patton, *The Inspiration of the Scriptures;* Orr, *Revelation and Inspiration*, pp. 159-218; Warfield, *Revelation and Inspiration*, pp. 169-226.

THE DOCTRINE OF GOD AND HIS CREATION

THE DOCTRINE OF GOD AND HIS CREATION

THE BEING OF GOD

The Essential Nature of God

A. **The knowledge of (respecting) God.** The possibility of knowing God has been denied on several different grounds. In some cases, however, this denial is simply equivalent to the assertion that man cannot comprehend God. And this is, of course, very true. It is not possible for man to know God with an absolutely all-comprehensive knowledge, to fathom the infinite depths of the divine being. But while we can know God only in part, his knowledge is nevertheless real and true knowledge. Man's knowledge of God is generally said to be twofold:

1. Innate or Inborn Knowledge. The statement that man has an innate knowledge of God does not *merely* mean that he has an inborn capacity to know God. It indicates something more than that. At the same time it does not imply that man at birth brings a certain knowledge of God with him into the world. The innate knowledge of God is inborn in the sense that, under normal conditions, it develops spontaneously in man as soon as he comes in contact with God's revelation. It is a knowledge which man, as he is constituted, develops of necessity and not as the result of any choice on his part. Naturally such knowledge is of a rather general nature.

2. Acquired Knowledge. Acquired knowledge, on the other hand, is derived from God's general and special revelation. It does not arise spontaneously in the mind, but results from the conscious and sustained pursuit of knowledge. It can be obtained only by the wearisome process of perception and reflection, reasoning and argumentation, and therefore depends on the voluntary direction of the will and on the persistent efforts of man. While it is possible only because man is born with the capacity to know God, it carries him far beyond the limits of his innate knowledge of God.

It is sometimes said that our knowledge of God is limited to the relations in which He stands to His creatures, and does not extend to His essential being; but this is hardly correct. It would not even be possible to know these relations without knowing something of the very nature of God and man. In virtue of God's self-revelation it is possible for man to have true and real knowledge of the being of God, though this knowledge is necessarily limited.

B. **The being of God as known from God's revelation.** While it is not possible to give a definition of God in the strict sense of the word, it is possible to give a general description of His being. Many so-called definitions have been given of God, but it is perhaps best to describe Him simply as *a pure Spirit of infinite perfections.* This description contains the following elements:

1. God Is A Pure Spirit. The Bible does not attempt to define the being of God. The nearest approach to anything like it is found in the word of

Christ to the Samaritan woman: "God is spirit," John 4:24. This means that He is essentially spirit, so that all the qualities which belong to the perfect idea of spirit are necessarily found in Him; that He is a self-conscious and self-determining being. The fact that He is *pure* spirit of necessity excludes the notion of the early Gnostics and medieval Mystics, that He has some sort of an ethereal or refined body. It also rules out the idea that He is visible and can be discerned by the bodily senses.

2. God Is Personal. The fact that God is spirit also involves his personality, for a spirit is an intelligent and moral being, and when we ascribe personality to God, we mean exactly that He is a rational being capable of self-determination. In the present day many deny the personality of God and speak of Him as the unconscious cause of all existing things, as the all-pervasive principle of the world, or as the all-inclusive purpose of the universe. The personality of God is clearly indicated, however, in the traces of intelligent and purposeful action in the world; in the rational, moral, and religious nature of man, all of which can only be the product of a personal God; and above all in the representations of God in Scripture. The presence of God, as it is described in the Old and New Testament, is clearly a personal presence. He is represented as a personal God, who comes and goes, with whom men can converse, whom they can trust, who enters into their experiences, who sustains them in their trials and difficulties, and who fills their hearts with the joy of victory. Moreover, the highest revelation of God in the New Testament is a personal revelation.

Jesus Christ reveals the Father in such a perfect way that He could say to Philip: "He who hath seen me hath seen the Father," John 14:9.

3. God Is Infinitely Perfect. God is distinguished from all His creatures by infinite perfection. He possesses His being and His virtues without any limitation or imperfection. As the infinitely perfect God, He is not only boundless or limitless, but is exalted above all His creatures in grand sublimity and in ineffable majesty. This infinity is characteristic of all the divine perfections, and distinguishes these from the attributes of all creatures, however exalted they may be. It is extolled in the song of Moses at the Red Sea: "Who is like unto thee, O Jehovah, among the gods? Who is like thee, glorious in holiness, fearful in praises, doing wonders," Ex. 15:11. Further references to it are found in such passages as I Kings 8:27; Ps. 96:4-6; 97:9; 99: 2, 3:147:5; Isa. 57:15; Jer. 23: 24. Some modern scholars, such as William James and H. G. Wells, deny the infinity of God. They conceive of God as "finite, developing, struggling, suffering, sharing with man his defeats and victories."

4. God and His Perfections Are One. Simplicity is one of the fundamental characteristics of God. This means not only that, as a spirit, He is not composed of different parts, but also that His essence and properties are one. The being of God is not something existing by itself, to which His attributes are added; the whole of His essence is in each one of the attributes. It is generally said that God's perfections are God Himself as He has revealed Himself

to man. They serve but to give a more detailed description of His divine essence. Hence the Bible says that God is truth, life, light, love, etc.

Questions for Review:

In what sense is God knowable, and in what sense unknowable? What is innate knowledge of God? What is acquired knowledge? Is it possible to know something of the very being of God? Is it possible to define God? What is involved in God's spirituality? What do we mean when we ascribe personality to God? How can His personality be proved? What is the divine infinity? How are the being of God and His perfections related?

References for Further Study:

Berkhof, *Reformed Dogmatics*, I, pp. 22-27; McPherson, *Christian Dogmatics*, pp. 104-123; Shedd, *Dogmatic Theology*, I, pp. 151-194; Snowden, *The Personality of God.*

The Names of God

A. **The Name of God in General.** The Bible often speaks of the name of God in the singular, as, for instance in Ex. 20:7 and Ps. 8:1. When it does this, it does not refer to any special designation of God, but uses the term in a very general sense to denote His self-revelation. The one general name of God is split up into many special names, which are expressive of His many-sided being. It is only because God has revealed Himself in His name, that is, in His self-revelation in nature and in Scripture, and also in the special names by which He is designated in the Bible, that we can now ascribe these names to Him. These names are of divine origin and not of human invention, though they are derived from human language. From what was said about the name of God in general it follows that not only the proper names of God, but also his attributes and the personal designations of Father, Son, and Holy Spirit may be included under the general heading, *"The Names of God."* In the present chapter we limit ourselves, however, to a discussion of the personal names of God.

B. **The Old Testament Names of God.** Of the Old Testament names the following are the most important:

1. There are certain names which direct attention to the fact that God is the high and exalted One, the transcendent God. *'El* and *'Elohim* stress the fact that He is strong and mighty, and therefore to be feared, while *'Elyon* directs attention to His exalted nature

as the Most High, the object of reverence and worship. Another name belonging to this class is *'Adonai,* which is usually rendered "Lord." It was frequently used in addressing God and was an explicit recognition of the fact that He is the owner and ruler of all men. Among Israel, the ancient covenant people, it was largely supplanted by the name Jehovah.

2. There are other names which point to the fact that this exalted being condescended to enter into relations of friendship with His creatures. In patriarchal times it was especially the name *Shaddai* or *El-Shaddai* that served this purpose, Ex. 6:3. This name also stresses the divine greatness, but primarily as a source of blessing and comfort for the people of God. It indicates the fact that God controls all the powers of nature and makes them subservient to his gracious purposes. It is especially in the name *Jehovah* (Yahweh), however, that God reveals Himself as the God of grace. This name has always been regarded as His most sacred and most distinctive name. On the basis of Ex. 3:14 it may be said that the name is derived from the Hebrew verb "to be," and that it serves to designate the unchangeableness of God. It implies the immutability of the divine being, but points more directly to the fact that God is unchangeable in His covenant relationship, that He is mindful of His promises and faithful in keeping His word, Mal. 3:6. The name often appears in the strengthened form *"Jehovah of hosts."* The hosts referred to are nor the stars, but rather the angelic hosts. Jehovah

of hosts is God as the King of glory, who is surrounded by angelic hosts, who rules heaven and earth in behalf of his people, and receives glory from all His creatures.

C. **The New Testament Names of God.** The New Testament simply uses the Greek equivalents for the Hebrew names of the Old Testament. The following should be noted particularly:

1. Theos. This is simply the word for "God," and is the most common name employed in the New Testament. It is the common rendering of *'El, 'Elohim,* and *'Elyon,* though the latter is sometimes rendered "the Most High" or "the Most High God." The names *Shaddai* and *El-Shaddai* are simply rendered by their Greek equivalents, meaning "the Almighty" or "the Almighty God." The simple Theos is frequently found with a genitive of possession, as "my God," "thy God," 'our God," "your God," because in Christ God may be regarded as the God of all and of each one of His children. The national idea has made place for the individual in religion.

2. Kurios. This is the word for "Lord," a name that is applied not only to God but also to Christ. It takes the place of both 'Adonai and Jehovah, though it does not have exactly the same meaning as the latter, but designates God as the possessor and the ruler of all things but particularly of His people, as the one who has regal power and authority. The fundamental idea of Jehovah is sometimes reproduced in such descriptions as "the Alpha and the

Omega," "who is and who was and who is to come," "the beginning and the end," "the first and the last."

3. PATER. It is often said that the New Testament introduced a new name in *Pater* (Father). But this is hardly correct, for it is also found in the Old Testament as expressive of the special relation in which God stands to Israel. God is the Father of Israel, Deut. 32:6, Isa. 63:16, and Israel is the son of God, Ex. 4:22, Deut. 14:1; Isa. 1:2. The name is not always used in the same sense in the New Testament. Occasionally it serves to designate God simply as originator and creator, I Cor. 8:6; Eph. 3:14; Heb. 12:9; James 1:17. In all other places it is expressive either of the special relation in which the first person of the Trinity stands to Christ, or of the ethical relation of God to believers as his spiritual children.

Questions for Review:

What does Scripture mean when it speaks of the name of God in the singular? Are the special names of God of human origin? What is the general difference between the names *'El, 'Elohim, 'Elyon, 'Adonai*, on the one hand, and *Shaddai, 'El-Shaddai*, and *Jehovah*, on the other? What is the specific meaning of each one of these names? What is the meaning of the name *Kurios* (Lord)? Is the name *Father* ever used of God in the Old Testament? In what different senses is it used in the New Testament?

References for Further Study:

Berkhof, *Reformed Dogmatics*, I, pp. 28-34; Bavinck, *Gereformeerde Dogmatiek*, II, pp. 124-137; Girdlestone, *Old Testament Synonyms*, pp. 32-73.

The Attributes of God

God reveals Himself not only in His names, but even more particularly in His attributes, that is, in the perfections which are ascribed to the divine being in Scripture, or are visibly exercised by Him in the works of creation, providence and redemption. Of the various divisions applied to the attributes of God we follow the one that is most commonly used.

A. **The Incommunicable Attributes.** The incommunicable attributes are those divine perfections which have no analogies in the creature. They emphasize the absolute distinctness of God, His transcendent greatness. The following attributes belong to this class:

1. The Independence or Self-Existence of God. When we ascribe independence or self-existence to God we thereby assert that He exists by the necessity of His own being and therefore necessarily, and does not, like man, depend for his existence on anything outside of Himself. This means not only that He is independent in His being, but also that He is independent in all His virtues and actions, and causes all his creatures to depend on Him. This idea is contained in the name Jehovah, finds expression in John 5:26, is indicated in passages which clearly imply that God is independent in His thought, Rom. 11:33, 34, in His will, Dan. 4:35; Rom. 9:19; Eph. 1:5; Rev. 4:11, in His power, Ps. 115:3, and in His counsel Ps. 33:11, and is also implied in the declaration that He is independent of all

things, and that all things exist only through Him. Ps. 84:8ff.; Isa. 40:18ff.; Acts 17:25.

2. The Immutability of God. Scripture teaches not only the independence but also the unchangeableness of God. He is forever the same, and therefore devoid of all change in His being, His perfections, His purposes, and His promises. This is clearly taught in such passages as Ps. 102:27; Mal. 3:6; James 1:17. At the same time there are many passages which seem to ascribe change to God. He is represented as revealing and hiding Himself, as coming and going, as repenting and changing His intention, and soon, Ex. 32:10-15; Jonah 3:10; Prov. 11:20; 12:22; Ps. 18:26, 27. But the unchangeableness of God, as taught in Scripture, clearly does not imply that there is no movement in God. He is unchangeable in His inner being, His attributes, His purposes, His motives of action, and His promises. And when the Bible speaks of Him as repenting and changing His intention, this is evidently only a human way of speaking. In reality the change is not in God but in man and in man's relations to God.

3. The Infinity of God. The infinity of God in general is *that perfection of His nature by which everything that belongs to His being is without measure or quantity.* It may be considered from various points of view:

a. His Absolute Perfection. This is the infinity of God with respect to His divine being or essence, and as such qualifies all the communicable attributes of God. God is infinite in His knowledge and wisdom, in His goodness and love, in His righteousness and holiness, and also in His sovereignty and power. All His perfections are free from limitation and defect. Scripture proof for it is found in Job 11:7-11; Ps. 145:3.

b. *His Eternity.* God's infinity viewed in relation to time is called His eternity. Scripture usually represents it as endless duration, Ps. 90:2; 102:12; Eph. 3:21, but in doing this it uses popular language, and not the more specific language of philosophy. Strictly speaking, it denotes that God transcends time and possesses the whole of His life all at once. There is with Him only an eternal present, and no past or future.

c. *His Immensity.* Viewed with reference to space, the infinity of God is called His immensity. In virtue of this perfection He transcends all space, and at the same time is present in every point of space *with His whole being.* He is not partly in our country and partly in other countries, but fills every part of space with His entire being. This is also called His omnipresence. God is immanent in all His creatures and in His entire creation, but is in no way bounded by it. This perfection of God is also clearly revealed in Scripture, I Kings 8:27; Isa. 66:1; Ps. 139:7-10; Jer. 23:23, 24; Acts 7:48, 49; 17:27, 28.

4. THE SIMPLICITY OF GOD. By ascribing simplicity to God we assert that He is not composite, and is not susceptible of division in any sense of the word. It implies, among other things, that the three persons in the Godhead are not so many parts of which the divine essence is composed, that God's essence

and attributes are not distinct, and that the attributes are not superadded to the essence of God. While the simplicity of God is not directly asserted by Scripture, it clearly follows from His self-existence and immutability. That which is composed of different parts never can be self-existent, just because it is composed of *previously existing* parts; neither can it be unchangeable, because every part that is added effects a change.

B. **The Communicable Attributes.** The communicable attributes of God are those to which the attributes of man bear some analogy. It should be borne in mind, however, that what is found in man is only a finite and imperfect analogy of what is infinite and perfect in God. In this connection it should be noted that the incommunicable attributes of God qualify His communicable attributes. God is independent and infinite and unchangeable in His knowledge and wisdom, and in His love and holiness.

1. THE KNOWLEDGE OF GOD. The knowledge of God may be defined as *that perfection by which He, in an entirely unique manner, knows Himself and all things possible and actual.* This knowledge is inherent in God and is not obtained from without. Moreover, it is always complete and stands out clearly in the consciousness of God. It is called *omniscience,* because it is all-comprehensive. God knows Himself and all that is contained in His plan. He knows all things as they actually come to pass, past, present, and future, and knows them in their real relations. He is fully acquainted with the hidden essence of things, to which the knowledge

of man cannot penetrate. The actual as well as the possible is present to His mind. The omniscience of God is clearly taught in such passages of Scripture as I Kings 8:39; Ps. 139:1-16; Isa. 46:10; Ezek. 11:5; Acts 15:18; John 21:17; Heb. 4:13.

2. THE WISDOM OF GOD. The wisdom of God may be called a particular aspect of His knowledge. *It is the intelligence of God as manifested in the adaptation of means to ends.* In virtue of it God chooses the best means for the attainment of the ends He has in view. The final end to which He makes all secondary ends subservient is the glory of His name, Rom. 11:33 14:7, 8; Eph. 1:11, 12; Col. 1:16. The wisdom of God is seen in creation, Ps. 19:1-7; 104:1-34; in providence, Ps. 33:10, 11; Rom. 8:28, and in the work of redemption, I Cor. 2:7; Rom. 11:33; Eph. 3:10.

3. THE GOODNESS OF GOD. God is good in Himself; that is, He is perfectly holy; but this is not the goodness which comes into consideration here. It is God's goodness in action, which reveals itself in doing well unto others, that is now under contemplation. It may be defined as *that perfection of God which prompts Him to deal bounteously and kindly with all His creatures.* It is the affection which the Creator feels toward the sentient creatures as such. As manifested towards His rational creatures, it is sometimes called His love of benevolence or His common grace, to designate the fact that its bounties are undeserved. The Bible refers to it in many places, such as Ps. 36:6; 104:21; 145:8, 9, 16; Matt. 5:45; 6:26; Acts 14:17.

4. THE LOVE OF GOD. In the present day this is frequently regarded as the most central attribute in God, in the light of which all the other divine perfections should be interpreted. But there is no sufficient reason for regarding it as more central than any of the other virtues of God. We have in mind here particularly God's love of complacency, which is His delight in the contemplation of His own infinite perfections and of the creatures who reflect His moral image. This love may be considered from various points of view as:

a. *The Grace of God.* In the specific language of Scripture the grace of God is the unmerited love of God toward those who have forfeited it, and are by nature under a judgment of condemnation. It is the source of all the spiritual blessings that are bestowed upon unworthy sinners, Eph. 1:6, 7; 2:7-9; Tit. 2:11; 3:4-7.

b. *The Mercy of God.* Another aspect of the love of God is His mercy or tender compassion. It is the love of God toward those who are in misery or distress, irrespective of their desires. It contemplates man as one who is bearing the consequences of sin, and is therefore in a pitiable condition. It is exercised only in harmony with the strictest justice of God, in view of the merits of Jesus Christ, Luke 1:54, 72, 78; Rom. 15:9; 9:16, 17; Eph. 2:4.

c. *The Longsuffering of God.* When the love of God is considered as bearing with the froward and evil, it is called His longsuffering or forbearance. This contemplates the sinner as continuing in sin, notwithstanding repeated admonitions and warnings, and reveals itself especially in postponing the merited judgment, Rom. 2:4; 9:22; I Pet. 3:20; II Pet. 3:15.

5. The Holiness of God. The holiness of God is first of all that divine perfection by which He is absolutely distinct from all His creatures, and is exalted above them in infinite majesty. This is the meaning which it has in Ex. 15:11; I Sam. 2:2; Isa. 57:15; Hos. 11:9. We have in mind here more particularly, however, the ethical holiness of God, which consists in His separation from moral evil, that is, from sin. While the fundamental idea in this holiness is that of separation, it also denotes something positive, namely, the moral excellence or ethical perfection of God. In its presence man feels himself burdened with a consciousness of sin. Job 34:10; Hab. 1:13; Isa. 6:5. It may be defined as *that perfection of God in virtue of which He eternally wills and maintains His own moral excellence, abhors sin, and demands purity in His moral creatures.*

6. The Righteousness of God. This attribute of God is closely related to the immediately preceding one. It is *that perfection of God by which He maintains Himself over against every violation of His holiness, and shows in every respect that He is the Holy One.* Different aspects of it should be distinguished.

   a. *His Rectoral Justice.* This is the rectitude which God manifests as the Ruler of both the good and the evil. In virtue of this He institutes a moral government in the world, and imposes a just law upon man, with promises of reward for the obedient and threats of punishment for the disobedient, Ps. 99:4; Isa. 33:22; Rom. 1:32.

b. *His Remunerative Justice.* This manifests itself in the distribution of rewards to both men and angels, Deut. 7:9, 12, 13; Ps. 58:11; Mic. 7:20; Rom. 2:7; Heb. 11:26. It is really an expression of the divine love, dealing out its bounties, not on the basis of strict merit, but according to promise and agreement, Luke 17:10; I Cor. 4:7.

c. *His Retributive Justice.* This relates to the infliction of penalties, and is an expression of the divine wrath. In a sinless world there would be no place for its exercise, but in a world full of sin it necessarily holds a very prominent place. While the Bible stresses the reward of the righteous more than the punishment of the wicked, even the latter stands out boldly in Scripture, Rom. 1:32; 2:9; 12:19; II Thess. 1:8.

7. THE VERACITY OF GOD. The veracity of God may be described as *that perfection in virtue of which He is true in His inner being, in His revelation, and in His relation to His people.* It implies that He is the true God as over against the idols, which are lies and vanity; that He knows things as they really are and also enables man to know the reality of things; and that He faithfully fulfils all His covenant promises. This last aspect of God's veracity is usually called His *faithfulness.* It is the ground of His people's confidence, the foundation of their

hope, and the cause of their rejoicing, Num. 23:19; I Cor. 1:9; II Tim. 2:13; Heb. 6:17; 10:23.

8. The Sovereignty of God. Under this general heading we consider God's sovereign will, or His sovereignty in planning and directing the affairs of the world and of His rational creatures; and God's sovereign power, His omnipotence, or the sovereignty of God in executing His will.

a. *The Sovereign Will of God.* The will of God is represented in Scripture as the final cause of all things: of creation and preservation, Rev. 4:11, of government, Prov. 21:1; Dan. 4:35; Eph. 1:11, of the sufferings of Christ, Luke 22:42; Acts 2:23, of election and reprobation, Rom. 9:15, 16, of regeneration, Jas. 1:18, of sanctification, Phil. 2:13, of the sufferings of believers, I Pet. 3:17, of man's life and destiny, Acts 18:21; Rom. 15:32; Jas. 4:15, and even of the smallest things of life, Matt. 10:29.

1) *The secret and the revealed will of God.* Several distinctions are applied to the will of God, of which the most common is that between the secret and the revealed will of God. The former is the will of God's decree, which is largely hidden in God, while the latter is the will of His precept, which is revealed in the law and in the gospel. This distinction is based on Deut. 29:29. The secret will of God is mentioned in Ps. 115:3; Dan. 4:17; Rom. 9:18, 19; 11:33, 34; Eph. 1:5, 9, 11; and His revealed will in Matt. 7:21; 12:50; John 4:34; 7:17; Rom. 12:2. The former pertains

to all things which God wills either to effect or to permit, and which are therefore absolutely certain. The latter has reference to the duties which God prescribes to man, represents the way in which man can enjoy the divine blessing, and is frequently frustrated.

2) *The freedom of God's will.* There are certain things which God necessarily wills. He cannot but love Himself and take delight in the contemplation of His own perfections. And yet He is under no compulsion even here, but acts according to the law of His inner being. No such necessity characterizes God's will with reference to His creatures. God chooses voluntarily what and whom He will create, and the times, places, and circumstances of their lives. He marks out the paths of all His rational creatures, determines their destiny, and uses them for His purposes. And while He endows them with freedom, yet His will controls their actions. The Bible speaks of the freedom of God's will in the most absolute terms, Job 11:10; 33:13; Ps. 115:3; Prov. 21:1; Isa. 10:15; Matt. 20:15 Rom. 9: 15-18; Rev. 4:11.

3) *The will of God in relation to sin.* Serious problems arise in connection with the relation of God's will to sin. If God planned all things. then He also planned the entrance of sin into the world. Does not this make Him the author of sin? It should be borne in mind, however, that God did not decide to effect sin Himself

nor procure its commission efficaciously. He decreed to permit His rational creatures to sin, thereby rendering the entrance of sin into the world certain, without Himself becoming its author. This statement of the matter does not solve the problem altogether, but safeguards the idea of the moral purity of God. Another problem arises from the relation of the secret and the revealed will to each other. They are often said to be contradictory. His secret will comprises many things which He forbids in His revealed will, and excludes many things which He commands in His revealed will, Gen. 22; Ex. 4:21-23; II Kings 20:1-7. God decreed that the Jews should crucify Jesus; yet in doing this they went contrary to the revealed will of God, Acts 2:23. It should be borne in mind, however, that in making the distinction under consideration we are using the word "will" in two different senses. By His secret will God has determined what He will do or what shall come to pass; in His revealed will, on the other hand, He reveals to us what we must do. Moreover, the situation is not such that, according to His secret will He does, and, according to His revealed will, He does not take pleasure in sin. The fact that He decreed that sin should enter the world does not imply that He takes delight in it.

b. *The Sovereign Power or Omnipotence of God.* The sovereignty of God also finds expression in the divine power or omnipotence, the power to execute His will. The omnipotence of God should not be understood to imply that God can do everything. The Bible teaches us that there are many things which God cannot do. He cannot lie, sin, change, nor deny Himself, Num. 23:19; I Sam. 15:29; II Tim. 2:13; Heb. 6:18; Jas. 1:13, 17. The Scholastics were wrong when they taught that He could do all kinds of things which are inherently contradictory and could even annihilate Himself. It is more correct to say that, in virtue of His omnipotence, God can, through the mere exercise of His will, realize whatsoever He has decided to accomplish. And if He so desired, He could do more than He actually brings to pass, Gen. 18:14; Jer. 32:27; Zech. 8:6; Matt. 3:9; 26:53. The omnipotence of God finds expression in the name *El-Shaddai,* and is clearly mentioned in several passages of Scripture, Job 9:12; Ps. 115:3; Jer. 32:17; Matt. 19:26; Luke 1:37; Rom. 1:20; Eph. 1:19.

Questions for Review:

How do we divide the attributes of God? Which belong to each one of these classes? What is the independence of God? His immutability? How can we explain that the Bible apparently ascribes change to God? What is God's eternity and immensity? How can we prove the simplicity of God? What is the nature and extent of God's knowledge? How is His wisdom related to His knowledge? What is the goodness of God, and what other names are used for it? Should we speak of love as central in God? How do we distinguish God's grace, mercy, and longsuffering? What is the holiness of God? Under what different aspects can the righteousness of God be considered?

What is included in the veracity of God? What distinction do we apply to the will of God? Is His will free or necessary? Does God's decree make Him the author of sin? Do the secret and revealed will of God conflict? Does God's omnipotence imply that He can do everything?

References for Further Study:

Berkhof, *Reformed Dogmatics*, I, pp. 35-61; McPherson, *Christian Dogmatics*, pp. 123-139; Hodge, *Outlines of Theology*, pp. 135-163; Orr, *Side-Lights on Christian Doctrine*, pp. 21-34; Clarke, *The Christian Doctrine of God.*

The Trinity

A. **The Trinity in General.** The Bible teaches us that the one God consists in three persons. This is decidedly a doctrine of special revelation, a doctrine that is not revealed in nature, and that could not be discovered by human reason.

1. Statement of the Doctrine. God is one in His essential being, but in this one being there are three persons, called, Father, Son, and Holy Spirit. These persons are not, however, like so many persons among men three entirely separate and distinct individuals. They are rather three modes or forms in which the divine essence exists. At the same time it should be borne in mind that these self-distinctions in the divine being are of such a nature that they can enter into personal relations. The Father can speak to the Son and can send forth the Holy Spirit. The real mystery of the Trinity consists in this that the three persons are one in their essential being. And this does not mean that the divine essence is divided among the three persons. It is wholly, with all its perfections, in each one of the persons, and has no existence outside of and apart from the persons. Moreover, the persons are not subordinate the one to the other in their essential being. It may be said, however, that in order of existence the Father is first, the Son second, and the Holy Spirit third, and this order also reflects itself in the work of creation and redemption. The three persons are distinguished by certain personal

distinctions: the Father generates the Son, the Son is generated by the Father, and the Holy Spirit proceeds from both Father and Son. This doctrine is one of the great mysteries of faith, and as such is far beyond our human comprehension.

2. Scripture Proof for the Trinity.

a. *In the Old Testament.* Some are of the opinion that the Old Testament contains no indications of the Trinity, but this is not correct. There are passages which indicate that there is more than one person in God, as for instance, where God speaks of Himself in the plural, Gen. 1:26; 11:7, when the angel of Jehovah is represented as a divine person, Gen. 16:7-13; 18:1-21; 19:1-22, and where the Spirit is spoken of as a distinct person, Isa. 48:16; 63:10. In addition to these there are some in which three persons are more or less clearly indicated, Isa. 48:16; 61:1; 63:9, 10.

b. *In the New Testament.* It is perfectly natural that the New Testament proofs should be clearer than those of the Old, since it records the incarnation of the Son of God and the outpouring of the Holy Spirit. There are several passages in which the three persons are expressly mentioned, as in connection with the baptism of Jesus, Luke 3:21, 22, in the farewell discourses of Jesus, John 14—16, in the great commission, Matt. 28:19, in the apostolic blessing, II Cor. 13:13, and also in such passages as Luke 1:35; I Cor. 12:4-6, and I Peter 1:2.

3. Erroneous Representations of the Trinity. In the early Christian Church some represented the three persons in the Trinity as three divine beings, virtually three gods. The Sabellians regarded the three persons merely as so many modes of divine action or manifestation, which God successively assumes, revealing Himself as Father in creation and in the giving of the law, as Son in the incarnation, and as Holy Spirit in regeneration and sanctification. Thus the three persons were reduced to one. Paul of Samosata, the Socinians of the days of the Reformation, and the Unitarians and Modernists of the present day, all represent the Trinity as consisting of God the Father, the man Jesus Christ, and a divine influence which is called the Spirit of God. This view also represents God as one, not only in being, but also in person, and therefore virtually destroys the Trinity.

B. The Three Persons Considered Separately.

1. The Father. The name "Father," as applied to God, is not always used in the same sense in Scripture. It may denote the triune God (*a*) as the origin of all created things, I Cor. 8:6; Eph. 3:14, 15; Heb. 12:9; Jas. 1:17; (*b*) as the Father of the chosen nation of Israel, Deut. 32:6; Isa. 63:16; 64:8; Jer. 3:4; Mal. 1:6; 2:10; and (*c*) as the Father of believers as His spiritual children, Matt. 5:45; 6:6-15; Rom. 8:15; I John 1:3. In a far more fundamental sense, however, the name is applied to the first person in the Trinity in His relation to the second person, John 1:14, 18; 5:17-26; 8:54; 14:12, 13. This is the original Fatherhood

of God, of which all earthly fatherhood is but a faint reflection. The distinctive property of the Father is that He generates the Son from all eternity. Certain works are ascribed particularly to the Father, though the other persons also participate in them, such as planning the work of redemption, the works of creation and providence, and the work of representing the Trinity in the Counsel of Redemption.

2. The Son. The second person of the Trinity is called "Son" or "Son of God." This name is not always applied to Him in the same sense, however. Considered purely as the second person in the Trinity, He is called "the Son" because of His eternal generation by the Father, John 1:14, 18; 3:16, 18; Gal. 4:4. He also bears that name as the incarnate Son of God in an official sense, to designate Him as the Messiah chosen of God, Matt. 8:29; 27:40; 26:63; John 1:49; 11:27. And, finally, He is called "the Son of God," at least in one passage, in virtue of the fact, that at His birth He was begotten by the special operation of the Holy Spirit, Luke 1:32, 35. In connection with the Son the following points deserve particular attention:

a. *His Eternal Generation.* The personal property of the Son is that He is eternally begotten of the Father. The doctrine of the generation of the Son is naturally suggested by the Biblical representation of the first and the second person in the Trinity as standing in the relation of Father and Son to each other, and is further based on Ps. 2:7; Acts 13:33; Heb. 1:5. By means of this generation the Father does not call the essential nature of the Son into being, but becomes the cause of the personal subsistence of the Son — a second mode of existence — within the divine being. This generation of the Son should not be regarded as an act completed in the past, but as a necessary and therefore eternal act of the Father. It is timeless, always continuing, and yet ever completed.

b. *The Divinity of the Son.* The divinity of the Son is denied by several sects in the early Christian Church, by a host of liberal scholars during the last two centuries, and by the Unitarians and the real Modernists and Humanists of the present day. It can only be denied, however, by setting aside the explicit testimony of the Word of God. There are passages which expressly assert the divinity of the Son, such as John 1:1; 20:28; Rom. 9:5; Phil. 2:6; Tit. 2:13; I John 5:20. Moreover, divine names are applied to Him, Jer. 23:5, 6; Joel 2:32 (comp. Acts 2:21); Isa. 9:6; I Tim. 3:16; divine attributes are ascribed to Him, Isa. 9:6; Rev. 1:8; Matt. 18:20; 28:20; John 2:24, 25; 21:17; Phil. 3:21; Rev. 1:8; divine works are done by Him, Matt. 9:2-7; Luke 10:22; John 1:3, 10; 3:35; Eph. 1:22; Col. 1:17; Heb. 1:10-12; Phil. 3:21; John 5:22, 25-30; and divine honour is accorded Him, John 5:22, 23; 14:1; I Cor. 15:19; II Cor. 13:13; Heb. 1:6.

c. *The Works More Particularly Ascribed to the Son.* The order of the existence of the persons in the Trinity is reflected in the order of their works

If all things are *out of* the Father, they are *through* the Son. If the former is the final, the latter is the mediating cause of all both in creation and in redemption. All things are created and maintained through the Son, John 1:3, 10; Heb. 1:2, 3. He is the light which lighteth every man coming into the world, John 1:9. More particularly the work of redemption is carried out by the Son in His incarnation, sufferings, and death, Eph. 1:3-14.

3. THE HOLY SPIRIT. With reference to the Holy Spirit the following points demand special consideration:

a. *The Personality of the Holy Spirit.* It is not so much the divinity as the personality of the Holy Spirit that is called in question by many. It is denied by several sectarians in the early Church, by the Socinians in the days of the Reformation, and by the Unitarians, the Modernists, and all kinds of Sabellians in the present time. They prefer to regard the Holy Spirit merely as a power or influence of God. Yet He is clearly designated as a person, John 14:16, 17, 26; 15:26; 16:7-15; Rom. 8:26. Personal characteristics are ascribed to Him, such as intelligence, John 14:26; 15:26; Rom. 8:16, affections, Isa. 63:10; Eph. 4:30, and will, Acts 16:7; I Cor. 12:11. Moreover, He performs acts proper to personality, such as speaking, searching, testifying, commanding, revealing, striving, making intercession, Gen. 1:2; 6:3; Luke 12:12; John 14:26; 15:26; 16:8; Acts 8:29; 13:2; Rom. 8:11; I Cor. 2:10, 11.

Finally, there are passages in which the Holy Spirit is distinguished from His own power, Luke 1:35; 4:14; Acts 10:38; Rom. 15:13; I Cor. 2:4.

b. *The Relation of the Holy Spirit to the Other Persons in the Trinity.* While it was asserted from the beginning on the basis of John 15:26 that the Holy Spirit proceeds from the Father, it was not until the year 589 A. D. that the western Church officially took the position that He also proceeds from the Son. This doctrine is based on the fact that the Spirit is also called the Spirit of Christ and of the Son, Rom. 8:9; Gal. 4:6, and is said to be sent by Christ, John 15:26; 16:7. In virtue of this procession from the Father and the Son, the Holy Spirit stands in the closest possible relationship to the other persons. He searches the deep things of God, I Cor. 2:10, 11, and is to a certain extent identified with Christ, II Cor. 3:17. In the Spirit Christ Himself returns to His disciples, John 15:16-18. Moreover, in the Epistles of Paul it is sometimes Christ, and sometimes the Spirit of God who is said to dwell in believers, Rom. 8:9, 10; Gal. 2:20; I Cor. 3:16.

c. *The Divinity of the Holy Spirit.* The divinity of the Holy Spirit may be established from Scripture by a line of proof quite similar to that employed in connection with the Son. Divine names are given to Him, Acts 5:3, 4; I Cor. 3:16; II Tim. 3:16; divine perfections are ascribed to Him, Ps. 139:7-10; Isa. 40:13, 15; I Cor. 2: 10, 11; 12:11; Rom. 15:19; Heb. 9:14; divine works are performed by Him, Gen. 1:2; Job 26:

13; 33:4; Ps. 104:30; John 3:5, 6; Tit. 3:5; Rom. 8:11; and divine honour is accorded Him, Matt. 28:19; Rom. 9:1; II Cor. 13:14.

d. *The Works More Particularly Ascribed to the Holy Spirit.* There are certain works which, while works of the triune God, are more particularly ascribed to the Holy Spirit. In general it may be said that it is His special task to bring the work of God to completion both in creation and redemption. In the natural sphere He generates life and thus puts the finishing touch to the work of creation, Gen. 1:3; Job 26:13; Ps. 33:6; Ps. 104:30; and He inspires and qualifies men for special tasks, Ex. 28:3; 31:2, 3, 6; 35:35; I Sam. 11:6; 16:13, 14. And in the sphere of redemption He prepares and qualifies Christ for His redemptive work, Luke 1:35; 3:22; John 3:34; Heb. 10:5-7; He inspires Scripture, I Cor. 2:13; II Pet. 1:21; He forms and augments the Church and dwells in it as the principle of a new life, Eph. 1:22, 23; 2:22; I Cor. 3:16; 12:4 ff.; and He teaches and guides the Church, leading it in all the truth, John 14:26; 15:26; 16:13, 14; Acts 5:32; Heb. 10:15; I John 2:27.

Questions for Review:

Can we discover the doctrine of the Trinity from nature? How do the persons in God differ from three persons among men? Is there any subordination of the persons in God? How can we prove the Trinity from the Old Testament? From the New? Against what errors should we guard in this doctrine? In how many different senses is the name "Father" applied to God? What works are especially ascribed to the Father? In how many different senses is the name "Son" applied to Christ? Is the generation of the Son a past act? What works are especially ascribed to the Son? How can you prove the divinity of the Son and of the Holy Spirit? How can you prove that the Holy Spirit is a person, and not merely a power or influence? How is the Spirit related to the other persons? What works are especially ascribed to the Holy Spirit? What is the characteristic property of the Father, of the Son, and of the Holy Spirit?

References for Further Study:

Berkhof, *Reformed Dogmatics*, I, pp. 62-81; McPherson, *Christian Dogmatics*, pp. 139-162; Hodge, *Outlines of Theology*, pp. 164-199; Orr, *Side-Lights on Christian Doctrine*, pp. 37-51; Steenstra, *The Being of God as Unity and Trinity.*

THE WORKS OF GOD

The Divine Decrees In General

A. **The Nature of the Divine Decrees.** The decree of God is His eternal plan or purpose, in which He has foreordained all things that come to pass. It is but natural that God, who controls all things, should have a definite plan according to which He works, not only in creation and providence, but also in the process of redemption. This plan includes many particulars, and therefore we often speak of the divine decrees in the plural, though in reality there is but a single decree. For the material contents of His decree God drew on the boundless knowledge which He has of all kinds of possible things. Of this great store of possibilities He embodied in His decree only those things which actually come to pass. Their inclusion in the decree does not necessarily mean that He Himself will actively bring them into existence, but means in some cases that, with the divine permission and according to the divine plan, they will certainly be brought to realization by His rational creatures. The decree covers all the works of God in creation and redemption, and also embraces the actions of His free moral beings, not excluding their sinful actions. But while the entrance of sin into the world and its various manifestations in the lives of angels and men were thus rendered certain, this does not mean that God decided to effectuate these Himself. God's decree with reference to sin is a permissive decree.

B. **The Characteristics of the Divine Decree.** The decree of God has several characteristics:

1. IT IS FOUNDED IN DIVINE WISDOM. This is implied in the statement that God's purpose is "according to the counsel of His will," Eph. 1:11. Though there is a great deal in it that we do not understand, it is certain that God formed His plan with wisdom.

2. IT IS ETERNAL. This does not merely mean that the decree was formed before the beginning of time, but also that, while it relates to things which come to pass in the course of history, its formation is and remains an act within the divine being, and therefore in the strictest sense eternal.

3. IT IS EFFICACIOUS. The fact that God made a divine plan does not mean that He has decided to bring to pass by His own act all that is included in it; but it does mean that what He has decided will certainly come to pass, and that nothing can thwart His purpose, Ps. 33:11; Prov. 19:21; Isa. 46:10.

4. IT IS UNCHANGEABLE. Man often changes his plans for various reasons. It may be that on second thought he considers them unwise, or that he is wanting in the power to carry them out. But neither the one nor the other is conceivable in God. He does not change His plan, because He is faithful and true, Job 23:13, 14; Isa. 46:10; Luke 22:22; Acts 2:23.

5. IT IS UNCONDITIONAL. The decree is not in any of its particulars dependent on anything outside of it, as, for instance, on the free actions of God's moral and rational creatures, on their foreseen disobedience or foreseen faith. God has determined not

only what will come to pass, but also the conditions under which it will be realized, Acts 2:23; Eph. 2:8; I Pet. 1:2.

6. It Is All-Comprehensive. It includes the good actions of men, Eph. 2:10, their wicked actions, Prov. 16:4; Acts 2:23; 4:27, 28, contingent events, Gen. 45:8; 50:20; Prov. 16:33, the means as well as the end, II Thess. 2:13; Eph. 1:4, the duration of man's life, Job 14:5; Ps. 39:4, and the place of his habitation, Acts 7:26.

7. With Reference to Sin it is Permissive. The decree of God with reference to sin is usually called a permissive decree. It renders the future sinful act absolutely certain, but this does not mean that God will by His own act bring it to pass. God decreed not to hinder the sinful act of the creature's self-determination, but nevertheless to regulate and control its result, Ps. 78:29; 106:15; Acts 14:16; 17:30.

C. **Objections to the Doctrine of the Decrees.** Outside of Reformed circles the doctrine of the decrees meets with very little favour. Pelagians and Socinians reject it as un-Scriptural and unreasonable, and Arminians either ignore it altogether, or represent the decree of God as based on His foreknowledge. There are especially three objections to the doctrine:

1. It Is Declared to Be Inconsistent with the Moral Freedom of Man. If God has decreed all the actions of man, then man must necessarily act as he acts and do what he does, and cannot be held

responsible for his actions. But the Bible teaches not only that God has decreed the free acts of man, but also that man is none the less free and responsible for his acts, Gen. 50:19, 20; Acts 2:23; 4:27, 28; and it makes no attempt to reconcile the two. We may not be able to harmonize them, but that does not necessarily mean that they are inherently contradictory. Some conceive of the freedom of the will in a way that makes it inconsistent with the divine decree, but theirs is not the proper conception of the free agency of man. Moral freedom is the power of man to determine his moral actions freely in harmony with his previous thoughts and judgments, with his inclinations and desires, and even with his very character. This freedom has its laws, and the better they are understood the more certain it is what a man will do under certain circumstances. God fully understands these laws, and therefore it is quite conceivable that He should determine the future actions of man in such a way as not to impinge on the moral freedom of man, even if we do not fully understand how this can be done.

2. It Is Said to Rob Men of all Motives for Seeking Salvation. If all things happen as God has decreed, people will naturally feel that they need not give themselves any concern for the future, nor make any efforts to obtain salvation. If their destruction is predetermined, they will be lost in spite of their best efforts; and if their salvation is decreed, they will be saved, though they neglect all the means of salvation. In answer to this objection it may be

said, (*a*) That the hidden decree of God cannot possibly be man's rule of action; this is found only in the law and the gospel. (*b*) That God has not only decreed the final destiny of man, but also the means leading up to it. It was absolutely certain that all who were in the vessel with Paul were to be saved, but it was equally certain that, in order to secure this end, the sailors had to remain aboard. (*c*) That, since the decree connects means and ends together, and ends are decreed only as the result of means, it encourages effort instead of discouraging it, Eph. 2:10; Phil. 2:13.

3. IT MAKES GOD THE AUTHOR OF SIN. If God has decreed sin, He must be regarded as the author of sin; and yet this cannot be in view of the fact that He is holy, that He himself forbids sin, and that Scripture stresses His moral purity, Ps. 92:15; Eccl. 7:29; Hab. 1:13; Jas. 1:13; I John 1:5. It may be said, however, that the decree merely makes God the author of free moral beings who are themselves the authors of sin. The decree with reference to sin is not an efficient but a permissive decree. God did not decree to produce sin by direct divine efficiency. This consideration, it is true, does not fully remove the difficulty. The problem of God's relation to sin remains a mystery for us, which we cannot fully solve.

Questions for Review:

What is the divine decree? Why do we sometimes speak of decrees in the plural? Which are the characteristics of the divine decree? In what sense is it eternal? What does it imply that the decree is efficacious? In what sense is it unconditional? What is included in the decree? What is the nature of God's decree respecting sin? What objections are raised against the doctrine of the decrees? What can be said in answer to these objections?

References for Further Study:

Berkhof, *Reformed Dogmatics*, I, pp. 82-92; Hodge, *Outlines of Theology*, pp. 200-213; Shedd, *Dogmatic Theology*, I, pp. 393-415; Girardeau, *The Will in its Theological Relations*, pp. 17-409.

Predestination

When we pass from the discussion of the decrees in general to that of predestination, we are proceeding from the general to the particular. Predestination is simply — to express it in general terms — the purpose of God respecting His moral creatures.

A. **The Objects of Predestination.** Predestination in the broader sense of the term refers to all God's rational creatures. It bears on all men both good and evil, and that not merely as groups but as individuals, Acts 4:28; Rom. 8:29, 30; 9:11-13; Eph. 1:4-6. Moreover, this decree also includes the angels, both good and evil. The Bible speaks not only of "holy angels," Mark 8:38; Luke 9:26, and of wicked angels who kept not their first estate, II Pet. 2:4; Jude 6; but also makes explicit mention of elect angels, I Tim. 5:21, thus implying that there are also non-elect angels. Since many of the angels never fell, the predestination of the angels cannot be conceived of in the same way as that of men. God did not choose a certain number of the angels out of the common fallen mass, leaving the others to perish in their sin. Their predestination consists in this that God decreed, for reasons sufficient unto Himself, to give unto some angels, in addition to the grace with which they were endowed by creation and which included sufficient power to remain holy, a special grace of perseverance, and to withhold this from others. Finally, Christ as the Mediator was also the object of divine predestination. This simply means that, as Mediator, He was the special object of God's good pleasure, I Pet. 1:20; 2:4.

B. **The Two Parts of Predestination.** Predestination includes two parts, namely, election and reprobation.

1. ELECTION. The Bible speaks of election in more than one sense: (*a*) the election of Israel as a people for special service and also for special privileges, Deut. 4:37; 7:6-8; 10:15; Hos. 13:5; (*b*) the election of individuals to some office or special service, Deut. 18:5; I Sam. 10:24; Ps. 78:70; Jer. 1:5; John 6:70; Acts 9:15; and (*c*) the election of individuals to be children of God and heirs of eternal glory, Matt. 22:14; Rom. 11:5; I Cor. 1: 27, 28; Eph. 1:4. The last is the election that comes into consideration here as a part of predestination. It may be defined as *God's eternal purpose to save some of the human race in and by Jesus Christ.*

2. REPROBATION. The doctrine of election naturally implies that some of the human race were not elected. If God purposed to save some, He also purposed not to save others. This is also in perfect agreement with the teachings of Scripture on this point, Matt. 11:25, 26; Rom. 9:13, 17, 18, 21, 23; 11: 7; Jude 4; I Pet. 2:8. Reprobation may be defined as *that decree of God whereby He has determined to pass some men by with the operation of His special grace and to punish them for their sin to the manifestation of His justice.* From this definition reprobation appears to be really a twofold purpose namely, (*a*) to pass by some in the bestowal of regenerating and saving grace; and (*b*) to assign them to dishonour and to the wrath of God for their sins.

The objection is sometimes raised that this doctrine exposes God to the charge of injustice. But this is hardly correct. We can speak of injustice only when one party has a claim on another. If God owed forgiveness of sin and eternal life to all men, it would be an injustice if He saved only a limited number of them. But the situation is quite different where all have forfeited the blessings of God. No one has a right to call God to account for electing some and passing by others. He would have been perfectly just, if He had not saved any, Matt. 20:14, 15; Rom. 9:14, 15.

C. **The Question of Supra- and Infralapsarianism.** The doctrine of predestination has not always been presented in exactly the same form. Supra- and Infralapsarians were pitted against each other, and even now exist alongside of each other in Reformed circles. The limitations of this Manual do not permit us to discuss the relative merits of Supra- and Infralapsarianism, and therefore we limit ourselves to a bare statement of the difference between the two views. The difference pertains primarily to the order of the divine decrees. The question is, whether in the plan of God the decrees of election and reprobation precede or follow the decrees to create the world and to permit the fall. This naturally involves another question, namely, whether in the decree of predestination God regarded man as already created and fallen, or as an object still to be created and certain to fall. The resulting order in both cases is as follows:

1. The Supralapsarian Order. The supralapsarian order may be stated thus:

a. God first decreed to glorify Himself in the salvation of some and in the damnation of other men, who at this stage existed in His mind only as possibilities.

b. As a means to that end, He decreed to create those already elected or reprobated.

c. For the consummation of the plan so far formed, He further decreed to permit man to fall.

d. Finally, He decreed to open up a way of salvation for the elect and to lead them to everlasting glory, passing the others by and consigning them to everlasting destruction for their sin.

2. The Infralapsarian Order. While the supralapsarian order may be regarded as the more ideal of the two, the infralapsarian is more historical.

a. God first decreed to create man.

b. Then He decreed to permit the fall of man.

c. Next He decreed to elect a certain number of the fallen and justly condemned race to eternal life, and to pass the others by, consigning them to everlasting destruction for their sin.

d. Finally, He decreed to provide a way of salvation for the elect.

This is the order officially adopted by the Reformed Churches in the Canons of Dordt.

Questions for Review:

How is predestination related to the decree of God in general? Who are the objects of the decree of predestination? How should we conceive of the predestination of the angels? In what sense is Christ the object of predestination? Which are the parts of predestination? In how many different senses does the Bible speak of election? What is election as distinguished from reprobation? What does the decree of reprobation include? What Scripture proof is there for the doctrine of reprobation? Does this doctrine involve injustice on the part of God? What is the difference between Infra- and Supralapsarianism?

References for Further Study:

Berkhof, *Reformed Dogmatics*, I, pp. 93-111; Hodge, *Outlines of Theology*, pp. 214-236; Shedd, *Dogmatic Theology*, I, pp. 415-462; Girardeau, *The Will in its Theological Relations;* Dijk, *Om 't Eeuwig Welbehagen*, pp. 265-456.

Creation

A. **Creation in General.** The discussion of the decrees naturally leads on to the consideration of their execution, which begins with the work of creation. Creation is the beginning and basis of all divine revelation, and also the foundation of all ethical and religious life. The doctrine of creation can be learned from no other source than Scripture and can be accepted only by faith.

1. The Idea of Creation. The word "creation" is not always used in the same sense, and as a result the definitions of creation vary. It may be defined as *that act of God by which He produces the world and all that is in it, partly without the use of pre-existent materials, and partly out of material that is by its very nature inadequate, for the manifestation of His glory*. Though it is often ascribed to the Father, it is also clearly represented as a work of the triune God, Gen. 1:2; Job 26:13; 33:4; Ps. 33:6; 104:30; Isa. 40:12, 13; John 1:3; I Cor. 8:6; Col. 1:15-17. Moreover, it was a free act of God and not a necessary act. He is the self-sufficient One, and therefore did not need the world. His production of the universe was not dependent on an inherent necessity in the divine being, but only on a perfectly voluntary decision of His sovereign will. This must be maintained over against all sorts of pantheistic theories. The Bible clearly teaches that God created all things, according to the counsel of His will, Eph. 1:11; Rev. 4:11. By His

creative work He gave the world a separate existence, distinct from His own being, so that the universe cannot be regarded as itself God or even a part of God. At the same time He constituted the world so that it is always dependent on Him and must be upheld from day to day by His almighty power. He is never distant from, but ever present in His entire creation,, Ps. 139-7-10; Jer. 23:24.

2. The Time of Creation. In speaking of the time of creation the Bible employs the ordinary language of daily life. It begins with the very simple statement: "In the beginning God created the heavens and the earth," Gen. 1:1. The "beginning" to which this statement refers is the beginning of all temporal things, and even of time itself. It would not be correct to assume that time was already in existence when God created the world, and that He at some point in that existing time, called "the beginning," brought forth the universe. The world was created *with* time rather than *in* time. Back of the beginning mentioned in Gen 1:1 lies a beginningless eternity.

3. The Manner of Creation. In the strictest sense of the word "to create" means to bring forth something out of nothing or without the use of preexistent materials. The expression "to create or bring forth out of nothing" is not found in Scripture, but only in one of the apocryphal books, namely, II Macc. 7:28. Some have interpreted it to mean that the world came into existence without a cause. But this interpretation is wide of the mark. The expression simply means that in the

work of creation God did not make use of pre-existent materials. The world could not come into existence without a cause. God Himself or, more specifically, the will of God, should be regarded as its cause. Scriptural warrant for the doctrine that God created the world without the use of pre-existent materials is found in such passages as Ps. 33:9; 148:5, and Heb. 11:3, which is the strongest Scriptural expression. The statement found in Rom. 4:17 does not speak of the work of creation, but may yet be brought to bear on the subject under consideration. It should be borne in mind, however, that the expression, "to create" does not always mean to bring forth something out of nothing. It may also mean to bring forth something out of some pre-existent material which is by its very nature unfit. God created the body of Adam out of the dust of the ground, and the body of Eve out of a rib of Adam.

4. The Final End of Creation. The question of the final end of God in the work of creation has frequently been debated. There are especially two answers that have been given to this question:

   a. *That the Happiness of Man is the Final End.* Some of the early Greek and Roman philosophers, the Humanists of the days of the Reformation, and the Rationalists of the eighteenth century, found the final end of creation in the happiness of man. The best form in which this theory is stated, is to the effect that God could not make Himself the end of creation, because He is sufficient unto Himself and has absolutely no need of His creatures. And if He could not make Himself the end, then this can be found only in the creature, and ultimately in its supreme happiness. But it would seem to be perfectly self-evident that God does not exist for the sake of man, but man for the sake of God. The creature cannot be the final end of creation. Moreover, it can hardly be said that everything in creation ministers to human happiness.

b. *That the Declarative Glory of God is the Final End.* According to Scripture the true end of creation is not found in anything outside of God, but only in God Himself, and more particularly in the manifestation of His inherent excellency. This does not mean that God created the world primarily to receive glory from His creatures in adoration and praise, but especially to manifest His glory. The glorious perfections of God are seen in the entire creation. But this final end includes other subordinate ends. The manifestation of the glory of God in nature is not intended as empty show, a mere exhibition to be admired by the creature, but also aims at promoting their welfare and perfect happiness. It seeks to attune their hearts to the praises of the Creator, and to elicit from their souls the expressions of their gratefulness, their love, and adoration. This doctrine is abundantly supported by Scripture, Isa. 43:7; 60:21; 61:3; Ezek. 36:21, 22; 39:7; Luke 2:14; Rom. 9:17; 11:36; I Cor. 15:28; Eph. 1:5, 6, 12, 14; 3:9, 10; Col. 1:16.

5. Suggested Substitutes for the Doctrine of Creation. Those who reject the doctrine of creation naturally resort to some other theory as to the origin of the world. Three theories deserve brief mention here:

a. *The Dualistic Theory.* This theory is to the effect that both God and matter are eternal. Original matter is frequently represented as the rude material out of which God formed the world. On this view God is not the Creator but merely the Framer of the universe. There are serious objections to this theory, however. It involves the impossible, namely, that two eternals, and therefore two infinites, exist alongside of each other. Moreover, matter shows clear traces of composition and arrangement, and therefore cannot be regarded as self-existent.

b. *The Emanation Theory.* According to this theory God and the world are essentially one, and the world is a necessary emanation or outflowing out of the divine being. This idea is characteristic of all pantheistic theories. The objections to this view are very serious. It applies to God a principle of change, of growth, and of progress, which characterizes only the finite and imperfect. It robs God of the power of self-determination, and men of their freedom and of their moral and responsible character. And in addition to that, it makes God responsible for all that transpires in the world, the evil as well as the good.

c. *The Theory of Evolution.* The theory of evolution is sometimes spoken of as if it could be a substitute for the doctrine of creation. But this is clearly a mistake. Evolution presupposes something that evolves, and this must be in the last resort either eternal or created, so that the evolutionist must choose between the theory that matter is eternal and the doctrine of creation. Some seek to escape the difficulty by adopting what they call theistic or creative evolution. But this is really a contradiction in terms. It is neither the Biblical doctrine of creation, nor a consistent theory of evolution.

B. **The Spiritual World.** God created not only a material but also a spiritual world, consisting of the angels, which calls for a brief consideration at this point.

1. THE EXISTENCE AND NATURE OF THE ANGELS. All religions recognize the existence of a spiritual world. Many prominent philosophers even admitted the possibility of the existence of a world of angels and sought to prove this by pure reason. This is quite impossible, however, and therefore modern liberal theology has largely discarded the belief in such spiritual beings. The Bible assumes the existence of angels throughout and ascribes to them real personality. They are represented as having intelligence, II Sam. 14:20; Matt. 24:36, and a moral character, Jude 6; Rev. 14:10. Moreover, personal actions are ascribed to them: they love and rejoice, Luke 15:10, desire, I Pet. 1:12, contend, Jude 9; Rev. 12:7, worship, Heb. 1:6, talk, Zech. 1:9; Luke 1:13, come and go, Gen. 19:1; Luke 9:26, and so on. Some have ascribed to them airy or

ethereal bodies, but this is quite contrary to Scripture, which clearly represents them as pure spiritual beings, Matt. 8:16; 12:45; Luke 7:21; 8:2; 11:26; Acts 19:12; Eph. 6:12; Heb. 1:14. They do not marry, Matt. 22:30, are invisible, Col. 1:16, have no flesh and bone, Luke 24:39, and can be present in great numbers in a very limited space, Luke 8:30. Some of them are represented as good, holy, and elect, angels of light, I Tim. 5:21; Mark 8:38; Luke 9:26; Rev. 14:10; II Cor. 11:14; and others as fallen from their original estate, and therefore evil, John 8:44; II Pet. 2:4; Jude 6.

2. The Angelic Orders. Besides the general name "angels," there are several specific names which point to different classes of angels:

a. *Cherubim.* The Bible repeatedly speaks of cherubim. They guard the entrance of paradise, Gen. 3:24, are represented as looking down on the mercy-seat, Ex. 25:18, and constitute the chariot on which God descends to the earth, II Sam. 22:11; Ps. 18:10. God is said to dwell between the cherubim in tabernacle and temple, Ps. 80:1; 99:1; Isa. 37:16. They reveal the power, majesty, and glory of God, and guard His holiness in the garden of Eden, in tabernacle and temple, and at the descent of God to the earth.

b. *Seraphim.* A related class of angels are the seraphim, mentioned in Isa. 6:2, 3, 6. Like the cherubim, they are also represented symbolically in human form. In distinction from the latter, however, they stand as servants round about the throne of the heavenly King, sing His praises, and are ever ready to do His bidding. While the cherubims are the mighty ones, they may be called the nobles among the angels. While the former guard the holiness of God, they serve the purpose of reconciliation and thus prepare men for the proper approach to God.

c. *Gabriel and Michael.* There are two angels which are mentioned by name in Scripture, namely, Gabriel and Michael. The former is mentioned in Dan. 8:16; 9:21; Luke 1:19, 26. Some regard him as an uncreated being, and even suggest that he might be the third person in the Trinity; but the passages referred to show this to be an untenable position. Evidently it was his special task to convey divine revelations to men and to interpret them. Michael is mentioned in Dan. 10:13, 21; Jude 9; Rev. 12:7. Some regard his name as a designation of the second person in the Trinity, but this position is also untenable. In view of Jude 9, where he is called the archangel, and of Rev. 12:7 it would seem that he occupies a unique place among the angels. We see in him the valiant warrior fighting the battles of Jehovah against the enemies of Israel and against the evil powers in the spirit-world.

d. *Principalities, powers, thrones, dominions.* These names, found in Eph. 1:21; 3:10; Col. 1:16; 2:10; I Pet. 3:22, also serve to designate angels. They do not point to different *kinds* of angels, but simply to the fact that there are differences of rank and dignity among the angels.

3. The Service of the Angels. The angels are represented in Scripture as praising God day and night, Job 38:7; Isa. 6; Ps. 103:20; 148:2; Rev. 5:11. Since the entrance of sin into the world, they are "sent forth to do service for the sake of them that shall inherit salvation," Heb. 1:14. They rejoice at the conversion of a sinner, Luke 15:10, watch over believers, Ps. 34:7; 91:11, protect the little ones, Matt. 18:10, are present in the Church, I Cor. 11:10; I Tim. 5:21, learning from her the manifold riches of the grace of God, Eph. 3:10; I Pet. 1:12, and convey believers into the bosom of Abraham, Luke 16:22. They also frequently mediate the special revelations of God, Dan. 9:21-23; Zech. 1:12-14; Acts 7:38, communicate blessings to His people, Ps. 91:11, 12; Isa. 63:9; Dan. 6:22; Acts 5:19, and execute judgments upon His enemies, Gen. 19:1, 13; II Kings 19:35; Matt. 13:41.

4. The Evil Angels. Besides the good there are also evil angels, who delight in opposing God and destroying His work. They were created good, but did not retain their original position, II Pet. 2:4; Jude 6. The special sin of these angels is not revealed, but probably consisted in this that they exalted themselves over against God and aspired to supreme authority. Satan, who was evidently one of the princes among the angels, became the recognized head of those that fell away, Matt. 25:41; 9:34; Eph. 2:2. He is represented as the originator of sin, Gen. 3:1; John 8:44; II Cor. 11:3;

I John 3:8; Rev. 12:9; 20:2, 10. They also possess superhuman power, but employ this in cursing God, in battling against Him and His Anointed, and in destroying His work. They seek to blind and mislead even the elect, and encourage the sinner in his evil way.

C. **The Material World.** Besides the spiritual there is a material world, and this is contemplated here in relation to God, that is, as a work of God and as a revelation of His divine perfections.

1. THE NARRATIVE OF CREATION. The story of creation was revealed to Moses or to one of the earlier patriarchs. If it was pre-Mosaic, it must have passed in tradition, oral or written, from one generation to another, and was finally penned by Moses under the guidance of the Holy Spirit.

a. *The Original Creation.* Some regard Gen. 1:1 as the superscription or title of the whole narrative of creation. But in that case there would be no account whatever of the original creation, nor of the creation of heaven. For that reason it is better to regard Gen. 1:1 as the record of the original and immediate creation of the universe, called in Hebrew fashion "heaven and earth." In this expression the word "heaven" refers to that invisible order of things in which the glory of God reveals itself in the most perfect manner. The second verse describes the original condition of the earth (comp. Ps. 104:5, 6).

b. *The Completion of Creation in Six Days.* Some assume that the days of which Genesis 1 speaks were long periods of time, corresponding with the periods of Geology. They find that Scripture allows and even favors this interpretation, since (1) the word "day" sometimes denotes an indefinite period, Ps. 50:15; Eccl. 7:14; Zech. 4:10; (2) the sun was not created until the fourth day, so that the length of the previous days could not be determined by the earth's relation to the sun; and (3) the seventh day continues up to the present time, and is therefore already more than six thousand years long. However, the fact that the word "day" may denote a period of some length, does not prove that it is so used in Genesis 1. Neither does the absence of the sun prove that the days previous to its creation were long periods. And the seventh day of Gen. 2:2, 3, the day which God hallowed, does not continue up to the present, but terminated thousands of years ago. The literal interpretation of the word "day" is favored by the following considerations: (1) The Hebrew word *yom* (day) primarily denotes an ordinary day, and should be so understood unless the context demands another interpretation. (2) Genesis 1 would seem to shut us up to the literal interpretation by its repeated "and there was evening and there was morning." Each day had just one evening and one morning. If these days were the long periods of Geology, there must have been interminable nights of thousands of years. What would become of all vegetation during the long nights following the third day? (3) In Exodus 20:9-11 Israel is commanded to labour six days, because Jehovah made heaven and earth in six days. This would seem to imply that the word "day" should be taken in the ordinary sense. (4) The last three days were certainly ordinary days, for they were determined by the earth's relation to the sun. And if they were ordinary days, why not the others?

c. *The Work of the Separate Days.* The work of God on the separate days was as follows:

1) On the first day light was created, and by the separation of light and darkness day and night were constituted. This does not conflict with the idea that the sun and the stars were created on the fourth day; for these are not themselves lights, but light-bearers. The account of each day's work closes with the words, "and there was evening and there was morning." The days are reckoned from morning to morning. After twelve hours there was evening, and after another twelve hours there was morning.

2) The work of the second day was also a work of separation: the firmament was established by dividing the waters above and the waters below, that is, the clouds and the seas. Notice that the Hebrew word for "firmament" does not denote a solid vault, as some claim, but is equivalent to our word "expanse."

3) The work of separation is continued on the third day in the separation of the sea and the dry land, cf. Ps. 104:8. In addition to that the vegetable kingdom of plants and trees was established. By the word of His power God caused the earth to bring forth flowerless

plants, vegetables, and fruit-trees, each yielding fruit according to its kind. God evidently created the different species of plants, and each one of these could reproduce only its kind. The doctrine of evolution, of course, denies both of these assertions.

4) On the fourth day, sun, moon, and stars were created as light-bearers, to serve a variety of purposes: to divide day and night, to serve as signs of weather conditions and of important future events, to determine the succession of the seasons and of days and years, and to function as lights for the earth.

5) The fifth day brought the creation of birds and fishes, the inhabitants of the air and of the water. We should notice that these, too, were created after their kind, that is, the species were created.

6) Finally, the sixth day is marked by the climax of the work of creation. The higher classes of animals were created. They did not naturally develop out of the earth, but were clearly brought forth out of it by the creative fiat of God. The whole creative work was crowned by the creation of man, made in the image of God. His body was formed out of the dust of the earth, while his soul was an immediate creation of God.

7) God rested from His labours on the seventh day. This means first of all that He ceased from His creative work, but also that He took delight in what He had accomplished. His rest was like that of an artist who finds pro-

found satisfaction in the contemplation of his production. He rejoiced in the works of His hands, and radiated good-will towards His creatures.

2. THE DOCTRINE OF CREATION AND THE THEORY OF EVOLUTION. Some seem to think that the theory of evolution might take the place of the doctrine of creation in explaining the origin of the world. But this is clearly a mistake, for it offers no such explanation. Evolution is development, and all development presupposes the existence of something that develops. That which does not exist cannot develop into existence. For the explanation of the origin of the world, the evolutionist must either resort to the theory that matter is eternal, or to the doctrine of creation. We should distinguish between two forms of the doctrine of evolution:

a. *Naturalistic Evolution.* Naturalistic evolution assumes that from the simplest forms of matter and life all existing species of plants and animals (including man), and also the various phenomena of life, such as sentiency, intelligence, morality, and religion, developed by a perfectly natural process, purely as the result of natural forces resident in nature. It should be borne in mind, however, that this is as yet only an unproved assumption, and one that fails at several points. It cannot explain how the inorganic changed into the organic, nor how the brute changed into a rational, moral, and religious being. Some evolutionists themselves admit that it has failed to produce a single example of one species producing another distinct species. Moreover, it is absolutely in conflict with the narrative of creation as to the origin of species and of man, as to the original condition of man, and as to his fall in sin and consequent deterioration.

b. Theistic Evolution. Due to the failure of naturalistic evolution to give an adequate explanation of things, some Christian scholars take refuge in what is called "theistic" or "creative evolution." This postulates God as the almighty Worker back of the whole process of development. It amounts to this that God created the world by a process of evolution, a process of natural development, in which God does not miraculously intervene, except when this is absolutely necessary, as in the origination of life and of man. The very fact that it has a certain religious appeal makes this theory a dangerous hybrid. As a matter of fact it is no more in harmony with Scripture than naturalistic evolution. It, too, teaches that it took God millions of years to create the world, that God did not create the various species of plants and animals, that man at least on his physical side descended from the brute, and that there was no fall in the Biblical sense of the word.

Questions for Review:

What is creation? Was creation a free or a necessary act of God? How is God related to the world? What is meant by "the beginning" in Gen. 1:1? Is the word "create" always used in the same sense in Scripture? How can we prove that God created the world without the use of pre-existent material? What two views are there as to the final end of creation? In what sense is the glory of God the final end? What substitutes have been suggested for the doctrine of creation? What is the nature of the angels? What orders of angels are indicated in Scripture? What is the function of Gabriel and Michael? What is the work of the angels? What proof have we for the existence of evil angels? How should Gen. 1:1 be interpreted? Were the days mentioned in Gen. 1 ordinary days or long periods? Why? What did God create on each of the six days? Why is the doctrine of evolution inconsistent with the Biblical narrative of creation? Does the theory of creative evolution agree with Scripture?

References for Further Study:

Berkhof, *Reformed Dogmatics*, I, pp. 113-151; Hodge, *Outlines of Theology*, pp. 237-257; McPherson, *Christian Dogmatics*, pp. 163-174; Orr, *Side-Lights on Christian Doctrine*, pp. 55-66; Clarke, *The Christian Doctrine of God*, pp. 135-153; Price, *The Phantom of Organic Evolution;* Fairhurst, *Theistic Evolution.*

Christian faith is equally opposed to a pantheistic confusion of God and the world, and to a deistic separation of God from the world. This becomes evident in the doctrine of divine providence. The name "providence" is not found in Scripture, but the doctrine of providence is nevertheless eminently Scriptural. It concerns the provision which God makes for attaining the ends of His government, and the care which He manifests for all creatures.

A. **Providence in General.** Divine providence is *that work of God by which He preserves all His creatures, is active in all that transpires in the world, and directs all things to their appointed end.* This definition indicates that there are three elements in divine providence, namely, preservation, concurrence or cooperation, and government. The first has reference primarily to the *being,* the second to the *activity,* and the third to the *guidance* of all things.

1. Misconceptions of the Nature of Providence. In dealing with God's relation to the world we should be on our guard against two misconceptions:

a. *The Deistic Conception.* According to Deism God's concern with the world is of a very general nature. He created the world, established its law, set it in motion, and then withdrew from it. He looks on from a distance as the world runs its course according to the invariable laws of nature, and interferes with its regular operation at most only when something goes wrong.

Thus the world is like a machine which He has put into operation, and not at all like a vessel which He pilots from day to day.

b. *The Pantheistic Conception.* Pantheism does not recognize the distinction between God and the world. It identifies the two, and therefore really leaves no room for providence in the proper sense of the word. The whole course of nature is simply the self-revelation of God, a self-revelation that leaves no room for the independent operation of secondary causes. The so-called laws of nature are simply modes of the direct activity of God. He is in a very direct sense the author of all that transpires in the world. Even the acts which we ascribe to man are really acts of God. According to this system man is not a free moral being, and is not responsible for his acts.

2. THE OBJECTS OF DIVINE PROVIDENCE. It is customary to distinguish between general and special providence, the former denoting God's control of the universe as a whole, and the latter His care for each part of it. Some even speak of a very special providence respecting the children of God. Scripture clearly teaches God's providential government and control (*a*) over the universe at large, Ps. 103:19; Eph. 1:11; (*b*) over the physical world, Ps. 104:14; Matt. 5:45; (*c*) over the brute creation, Ps. 104:21, 28; Matt. 6:26; (*d*) over the affairs of nations, Job 12:23; Acts 17:6; (*e*) over man's birth and lot in life, Ps. 139:16; Gal. 1:15,

16; (f) over things seemingly accidental or insignificant, Prov. 16:33; Matt. 10:30; (*g*) in the protection of the righteous, Ps. 4:8; 121:3; Rom. 8:28; (*h*) in supplying the wants of God's people, Deut. 8:3; Phil. 4:19; (*i*) in giving answers to prayer, Ps. 65:2; Matt. 7:7; and (*j*) in the exposure and punishment of the wicked, Ps. 7:12, 13; 11:6. They who believe that nature is controlled entirely by an iron-clad system of laws, which ties even the hands of God, usually deny all special providences. They do not believe that God can perform miracles, nor that He can answer prayer. Others are of the opinion that, while He controls the big things of life, He pays no attention to the smaller ones. But if He does not heed the smaller things of life, He can never control the larger ones.

B. **The Elements of Providence in Particular.** The definition given of providence in the preceding clearly indicates that there are three elements in providence; and these deserve special consideration.

1. DIVINE PRESERVATION. *Preservation is that continuous work of God by which He upholds all things.* This does not mean, as some pantheists assume, that God continues to create the world from moment to moment, nor simply, as the deists think, that He withdraws His hand from the world and does not destroy it. It proceeds on the assumption that the world has a distinct existence apart from God, but that it nevertheless has the ground of its continued existence in God and not in itself.

It continues to exist in virtue of a continued exercise of divine power by which all things are maintained in being and action. God alone is sovereign and absolutely independent, and the creature is and always remains dependent on Him. This doctrine is clearly taught in the following passages, Ps. 63:8; Neh. 9:6; Acts 17:28; Col. 1:17; Heb. 1:3.

2. Divine Concurrence. Concurrence may be defined as *that work of God by which He co-operates with all His creatures and causes them to act precisely as they do.* This means that there are real causes in the world, such as the forces of nature and the will of man, but that these causes do not work independently of God. God is operative in every act of His creature, not only in their good but also in their evil acts. He stimulates them to action, accompanies their action at every moment, and makes this action effective. We should guard against the idea that God and man have an equal part in the work, for God ever remains the primary cause, without which man can do nothing; and against the notion that the two divide the work, God doing a part and man a part. The same deed is in its entirety both a deed of God and a deed of the creature. This should be so conceived, however, that where God co-operates with man the responsibility for the deed remains that of the moral creature. God cannot be held responsible for the sins of His creatures. This must be maintained in spite of the fact that we cannot fully explain what is certainly true, namely, that God's concurrent action involves no responsibility on His part for the evil of man. Scripture plainly teaches that God

works in the entire creation and in all His creatures, Ps. 104:20, 21, 30; Amos 3:6; Deut. 8:18; Matt. 5:45; 10:29; Acts 14:17. It is also clear that sinful acts are under divine control, Gen. 45:5; 50:20; Ex. 14:17; Isa. 66:4; Rom. 2:4; 9:22; II Thess. 2:11 that God restrains the sinful works of the sinner, Gen. 6:3; Job 1:12; 2:6; Ps. 76:10; Isa. 10:15; Acts 7:51; and that He overrules evil for good, Gen. 50:20; Ps. 76:10; Acts 3:13.

3. Divine Government. The divine government is *the continued activity of God whereby He rules all things, so that they answer to the purpose of their existence.* Both the Old and the New Testament teach us that God is King of the universe and rules all things according to His divine good pleasure. The notion that in the new dispensation the idea of God's sovereignty is supplanted by that of His Fatherhood, is not in agreement with such passages as Matt. 6:33; I Tim. 1:17; 6:15; Rev. 19:6; God adapts His rule to the nature of the creatures which He governs; His government of the physical world differs from that of the spiritual world. This government is universal, Ps. 103:19; Dan. 4:34, 35; Ps. 22:28, 29, but also relates to particulars. The most significant things, Matt. 10:29-31, that which is seemingly accidental, Prov. 16:33, the good deeds of man, Phil. 2:13, as well as their evil deeds, Acts 14:16 — they are all under divine control. God is King of Israel, Isa. 33:22, but He also rules among the nations, Ps. 47:9. Nothing can ever be withdrawn from His government.

C. **Extraordinary Providences or Miracles.** Among the special providences of God we may also reckon the miracles, in which God does not work through secondary causes or employs them in an unusual way. McPherson gives the following definition of a miracle: "A miracle is something done without recourse to the ordinary means of production, a result called forth directly by the first cause (God) without the mediation, at least in the usual way, of second causes." The distinctive thing in the miracle is that it results from the exercise of the supernatural power of God. And this means, of course, that it is not brought about in the usual way by means of secondary causes that operate according to the laws of nature. Some maintain that miracles are impossible on the ground that they imply a violation of the laws of nature. But this is not the case. The so-called laws of nature merely represent God's usual method of working in nature. It is His good pleasure to work ordinarily in an orderly way through secondary causes, that is, through the powers of nature or through the activity of man. But this does not mean that He cannot depart from the established order and produce extraordinary effects by a single act of His will, and that without violating the order of nature. Even man can counteract the laws of nature without disturbing them in any way. He can lift up his hand and throw a ball into the air in spite of the law of gravitation. And if this is possible for man, it is all the more possible for the omnipotent God.

Questions for Review:

How is the doctrine of providence related to that of creation? What is divine providence? What is the deistic view of God's relation to the world? How does the pantheist conceive of this relation? What is the difference between general and special providence? Why do some deny special providence? Which are the objects of divine providence? What is meant by divine preservation? By divine concurrence? How should we conceive of this concurrence? To what difficult problem does it give rise? How far does the divine government extend? What is a miracle? Why are miracles considered by some to be impossible?

References for Further Study:

Berkhof, *Reformed Dogmatics*, I, pp. 152-168: Hodge, *Outlines of Theology*, pp. 258-295; McPherson, *Christian Dogmatics*, pp. 174-184; Orr, *Side-Lights on Christian Doctrine*, pp. 66-71; Clarke, *The Christian Doctrine of God*, pp. 174-212; Thomson, *The Christian Miracles and the Conclusions of Science;* Bruin, *Het Christelijk Geloof en de Beoefening der Natuurwetenschap*, pp. 110-138.

THE DOCTRINE OF MAN IN RELATION TO GOD

THE DOCTRINE OF MAN IN RELATION TO GOD

MAN IN HIS ORIGINAL STATE

The Constitutional Nature of Man

From the discussion of the doctrine of God we pass on to that of man, the crown of God's handiwork. The study of man in theology should not be confused with the science of anthropology, though it bears the same name. It does not make man as such, but very particularly man *in relation* to God the object of its consideration and discussion. Under the present heading the essential constituents of human nature, and the origin of the soul in the individuals of the race will be considered.

A. **The Essential Elements of Human Nature.** There are especially two views respecting the number of elements that go to make up the essential nature of man.

1. Dichotomy or the View that Man Consists of Two Parts, Body and Soul. The usual view of the constitution of man is that he consists of two, and only two, distinct parts, namely, body and soul or spirit. This is in harmony with the self-consciousness of man, which clearly testifies to the fact that man consists of a material and a spiritual element. It is also borne out by the study of Scripture, which speaks of man as consisting of "body and soul," Matt. 6:25; 10:28, or of "body and spirit," Eccl. 12:7; I Cor. 5:3, 5. The two words, "soul" and "spirit" do not denote two different

elements in man, but serve to designate the one spiritual substance of man. This is proved by the following consideration: (*a*) There are several passages which clearly proceed on the assumption that man consists of only two parts, Rom. 8:10; I Cor. 5:5; 7:34; II Cor. 7:1; Eph. 2:3; Col. 2:5. (*b*) Death is sometimes described as the giving up of the soul, Gen. 35:18; I Kings 17:21; Acts 15:26; and in other cases as the giving up of the spirit, Ps. 31:5; Luke 23:46; Acts 7:59. (*c*) The immaterial element of the dead is in some instances termed "soul," Rev. 9:6; 20:4, and in others "spirit," I Pet. 3:19; Heb. 12:23. These two terms merely serve to designate the spiritual element of man from two different points of view. The word "spirit" contemplates it as the principle of life and action which controls the body; while the word "soul" refers to it as the personal subject in man, which thinks and feels and wills, and in some cases particularly as the seat of affections, Gen. 2:7; Ps. 62:1; 63:1; Ps. 103:1, 2.

2. Trichotomy, or the View that Man Consists of Three Parts, Body, Soul, and Spirit. Alongside of the usual view another one arose, which conceives of man as consisting of three parts, body, soul, and spirit. This conception of man did not result from the study of Scripture, but was born of the study of Greek philosophy. It was adopted by several German and English theologians. These do not agree, however, as to the nature of the soul, nor as to the relation in which it stands to the other parts of human nature. Some regard the

soul as the principle of the animal life in man, and the spirit as the principle of the higher rational and moral life. Others consider the soul to be a sort of intermediate element, which furnishes the point of contact between the body and the spirit. Biblical support for this view was sought particularly in I Thess. 5:23 and Heb. 4:12, but these do not prove the point. It is true that Paul speaks in the first passage of "spirit and soul and body," but this does not necessarily mean that he regards these as three distinct elements in man rather than as three different aspects of man. When Jesus summarizes the first table of the law by saying, "Thou shalt love the Lord thy God with all thy heart, and with all thy soul, and with all thy mind," in Matt. 22:37, He does not have in mind three distinct substances. Such expressions simply serve to emphasize the fact that the *whole man* is intended. Moreover, Hebrews 4:12 should not be taken to mean that the Word of God, penetrating to the inner man, makes separation between his soul and his spirit, which would naturally imply that these two are different substances; but simply that it brings about a separation in both of these aspects of man between the thoughts and intents of the heart.

B. **The Origin of the Soul in Each Individual.** There are three theories respecting the origin of the soul in each individual.

1. PRE-EXISTENTIANISM. Some speculative theologians advocated the theory that the souls of men

existed in a previous state, and that certain occurrences in that former state account for the condition in which those souls are now found. It was thought to afford the most natural explanation of the fact that all men are born as sinners. This theory meets with little favor at present.

2. TRADUCIANISM. According to Traducianism the souls of men are propagated along with the bodies by generation, and are therefore transmitted to the children by the parents. Scripture support for it is found in the fact that God ceased from the work of creation after He had made man, Gen. 2:2; that the Bible says nothing about the creation of Eve's soul, Gen. 2:23; I Cor. 11:8; and that descendants are said to be in the loins of their fathers, Gen. 46:26; Heb. 7:9, 10. Furthermore, it would seem to be favored (*a*) by the analogy of the animal world, where both body and soul are passed on from the old to the young; (*b*) by the inheritance of mental peculiarities and family traits which inhere in the soul rather than in the body; and (*c*) by the inheritance of moral depravity or sin, which is a matter of the soul rather than of the body. This theory is burdened with certain difficulties, however, of which the following are the most important: (*a*) It either makes the parents in some sense creators of the soul of the child, or proceeds on the assumption that the soul of the parents can split itself up into several souls, which is contrary to the doctrine that the soul does not admit of division. (*b*) It proceeds on the assumption that God works only in a mediate manner after He has finished the creation

of the world. But this is an unproved assumption. God often works immediately in the performance of miracles and in some parts of the work of redemption. (*c*) It makes it very difficult to guard the sinlessness of Jesus, if He derived both His body and soul from the sinful Mary.

3. CREATIONISM. The creationist view is to the effect that each individual soul is an immediate creation of God, which owes its origin to a direct creative act, of which the time cannot be precisely determined. The soul is supposed to be created pure, but to become sinful even before birth by entering into that complex of sin by which humanity as a whole is burdened. This theory is more in harmony with Scripture than the preceding one, since the Bible throughout represents body and soul as having different origins, Eccl. 12:7; Isa. 42:5; Zech. 12:1; Heb. 12:9; cf. Num. 16:22. Moreover, it is far more in harmony with the nature of the human soul than traducianism, since it safeguards the spiritual and therefore indivisible nature of the soul. And, finally, it also avoids the pitfalls in connection with the doctrine of Christ, since it enables us to guard the sinlessness of Jesus. This does not mean, however, that it is free from all difficulties. It makes it rather hard to account for the re-appearance of the mental and moral traits of the parents in the children. In addition to that it ascribes to the beast nobler powers of propagation than to man, for the beast multiplies itself after its kind. And, finally, it is in danger of making God at least indirectly responsible for sin, since He puts a pure

soul into a complex which will inevitably corrupt it. In spite of these difficulties, however, it deserves the preference.

Questions for Review:

What is the dichotomic view of the essential elements of human nature? How can this view be proved from Scripture? What is the trichotomic view? What Scriptural proof is advanced for it? What objections are there to this view? What theories are there as to the origin of the soul in the individual? What does Pre-existentianism teach? What is the traducianist view? What arguments can be advanced in favor of it? What objections are there to it? What is the theory of creationism? What considerations favor this view? What objections are there to it?

References for Further Study:

Berkhof, *Reformed Dogmatics*, I, pp. 179-190; Hodge, *Outlines of Theology*, pp. 299, 300, 351, 352; McPherson, *Christian Theology*, pp. 192-201; Laidlaw, *The Biblical Doctrine of Man*, pp. 49-138; Weidner, *The Doctrine of Man*, pp. 13-23, 28-35.

Man as the Image of God and in the Covenant of Works

In the discussion of the moral and spiritual condition of man, it is of the utmost importance to consider first of all his original state. The two subjects that call for special consideration here are man as the image of God, and man in the covenant of works.

A. **Man as the Image of God.**

1. The Scriptural Teaching Respecting Man as the Image-Bearer of God. The Bible represents man as the crown of God's handiwork, whose special glory consists in this that he is created in the image of God and after His likeness, Gen. 1:26, 27. Attempts have been made to distinguish sharply between the terms "image" and "likeness." Some were of the opinion that the former referred to the body, and the latter to the soul. Augustine held that they had reference respectively to the intellectual and to the moral qualities of the soul. And Roman Catholics regard "image" as an indication of the natural gifts bestowed on man, and "likeness" as a designation of the gifts with which he was supernaturally endowed, that is, his original righteousness. In all probability however, the words are used as synonyms and both refer to the same thing, though from a slightly different point of view. The following passages clearly show that they are used interchangeably, Gen. 1:26, 27; 5:1; 9:6; I Cor. 11:7; Col. 3:10; Jas. 3:9. The words

"after our likeness" in Gen. 1:26 apparently serve to stress the fact that the image is most like or very similar. The doctrine of man's creation in the image of God is of the greatest importance, for the image is that which is most distinctive in man, that which distinguishes him from the animals and from every other creature. As far as we know even the angels do not share that honour with him. They certainly are not the image-bearers of God in the sense and to the extent that man is.

2. Historical Conceptions of the Image of God in Man. There are especially three important historic conceptions of the image of God in man.

a. *The Roman Catholic View.* Roman Catholics believe that God at creation endowed man with certain natural gifts, such as the spirituality of the soul, the freedom of the will, and the immortality of the body. These natural endowments constitute the image of God. In this purely natural condition of man, however, there was a tendency of the lower appetites and passions to rebel against the higher powers of reason and conscience. This tendency was not in itself sin, but would naturally become sin as soon as the will yielded to it and it passed into voluntary action. In order to enable man to hold his lower nature in check, however, God endowed man with a supernatural gift, called original righteousness. And this is supposed to constitute man's likeness to God.

b. *The Lutheran View.* The Lutherans are not all agreed as to what constitutes the image of God.

The prevailing opinion, however, is that it consists only in those spiritual qualities with which man was endowed at creation, and which are generally called original righteousness. These qualities consist in true knowledge, righteousness, and holiness. In taking this view of the matter, they do not sufficiently recognize the essential nature of man, as distinct from that of the animals on the one hand, and that of the angels on the other hand. If the image of God, consisting in true knowledge, righteousness, and holiness, constitutes the very essence of man, the question arises, how can man lose this image, as he did by sin, and still remain man. And, again, if the image of God so understood determines the essential nature of man, what essential difference is there between men and the angels, who also possess these spiritual qualities?

c. *The Reformed View.* The Reformed have a far more comprehensive view of the image of God than either the Roman Catholics or the Lutherans. They usually distinguish between the image of God in a restricted, and the image of God in a more comprehensive sense. The former consists in the spiritual qualities with which man was created, namely, true knowledge, righteousness and holiness. That these belong to the image of God, follows from Eph. 4:24 and Col. 3:10. The image of God in the more comprehensive sense of the word is found in the fact that man is a spiritual being, rational, moral, and immortal, in the body, not as a material substance, but as the organ of the soul, and in his dominion over the lower creation. Notice that Scripture links up this dominion immediately with man's creation in the image of God, Gen. 1:26. It is only in virtue of the image of God in this broader sense that man, even after he has lost the image of God in the restricted sense, consisting in true knowledge, righteousness, and holiness, can still be called the image-bearer of God, Gen. 9:6; I Cor. 11:7; 15:49; Jas. 3:9.

B. **Man in the Covenant of Works.** The natural relationship between God and man was supplemented by a covenant relationship, in which God made the future perfection and bliss contingent on the temporary obedience of man. This covenant is known as the covenant of works.

1. Scripture Proof for the Covenant of Works. In view of the fact that some deny the existence of the covenant of works, it is highly desirable to examine its Scriptural basis. The Scripture proof for it is found in the following:

a. All the elements of a covenant are indicated in Scripture; and if the elements are present, we have not only the right but also the duty to combine them and to give the doctrine so construed an appropriate name. There are clearly two parties, God and man, entering into an agreement; there is a condition, the condition of obedience, which God imposes on man, Gen. 2:16, 17; and there is also a promise, the promise of eternal life. This is implied in the alternative of death as the result of disobedience, in such passages as Rom. 10:5 and Gal. 3:12, and in the symbolical significance of the tree of life, Gen. 3:22.

b. The parallel which Paul draws between Adam and Christ in Rom. 5:12-21, in connection with the imputation of sin on the one hand and the imputation of righteousness on the other hand, can only be explained on the assumption that Adam, like Christ, was the head of a covenant. If we share in the righteousness of Christ, because He is our representative, then it follows that we share in the guilt of Adam for the same reason.

c. There is one passage in Scripture which speaks of Adam as having transgressed the covenant. In Hosea 6:7 we read: "But they like Adam have transgressed the covenant." (Am. Rev.) This rendering of the text corresponds with that in the Dutch Bible. The Authorized Version, however, renders: "But they like men have transgressed the covenant." The other rendering is clearly to be preferred, and is also favored by the parallel passage in Job 31:33.

2. THE ELEMENTS OF THE COVENANT OF WORKS. The following elements must be distinguished.

a. The Covenanting Parties. A covenant is always a compact between two parties. In the case of the covenant of works there was, on the one hand, the triune God, the sovereign Lord of all creation, binding Himself by an act of condescending grace to give to man, on the condition of obedience, the blessings of eternal life and perfect happiness. And, on the other hand, there was Adam, the representative of the human race, absolutely dependent and without any claim on God, graciously permitted to covenant with God for himself and his posterity, and assuming the responsibility of obeying God implicitly.

b. *The Promise of the Covenant.* The great promise of the covenant was the promise of life in the fullest sense of the word, that is, not merely a continuance of the natural existence of man, but life raised to the highest development of perennial bliss and glory. Adam was indeed created in a state of positive holiness, and was not subject to the law of death. But he did not yet possess the highest privileges in store for man; he was not yet raised above the possibility of erring, sinning, and dying. He did not yet possess the highest degree of holiness, nor enjoy life in all its fulness.

c. *The Condition of the Covenant.* The promise in the covenant of works was not unconditional. The condition was that of perfect, unconditional obedience. The divine law can demand no less than perfect obedience, and the positive command not to eat of the fruit of the tree of knowledge of good and evil was clearly a test of pure obedience. In it the demands of the law of God converged, so to speak, in a single point. The great question had to be settled, whether man would obey God implicitly, or follow the guidance of his own insight.

d. *The Penalty of the Covenant.* The penalty that was threatened in case of transgression was death in the most inclusive sense of the word, physical, spiritual, and eternal. The fundamental idea of death is not that of extinction of being, but that of separation from the source of life, and the resulting dissolution of misery and woe. It consists in the separation of body and soul; but also, and this is even more fundamental, in the separation of the soul from God.

e. *The Sacrament (s) of the Covenant.* Opinions vary a great deal respecting the sacrament(s) of the covenant of works. Though some speak of two, three, or even four sacraments, the most prevalent opinion is that the tree of life was the only sacrament. This would seem to be the only one that finds any warrant in Scripture. In all probability the tree of life was an appointed symbol and pledge or seal of life. The words in Gen. 3:22 should then be understood sacramentally.

3. The Present Validity of the Covenant of Works. The Arminians of the seventeenth century maintained the position that the covenant of works was wholly abrogated by the fall of Adam, so that his descendants are entirely free from its obligations. In opposition to them the Reformed took the position that it is partly a thing of the past, and partly still in force.

a. *The Sense in Which it is Not Abrogated.* The demand for perfect obedience still holds. The curse and punishment pronounced on the transgressor still apply to all those who continue in sin. And the conditional promise is also still in effect. God might have withdrawn it, but did not, cf. Lev. 18:5; Gal. 3:12. It is evident, however, that after the fall no one can comply with the condition.

b. The Sense in Which it is Abrogated. The special obligations of this covenant have ceased for those who really live in the covenant of grace. This does not mean that these obligations are simply set aside and disregarded, but that they were met by the Mediator for all His people. Moreover, the covenant of works is abrogated as an appointed way or means to obtain eternal life, for as such it is powerless after the fall of man.

Questions for Review:

Why is the doctrine of the image of God in man important? Do the words "image" and "likeness" denote different things? What is the Roman Catholic view of the image and likeness of God in man? What the Lutheran view of the image of God in man? What objection is there to this view? What distinction do the Reformed apply to the image of God in man? What constitutes the image of God in the restricted sense? In the more comprehensive sense? What Bible proof have we for the covenant of works? Which are the parties of the covenant? What is the promise, the condition, the penalty, and the sacrament of the covenant? In what sense does the covenant still hold? In what sense is it abrogated?

References for Further Study:

Berkhof, *Reformed Dogmatics*, I, pp. 191-206; Hodge, *Outlines of Theology*, pp. 296-314; McPherson, *Christian Dogmatics*, pp. 201-210; Orr, *Side-Lights on Christian Doctrine*, pp. 75-89; Kuyper, *De Leer der Verbonden* (in the series, *Uit het Woord*), pp. 107-229; A. Kuyper, Jr., *De Vastigheid des Verbonds*, pp. 33-45.

MAN IN THE STATE OF SIN

The Origin and Essential Character of Sin

A. **The Origin of Sin in the Fall of Man.** The problem of the origin of sin is one that necessarily forces itself upon the attention of thoughtful men, and still continues to baffle those who are not satisfied with the Biblical account of it. Some earlier and later theologians simply pushed the problem back a step by saying that the souls of men sinned in some previous existence, and that consequently all men are now born as sinners. The great philosopher, Immanuel Kant, recognized the existence of radical evil in man, but despaired of explaining its origin. Evolutionists find its explanation in the tendencies, impulses, and passions inherited from the brute. The Bible, however, directs our attention to the fall of man. It teaches us that the root of all moral evil in the world lies in the first sin of Adam, the natural and representative head of the human race.

1. The Nature of the First Sin. The first sin consisted in man's eating of the tree of the knowledge of good and evil. This eating was sinful simply because God had forbidden it. We do not know what kind of tree this was. It was called "the tree of the knowledge of good and evil," because it was destined to reveal (*a*) whether man's future state would be good or evil; and (*b*) whether man would allow God to determine for him what was good and evil, or would undertake to determine this for

himself. The first sin was of a typical character, clearly revealing the essential nature of sin. This lies in the fact that man refused to subject himself to the will of God and to have God determine the course of his life, and decided to settle this for himself. Different elements can be distinguished in this first sin. In the intellect it revealed itself as unbelief and pride, in the will as the desire to be like God, and in the affections as an unholy satisfaction in eating of the forbidden fruit.

2. The Occasion of the First Sin. The fall of man was occasioned by the temptation of the serpent, who sowed in man's mind the seeds of distrust and unbelief. Though it was undoubtedly the intention of the tempter to cause Adam, the head of the covenant, to fall, yet he addressed himself to Eve, probably because she (*a*) was not the covenant head and therefore would not have the same sense of responsibility; (*b*) had not received the command of God directly but only indirectly, and would consequently be more susceptible to argumentation and doubt; and (*c*) would undoubtedly prove to be the most effective agent in reaching the heart of Adam. The speaking serpent has been a great stumbling-block for many and often led to a figurative or symbolical interpretation of the narrative of the fall. Scripture clearly intimates, however, that the serpent was but the instrument of Satan, and that Satan was the real tempter, who was working in and through the serpent, just as in the days of Jesus' ministry he worked in men and swine, John 8:44; Rom. 16:20; II Cor. 11:3; Rev. 12:9.

3. THE RESULTS OF THE FIRST SIN. In consequence of the first sin man lost the image of God in the restricted sense of the word, true knowledge of God, righteousness, and holiness; and, moreover, became totally depraved, that is, depraved in every part of his being and utterly incapable of doing any spiritual good. This change in the actual condition of man also reflected itself in his consciousness. There was a sense of pollution, revealing itself in a feeling of shame, and a sense of guilt, which found expression in an accusing conscience and in fear of God. In addition to that man became subject to the law of death in the fullest sense of the word, Gen. 3:19; Rom. 5:12; 6:23, though the full execution of the sentence was stayed. Finally, man was driven from paradise and barred from the tree of life, which symbolized the life that was promised in the covenant of works.

B. **The Essential Character of Sin.** .There are many erroneous conceptions of the real character of sin. It is only from Scripture that we can learn just what sin is. In connection with the Scriptural idea of sin several points should be emphasized.

1. SIN IS A SPECIFIC KIND OF EVIL. In the present day many people show a tendency to substitute the word "evil" for "sin." But this is a poor substitute. While it is perfectly true that all sin is evil, it cannot be said with equal truth that all evil is sin. Sickness may be regarded as an evil, but can hardly be called a sin. Moreover, the modern tendency to speak of evil rather than of sin finds its explanation largely in the fact that people prefer to

regard sin simply as a disease or as an imperfection, for which man can hardly be held responsible. The Bible teaches us to regard sin as a specific kind of evil, as a moral evil for which man is directly responsible and which brings him under a sentence of condemnation.

2. Sin Has an Absolute Character. In the ethical sphere the contrast between good and evil is absolute. There is no neutral condition between the two. This is the clear teaching of Scripture. He who does not love God from the heart, is thereby already characterized as evil. The Bible knows of no position of moral neutrality. It urges the wicked to turn to righteousness, and frequently speaks of the righteous as falling into evil; but it does not contain a single indication that either the one or the other ever lands in a neutral position. Man is either on the right or on the wrong side, Matt. 10:32, 33; 12:30; Luke 11:23; Jas. 2:10.

3. Sin Always Has Relation to God and His Will. Modern theology insists on interpreting sin in a social way, that is, with reference to one's fellowmen. Sin is wrong done to one's fellow-beings. But this misses the point entirely, for such a wrong can be called sin only in view of the fact that it is contrary to the will of God. Sin is correctly defined as "lack of conformity to the law of God," and this means that it is the opposite of that love to God which is required by the divine law. It is quite evident that Scripture always contemplates sin in relation to God, and the law, either as written on the tablets of man's heart or as given by Moses,

Rom. 1:32; 2:12-14; 4:15; 5:13; Jas. 2:9, 10; I John 3:4.

4. Sin Includes Both Guilt and Pollution. Sin is first of all guilt, that is, it is a transgression of the law, which makes men liable to the punishment of a righteous God. Many indeed deny that sin includes guilt, but this denial goes contrary to the fact that the sinner is threatened and actually visited with punishment, and to the plain statements of Scripture, such as Matt. 6:12; Rom. 3:19; 5:18; Eph. 2:3. Sin is also pollution, an inherent corruption to which every sinner is subject. Guilt always carries pollution with it. Everyone who is guilty in Adam is, as a result, also born with a corrupt nature. The pollution of sin is clearly taught in such passages as Job 14:4; Jer. 17:9; Matt. 7:15-20; Rom. 8:5-8; Eph. 4:17-19.

5. Sin Has Its Seat in the Heart. Sin does not reside in any one faculty of the soul, but in the heart, which in the psychology of Scripture is the central organ of the soul, out of which are the issues of life, Prov. 4:23. And from this center its influence and operations spread to the intellect, the will, the affections, in short, to the whole man, including his body. This view is clearly based on the representations of Scripture in such passages as the following: Prov. 4:23; Jer. 17:9; Matt. 15:19, 20; Luke 6:45; Heb. 3:12.

6. Sin Does Not Consist in Outward Acts Only. Over against Pelagians and Semi-Pelagians of every description the fact should be emphasized that sin consists not only in outward acts, but also in

sinful habits and in a sinful condition of the heart. These three are related to one another as follows: the sinful state is the basis of the sinful habits, and these, in turn, lead on to the sinful deeds. That the evil thoughts, affections, and intents of the heart should also be regarded as sinful follows from such passages as the following: Matt. 5:22, 28; Rom 7:7; Gal. 5:17, 24.

C. **Divergent Views of Sin.** There are several views of sin which are not at all in harmony with the Scriptural representation of it. Just a few of these can be briefly indicated here.

1. THE PELAGIAN VIEW OF SIN. The Pelagian does not believe in original sin, and therefore does not share the conviction that every man is born as a sinner. Adam was created, and every one of his descendants is born, in a state of moral neutrality, neither positively good nor positively bad. Sin is the result of the free choice of every man. No one need sin, if he does not want to. There is no such thing as a sinful nature or a sinful character; neither are there sinful dispositions. Sin consists only in a deliberate choice of evil by a will which is perfectly free, and can just as well choose and follow the good.

2. THE ROMAN CATHOLIC VIEW OF SIN. According to the Roman Catholics original sin is primarily a negative condition, consisting in the absence of that original righteousness with which man was supernaturally endowed. It is a state of aversion to

God, and therefore a state of sin. Actual sin consists only in those actions of man which are the result of a deliberate choice of the will. The unholy disposition, desires, and affections that lie back of these deeds may be of a sinful nature and tend to produce sin, but cannot themselves be considered as sin in the strictest sense of the word.

3. The Evolutionary View of Sin. In modern liberal theology the evolutionary view of sin is very popular, though it is not always presented in exactly the same way. It was developed particularly in the works of Tennant. According to him there are many impulses and qualities which man has inherited from the brute. These are not in themselves sin, but naturally become sin under certain conditions. There is a gradually awakening moral sense in man, which condemns those impulses and qualities. And these actually become sin, if man continues to yield to them in spite of the condemning voice of conscience. Sin consists in this, therefore, that man, as a moral being, still allows himself to be controlled by the appetites and passions of his sensual nature rather than by the aspirations of his higher nature.

Questions for Review:

What is the Biblical view of the origin of sin? Can you name any other views? What was the first sin? Why was the tree concerned called "the tree of the knowledge of good and evil"? What elements can be distinguished in the first sin? Why did the tempter approach Eve? Can you prove that Satan was the real tempter? Which were the results of the first sin? Why is it undesirable to substitute the word "evil" for "sin"? Is it possible for man to occupy a neutral position, neither good nor bad? Is it correct to interpret sin with reference to man?

How can we prove that sin includes guilt? Where does sin have its seat in man? How can we prove that sin does not consist exclusively in outward acts? What is the Pelagian, the Roman Catholic, and the evolutionary view of sin?

References for Further Study:

Berkhof, *Reformed Dogmatics,* I, pp. 207-225; Hodge, *Outlines of Theology,* pp. 315-324; McPherson, *Christian Dogmatics,* pp. 220-242; Orr, *Side-Lights on Christian Doctrine,* pp. 93-99; Candlish, *The Biblical Doctrine of Sin,* pp. 9-44.

Sin in the Life of the Human Race

A. **The Connection Between Adam's Sin and that of His Descendants.** The Pelagians deny that there is any necessary connection between the sin of Adam and that of his descendants. The earlier Arminians maintain that man has inherited his natural corruption from Adam, but is in no sense responsible for the sin of the latter, while the later or Wesleyan Arminians admit that man's inborn corruption also involves guilt. There are especially three different ways of explaining the connection between the sin of Adam and that of his descendants.

1. The Realistic Theory. The earliest of the three is the realistic theory, which is to the effect that God originally created one general human nature, which in course of time is divided into as many parts as there are human individuals. Adam possessed the whole of this general human nature; and as the result of his sin it became guilty and polluted. Consequently every individual part of it also shares in this guilt and pollution. This theory does not explain why we are responsible only for the first sin of Adam, and not for the rest of his sins, committed by the same human nature, nor for the sins of the rest of our forefathers. Neither does it give an answer to the question, why Christ was not held responsible for the sin of Adam, for He certainly shared the very nature that sinned in Adam.

2. The Theory of Immediate Imputation (Covenant of Works). According to this view Adam stood in a twofold relation to his descendants. He was the natural head of the human race, the progenitor of all the children of men. To this natural relationship God added the covenant relationship, in virtue of which Adam was also the representative head of all his descendants. When he sinned in this representative capacity, the guilt of his sin was naturally imputed to all those whom he represented; and as the result of this they are all born in a corrupt state. This theory explains why the descendants of Adam are responsible only for the one sin which he committed as head of the covenant, why they are not responsible for the sins of their forbears, and why Christ, who is not a human person, does not share in the guilt of Adam.

3. The Theory of Mediate Imputation. The last theory proceeds on the assumption that the guilt of Adam's sin is not directly imputed to his descendants, and advocates the following idea: Adam's descendants derive their innate corruption from him by the process of natural generation; and on the basis of that inherent depravity which they share with him they are also considered guilty of his apostasy. They are not born corrupt because they are guilty in Adam, but they are considered guilty because they are born corrupt. If this theory were consistent, it ought to teach the mediate imputation of the sins of all previous generations to those following, for their joint corruption is passed on by generation. Moreover, by holding that our moral

corruption is *imputed* to us as sin, it clearly implies that this corruption would not be guilt, if it were not so imputed; but there is no moral corruption that is not at the same time guilt and that does not make one liable to punishment.

B. **Original and Actual Sin.** In a general way sin is divided into original and actual sin.

1. ORIGINAL SIN. In virtue of their connection with Adam all men are, after the fall, born in a sinful state and condition. This state is called original sin and is the inward root of all the actual sins that defile the life of man. It contains two elements:

   a. *Original Guilt.* This means that the guilt of Adam's sin is imputed to us. Since he sinned as our representative, we are guilty in him. This means that the state in which we are born is one of wilful violation of the law, and that we are therefore by nature liable to punishment. The Arminians of the seventeenth century and the advocates of modern liberal theology both deny that original sin involves original guilt. Yet this is certainly the case according to the plain teachings of Scripture, Rom. 5:12-19; Eph. 2:3.

   b. *Original Pollution.* The descendants of Adam are not only burdened with his guilt, but also inherit from him their moral pollution. They are not only deprived of original righteousness, but also have an inherent positive disposition toward sin. This pollution may be considered from two different points of view:

1) *As total depravity.* This does not mean that every man is as bad as he can be, cannot do good in any sense of the word, and has absolutely no sense of admiration for the true, the good, and the beautiful; but simply that the inherent corruption extends to every part of man's nature, and that there is in him no spiritual good, that is good in relation to God, at all, but only moral perversion. The total depravity of man is denied by Pelagians, Socinians, and the earlier Arminians, but is clearly taught by Scripture, John 5:42; Rom. 7:18, 23; 8:7; II Cor. 7:1; Eph. 4:18; II Tim. 3:2-4; Tit. 1:15; Heb. 3:12.

2) *As total inability.* Here, again, it is necessary to distinguish. Reformed theologians generally maintain that the sinner is still able to perform (*a*) natural good; (*b*) civil good or civil righteousness; and (*c*) externally religious good. He may perform acts and manifest sentiments that deserve the sincere approval and gratitude of their fellow-men, and that even meet in a measure with the approval of God. Yet when these works are considered in relation to God, they are radically defective, since they are not prompted by love to God, nor by any regard for the will of God as requiring them. Moreover, man cannot change his fundamental preference for sin to love for God, nor even make an approach to such a change. There is abundant Scriptural support for this doctrine, John 1:13; 3:5; 6:44;

8:34; 15:4, 5; Rom. 7:18, 24; 8:7, 8; I Cor. 2:14; II Cor. 3:5; Eph. 2:1, 8-10; Heb. 11:6.

2. Actual Sin.

a. *The Difference Between Actual and Original Sin.* The term "actual sin" denotes not only sins consisting in outward acts, but also all those conscious thoughts and volitions which proceed from original sin. They are the sins which an individual performs, in distinction from his inherited nature and inclination. While original sin is one, actual sins are manifold. They may be sins of the inner life, such as pride, envy, hatred, sensual lusts and evil desires; or sins of the outer life, such as deceit, theft, murder, adultery, and so on. While the existence of original sin has met and is still meeting with widespread denial, the presence of actual sin, at least in some sense of the word, is generally admitted. At the present time, however, many deny that it constitutes guilt, and thus close their eyes to the real sinfulness of sin.

b. *The Unpardonable Sin.* There are passages of Scripture which speak of a sin that cannot be forgiven, after which a change of heart is impossible, and for which it is not necessary to pray, Matt. 12:31, 32; Mark 3:28-30; Luke 12:10; Heb. 4:4-6; 10:26, 27; I John 5:16. It is generally known as the sin or blasphemy against the Holy Spirit. This sin consists in the conscious, malicious, and wilful rejection and slandering, against evidence and conviction, of the testimony of the Holy Spirit respecting the grace of God in

Jesus Christ, attributing it out of hatred and enmity to the prince of darkness. It presupposes in those who commit it a rather profound knowledge of the truth, an inner illumination of the Holy Spirit, and an intellectual conviction of the truth so strong and powerful as to make an *honest denial* of it impossible. The sin itself then consists not simply in doubting the truth or in a simple denial of it, but in a contradiction of it that goes contrary to the conviction of the mind and to the illumination of the conscience. It is unpardonable, not because its guilt transcends the merits of Christ, or because the sinner is beyond the renewing power of the Holy Spirit; but because it is a sin that excludes all repentance, sears the conscience, and hardens the sinner. In those who have committed this sin we may therefore expect to find a pronounced hatred of God, a defiant attitude to Him and to all that is divine, delight in ridiculing and slandering that which is holy, and absolute unconcern respecting the welfare of their soul and the future life. In view of the fact that this sin is not followed by repentance, we may be reasonably sure that they who fear that they have committed it, who worry about it, and who desire the prayers of others for them, have not committed it.

C. **The Universality of Sin.** Scripture and experience both teach us that sin is universal. Even Pelagians do not deny this, though they ascribe it to external conditions, such as a bad environment, evil examples, and a wrong kind of education. According to Scripture, however, the explanation for it lies in the fall of Adam and in the imputation of his sin to all his descendants. It may be proved in various ways:

1. The universality of sin is asserted in several direct statements of Scripture. The following are some of the most important passages that come into consideration here: I Kings 8:46; Ps. 143:2; Prov. 20:9; Eccl. 7:20; Rom. 3:1-12, 19, 20, 23; Gal. 3:22; Jas. 3:2; I John 1:8, 10.

2. Several passages of Scripture teach that sin is the heritage of man from the time of his birth, and is therefore present in human nature so early that it cannot possibly be considered as the result of imitation, Ps. 51:5; Job 14:4; John 3:6.

3. Death as the penalty of sin is visited even upon those who have never exercised a personal and conscious choice, Rom. 5:12-14. This passage implies that sin exists, in the case of infants, prior to moral consciousness. Since infants die, and therefore the effect of sin is present in their case, it is but natural to assume that the cause is also present.

4. According to Scripture all men are under condemnation and therefore need the redemption which is in Christ Jesus. Children are never made an exception to this rule. This follows from the passages quoted under (1), and also from John 3:3, 5; Eph. 2:3; I John 5:12. They all need the regenerating power of the Holy Spirit unto salvation.

Questions for Review:

What different opinions are there respecting the connection between Adam's sin and that of his descendants? What is the realistic theory, and why is it objectionable? How does the doctrine of the covenant of works conceive of the connection between the sin of Adam and our sinful condition? What advantages has this view? What solution of the problem is suggested by the theory of mediate imputation? What objections are there to this solution? What is original sin? What two elements does it include? How should we conceive of man's total depravity? How must his total inability be understood? What is included in actual sin? How does actual sin differ from original sin? What is the nature of the unpardonable sin? Can there be any reasonable doubt as to the universality of sin? What explanation do some offer for this? How does the Bible account for it?

References for Further Study:

Berkhof, *Reformed Dogmatics*, I, pp. 226-242; Hodge, *Outlines of Theology*, pp. 325-366; McPherson, *Christian Dogmatics*, pp. 242-256; Orr, *Side-Lights on Christian Doctrine*, pp. 100-106; Candlish, *The Biblical Doctrine of Sin*, pp. 55-81, 90-128.

MAN IN THE COVENANT OF GRACE

The Covenant of Redemption

In the covenant of redemption we have an agreement between the Father, as the representative of the Trinity, and the Son, as the representative of His people, in which the latter undertakes to meet the obligations of those whom the Father has given Him, and the former promises the Son all that is necessary for His redemptive work. This eternal covenant is the firm foundation of the covenant of grace. If there had been no eternal counsel of peace between the Father and the Son, there could have been no agreement between God and the sinner. The covenant of redemption makes the covenant of grace possible.

A. **The Scriptural Basis for the Covenant of Redemption.** The covenant of redemption is frequently called *the counsel of peace,* a name that is derived from Zech. 6:13. The doctrine of this eternal counsel rests on the following Scriptural basis:

1. Scripture clearly points to the fact that the plan of redemption was included in the eternal decree or counsel of God, Eph. 1:4 ff.; 3:11; II Thess. 2:13; II Tim. 1:9; Jas. 2:5; I Peter 1:2, and other passages.

2. There are passages which point to the fact that the plan of God for the salvation of sinners was of the nature of a covenant. Christ speaks of promises made to Him before His advent, and repeatedly refers to a commission which He received from the

Father, John 5:30, 43; 6:38-40; 17:4-12. Moreover, in Rom. 5:12-21 and in I Cor. 15:22 He is clearly represented as a covenant head. The parallel between Adam and Christ leaves no doubt on this point.

3 The elements of a covenant are clearly indicated, such as contracting parties, a promise, and a condition. In Ps. 2:7-9 the parties are mentioned and a promise is indicated (comp. Acts 13:33; Heb. 1:5; 5:5). In another Messianic passage, Ps. 40: 7-9 (comp. Heb. 10:5-7) the Messiah expresses His readiness to do the Father's will in becoming a sacrifice for sin. Christ repeatedly speaks of a task which the Father has entrusted to Him, John 6:38, 39; 10:18; 17:4. Moreover, John 17:5, 6. 9, 24 (cf. also Phil. 2:9-11) refer to a reward which He receives from the Father.

4. There are two passages in the Old Testament, which connect the idea of the covenant immediately with the Messiah, namely, Ps. 89:3 and Isa. 42:6, which refers to the Servant of the Lord. The connection clearly shows that this servant is not merely Israel. Moreover, there are also passages in which the Messiah speaks of God as *his God,* which is covenant language, Ps. 22:1, 2; Ps. 40:8.

B. **The Son in the Covenant of Redemption.** There are a few things that should be stressed in connection with the place and work of Christ in the covenant of redemption.

1. The Official Position of Christ in the Covenant. Christ is both surety and head of the covenant of redemption. He is called "surety" in Heb.

7:22. A surety is a person who takes upon himself the legal obligations of another. Christ stepped into the place of the sinner and undertook to atone for sin by bearing the necessary punishment, and to meet the demands of the law for all His people. By taking the place of delinquent man He became the second or last Adam, and in that capacity is the head of the covenant, the representative of all those whom the Father has given Him.

2. THE COVENANT WAS FOR CHRIST A COVENANT OF WORKS. The covenant of redemption is indeed the eternal basis of the covenant of grace, and for sinners also its original pattern. But for Christ it is a covenant of works rather than a covenant of grace. For Him the law of the original covenant, the covenant of works applies, namely, that eternal life can only be obtained by meeting the demands of the law. As the last Adam, Christ obtains eternal life as a reward for faithful obedience, and not at all as an unmerited gift of grace.

3. CHRIST'S WORK IN THE COVENANT IS LIMITED BY ELECTION. The covenant of redemption has sometimes been confused with the decree of election, but the two are not identical. The decree of election determines the number of those who are destined to be heirs of eternal glory in Christ, while the covenant of redemption represents the way in which grace and glory are prepared for sinners. Logically, election precedes the counsel of redemption, because the surety of Christ in the covenant is particular

and not universal. Christ undertakes to save only those who are given Him by the Father.

4. The Covenant of Redemption and the Use of the Sacraments by Christ. Christ used the sacraments of both the Old and the New Testament. Clearly they could not mean for Him what they mean for believers; they could not be symbols nor seals of saving grace; neither could they be instrumental in strengthening saving faith. In all probability they were for Him signs and seals of the covenant of redemption. He used them in an official capacity, as the representative of His people. He was burdened with the guilt of His people, and the sacraments could signify and seal for Him the removal of this burden and the fulfilment of the promises of the Father. And in so far as He in the capacity of Mediator was called upon to exercise faith (not saving faith), they could also serve to strengthen this faith as far as His human nature was concerned.

C. Requirements and Promises in the Covenant of Redemption.

1. Requirements. The Father required of the Son as the surety and head of His people:

a. That He should assume human nature by being born of a woman, and should assume this nature with its present infirmities, though without sin, Gal. 4:4, 5; Heb. 2:10, 11, 14, 15; 4:15.

b. That He should place Himself under the law, in order to pay the penalty for sin and to merit everlasting life for the elect, Ps. 40:8; Matt. 5:17, 18; John 8:29; 9:4, 5.

c. That He should apply His merits to His people by regenerating them, leading them to conversion, endowing them with faith, and sanctifying them, through the powerful operation of the Holy Spirit, thus securing the consecration of their lives to God, John 16:13-15; 17:19-22.

2. Promises. The main promises of the Father, which correspond to the demands of the Son, were:

a. That He would prepare for Him a body uncontaminated by sin, Heb. 10:5, and would anoint Him by giving Him the Spirit without measure, thus qualifying Him for His Messianic offices, Isa. 42:1, 2; 61:1; John 3:34.

b. That He would support Him in the performance of His work, and thus enable Him to accomplish the destruction of Satan and the establishment of the kingdom of God, Isa. 42:6, 7; Luke 22:43.

c. That He would deliver Him from the power of death, and exalt Him to His own right hand in heaven, committing to Him all power in heaven and on earth, Ps. 16:8-11; Acts 2:25-28; Phil. 2:9-11.

d. That He would enable Him, as a reward for His accomplished atonement, to send out the Holy Spirit for the formation of His spiritual body by regeneration and sanctification, and for the instruction, guidance, and protection of the Church, John 14:26; 15:26; 16:13, 14.

e. That through the operation of the Holy Spirit all those given unto the Son would really come unto Him, so that none of them would be lost, John 6:37, 39, 40, 44, 45.

f. That a multitude which no man can number would thus be made partakers of redemption, so that ultimately the kingdom of the Messiah would embrace all the nations of the earth, Ps. 22:27; 72:17.

g. That in and through this wondrous work of redemption the glory of the divine perfections would become manifest to men and angels, and God would receive all the honor, Eph. 1:6, 12, 14.

Questions for Review:

What is the covenant of redemption? How is it related to the covenant of grace? By what other name is it known? What Scriptural evidence is there for the covenant of redemption? What is the official position of Christ in this covenant? Is it for Christ a covenant of works or a covenant of grace? Whom does Christ represent in this covenant? What was the significance of the use of the sacraments by Christ? What did the Father require of Christ in the covenant of redemption? What did He promise the Son?

References for Further Study:

Berkhof, *Reformed Dogmatics*, I, pp. 247-256; Hodge, *Systematic Theology*, II, pp. 359-362; Dabney, *Theology*, pp. 432-437.

The Covenant of Grace

On the basis of the covenant of redemption God established the covenant of grace, a covenant of friendship with man, which represents the way in which the blessings of redemption are mediated to the sinner. Under the present heading several particulars call for consideration.

A. **The Contracting Parties in the Covenant of Grace.** God is the first party in the covenant of grace, the party that takes the initiative and graciously determines the relation in which the second party will stand to Him. He appears in the covenant as a gracious and forgiving Father, willing to pardon sin and to restore sinners to His blessed communion. It is not so easy to determine precisely who the second party is, though in general it may be said that God established the covenant with fallen man. Though there was no historical limitation at first, it became evident in the days of Abraham that it was not intended to include all men. For that reason it does not satisfy to say that God made the covenant with the sinner. There must be some limitation, and therefore some hold that God made the covenant with Abraham and his seed, that is, his natural but especially his spiritual descendants; or, slightly different, with believers and their seed. The majority maintain, however, that He entered into covenant relationship with the elect or the elect sinner. To be perfectly clear in the matter, it is of great importance to make a very necessary distinction.

1. The Covenant as an End in Itself, A Covenant of Mutual Friendship or Communion of Life. The covenant of grace may be contemplated as an end which God had in view in the covenant of redemption, as an ultimate spiritual reality which He brings to realization in the course of history through the ministry of the Word and the powerful operation of the Holy Spirit, and which will be perfected at the time of the consummation of all things. From this point of view it is a relation sought and established, namely, a relation of friendship between God and man, a communion of life in which man is made to share in the divine life, the life of the resurrection. It represents a condition in which privileges are improved for spiritual ends, the promises of God are embraced by a living faith, and the promised blessings are brought to full fruition. If the covenant is regarded from this point of view, there would seem to be only one possible position with respect to the second party in the covenant, and that is that God established His covenant of grace with the elect. It is then that gracious agreement between God and the elect sinner, in which God gives Himself with all the blessings of salvation to the elect sinner, and the latter embraces God and all His gracious gifts by faith. In view of the fact that in Abraham the central blessing of the covenant was realized, he is called "the friend of God," Jas. 2:23. Jesus calls His disciples friends, because they share the covenant blessing of the new life and live in obedience to His commandments, John 15:14, 15. Several passages of Scripture speak of God's covenant mercies as realized in

those that fear Him, Deut. 7:9; II Chron. 6:14; Ps. 103:17, 18. The way in which this is done in the new dispensation is indicated in Jer. 31:31-34; Heb. 10:8-12. The final realization of the covenant is described in Rev. 21:3, "And I heard a great voice out of the throne saying, Behold, the tabernacle of God is with men, and He shall dwell with them, and they shall be His peoples, and God Himself shall be with them, and be their God."

2. THE COVENANT AS A MEANS TO AN END, A PURELY LEGAL RELATIONSHIP INDICATIVE OF THE SPIRITUAL END THAT SHOULD BE REALIZED. It is quite evident that the Bible also speaks of the covenant in a broader sense, as including many who do not share in the life of the covenant, and even some in whom the covenant promises are never realized. Ishmael and Esau were in the covenant; so were the wicked sons of Eli. The rebellious Israelites, who died in their sins, were covenant people, and even the Scribes and Pharisees, so strongly denounced by Jesus, shared in the privileges of the covenant. The covenant may be regarded as a purely legal agreement, in which God guarantees the blessings of salvation to all those who believe. This agreement may exist as a purely objective arrangement even where nothing is done to realize its purpose. The relation which it represents may exist independently of the attitude assumed by man to his covenant obligations. That is, a man may not meet the covenant requirements, may not believe in the Lord Jesus Christ, and yet stand in covenant

relationship to God. If we conceive of the covenant in this broader sense, as a purely legal relationship, as a means by which God realizes the blessings of salvation in the lives of those who meet the covenant requirements, — then we shall have to say that God established the covenant with believers and their children.

B. **The Promises and Requirements of the Covenant of Grace.** Every covenant has two sides: it offers certain privileges and imposes certain obligations. There are in it promises and requirements.

1. The Promises of the Covenant. The main promise of the covenant, which includes all other promises, is contained in the oft-repeated words, "I will be a God unto thee and to thy seed after thee." This promise in its full or in an abbreviated form is found in several Old and New Testament passages, especially in passages which speak of the introduction of a new phase of the covenant life, or which refer to a renewal of the covenant, Jer. 31:33; 32:38-40; Ezek. 34:23-25, 30, 31; 36:25-28; 37:26, 27; Heb. 8:10; II Cor. 6:16-18. The promise is fully realized when at last the new Jerusalem descends out of heaven from God, and the tabernacle of God is pitched among men, Rev. 21:3. This grand promise is re-echoed time and again in the jubilant exultation of those who stand in covenant relationship to God, "Jehovah is my God." This one promise really includes all other promises, such as (*a*) the promise of various temporal blessings, which often serve to symbolize those of a spiritual kind (*b*) the promise of justification, including

the forgiveness of sins, the adoption of children, and a claim to life eternal; (*c*) the promise of the Spirit of God for the application, full and free, of the work of redemption and of all the blessings of salvation; and (d) the promise of final glorification in a life that never ends, Job 19:25-27; Ps. 16:11; 73:24-26; Isa. 43:25; Jer. 31:33, 34; Ezek. 36:27; Dan. 12:2, 3; Gal. 4:5, 6; Tit. 3:7; Heb. 11:7; Jas. 2:5.

2. THE REQUIREMENTS OF THE COVENANT. It is sometimes said that the covenant of grace, in distinction from the covenant of works, contains no requirements and imposes no obligations on man. However, this is hardly correct in the absolute sense of the word. It is perfectly true that there are no requirements of a meritorious character. Man earns nothing by meeting the demands of the covenant. It is also true that all the requirements of the covenant are covered by the promises of God, that is, God promises to give man all that He requires of him. Hence the prayer of Augustine: "Lord, give what Thou commandest, and then command what Thou wilt." Bearing these things in mind, however, it is perfectly correct to speak of covenant requirements. There are especially two things which God demands of those who stand in covenant relationship to Him. He requires of them, (*a*) that they accept the covenant and covenant promises by faith, and thus enter upon the life of the covenant; and (*b*) that, from the principle of the new life born within them, they consecrate themselves to God in a new obedience.

C. **The Characteristics of the Covenant.** There are several characteristics of the covenant of grace.

1. IT IS A GRACIOUS COVENANT. This covenant may be called gracious, (*a*) because in it God allows a surety to meet our obligations; (*b*) because He Himself offers the surety in the person of His Son, who meets the demands of justice; and (*c*) because by His grace, revealed in the operation of the Holy Spirit, He enables man to live up to his covenant responsibilities.

2. IT IS A TRINITARIAN COVENANT. The triune God is operative in the covenant of grace. It has its origin in the elective love and grace of the Father, finds its legal foundation in the suretyship of the Son, and is fully realized in the lives of sinners only by the effective application of the Holy Spirit, John 1:16; Eph. 2:8; I Pet. 1:2.

3. IT IS AN ETERNAL AND THEREFORE UNBREAKABLE COVENANT. If we distinguish between the covenant of redemption and the covenant of grace, then we cannot say that the latter was established in eternity. We can maintain, however, that it will endure eternally, Gen. 17:19; II Sam. 23:5; Heb. 13:20. And because the covenant is eternal, it is also inviolable, Heb. 6:17. God remains forever true to His covenant and will invariably bring it to full realization in the elect. This does not mean, however, that man will never break the covenant relationship.

4. IT IS A PARTICULAR AND NOT A UNIVERSAL COVENANT. This means that the essence of the covenant, the relation of friendship with God and of life in

communion with Him, will be realized only in the elect, and that even the external covenant relationship does not extend to all men, but only to believers and their seed. The New Testament dispensation of the covenant may be called universal in the sense that in it the covenant is extended to all nations, and is no more limited to the Jews, as it was in the old dispensation.

5. THE COVENANT IS ESSENTIALLY THE SAME IN ALL DISPENSATIONS, THOUGH THE FORM OF ITS ADMINISTRATION CHANGES. The essential covenant promise is the same throughout, Gen. 17:7; Ex. 19:5; 20:1; Deut. 29:13; II Sam. 7:14; Jer. 31:33; Heb. 8:10. The gospel, which represents the contents of the covenant, is the same in both Testaments, Gen. 3:15; Gal. 1:8, 9; 3:8. The way in which Abraham obtained the realization of the covenant promise, is also the way in which the New Testament believers obtain this, Rom. 4:9-25; Gal. 3:7-9, 17, 18. Moreover, the Mediator is the same yesterday, today, and forever, Heb. 13:8; Acts 4:12.

6. THE COVENANT IS BOTH CONDITIONAL AND UNCONDITIONAL. The covenant is clearly conditional on the suretyship of Jesus Christ. Man's conscious entrance into the covenant as a communion of life is conditioned by faith and his continued enjoyment of its blessings by the persistent exercise of faith. At the same time there is no condition in the covenant that can be regarded as meritorious. In that sense it is unconditional. The sinner is called upon to repent and believe, but his faith and repentance

do not in any way merit the blessings of the covenant.

7. THE COVENANT CAN BE CALLED A TESTAMENT. The covenant is, of course, two-sided, that is, it is an agreement between two parties. An absolutely one-sided covenant is a contradiction in terms. Yet there is a sense in which the covenant of grace can be called one-sided. In origin the covenant is simply of the nature of a divine disposition or arrangement by which God communicates His blessings to man. Moreover, in the covenant God freely gives all that He demands. And because the covenant is a free and sovereign disposition on the part of God, it can also be called a testament, Heb. 9:16, 17. This name stresses the facts, (*a*) that the covenant is as a whole a gift of God; (*b*) that its New Testament dispensation was ushered in by the death of Christ; (*c*) that it is firm and inviolable; and (*d*) that in it God gives what He demands.

D. **The Relation of Christ to the Covenant of Grace.** Christ is represented in Scripture as the Mediator of the Covenant. A mediator in the general sense of the word is simply a person who mediates between two opposite parties in an attempt to bring them together. The Scriptural idea of Christ as our Mediator, however, is far more specific and more profound. Christ is Mediator in more than one sense. He intervenes between God and man, not merely to sue for peace and to persuade to it, but armed with full power to do all that is necessary for the actual establishment of peace. He is the Mediator who, as our surety, takes upon Himself the guilt of sinners, pays the penalty of sin, fulfils the law, and thus restores those whom He represents to the right relation to God, Heb. 7:22; 8:6; 9:15; 12:24. But He is also the Mediator of access, who reveals to men the truth concerning God and their relation to Him, and the conditions of acceptable service; who persuades and enables them to receive the truth, and directs and sustains them in all circumstances of life, so as to perfect their deliverance, Rom. 5:2. In doing all this He employs the ministry of men, II Cor. 5:20.

E. **Membership in the Covenant.** In speaking of membership in the covenant the distinction between the covenant as a purely legal agreement and the covenant as a communion of life should always be borne in mind.

1. ADULTS IN THE COVENANT. Adults can only enter the covenant as a legal agreement by faith and confession. And when they so enter it, they at the same time gain entrance into the covenant as a communion of life. The only case in which this does not hold is when the faith is pretended and the confession is false. They enter upon the full covenant life at once therefore, and this is the only way in which they can enter the covenant. They not only become participants in certain external privileges and engage in the performance of certain external duties, but confess that they accept the covenant with a living faith, and that it is their desire and intention to continue in this faith.
2. CHILDREN OF BELIEVERS IN THE COVENANT. Children of believers enter the covenant as a legal relationship by birth, but this does not necessarily mean

that they are also at once in the covenant as a communion of life. It does not even mean that the covenant relation will ever come to its full realization in their lives. At the same time there is in the case of these children a reasonable assurance that the covenant will in time become a living reality in their experience. This is based on the promise of God, which is absolutely reliable, that He will work in the hearts of the covenant seed with His saving grace and transform them into living members of the covenant. As long as they do not manifest the contrary, we shall have to proceed on the assumption that they are in possession of the covenant life. And when these children come to years of discretion, it is incumbent on them to accept their covenant responsibilities voluntarily by a true confession of faith. Failure to do this is, strictly speaking, a denial of their covenant relationship.

3. UNREGENERATE IN THE COVENANT. From the preceding it follows that even unregenerate and unconverted persons may be in the covenant as a legal agreement. They may claim the covenant promises, which God gave when He established the covenant with believers and their seed, Rom. 9:4. They are subject to the ministrations of the covenant, and are constantly admonished and exhorted to live according to its requirements. The Church treats them as covenant children, offers them the seals of the covenant and exhorts them to a proper use of these. They also share in the common blessings of the covenant, and are even subject to certain spe-

cial operations of the Holy Spirit. The Spirit strives with them in a special manner, convicts them of sin, enlightens them in a measure, and enriches them with the choicest blessings of common grace, Gen. 6:3; Matt. 13:18-22; Heb. 6:4, 5. Finally, they are also under covenant responsibility, and are in duty bound to repent and believe. If they do not turn to God and accept Christ by faith, they will be judged as breakers of the covenant.

F. **The Different Dispensations of the Covenant.** There are only two dispensations in the strict sense of the word, that of the Old and that of the New Testament. But in the old dispensation we may distinguish several periods or stages in the revelation of the covenant. A brief characterization of these stages must suffice here.

1. THE FIRST REVELATION OF THE COVENANT IN GEN. 3:15. The first revelation of the covenant is found in what is usually called the protevangel or the maternal promise. This does not yet refer to the formal establishment of the covenant. The revelation of such a formal establishment could only follow after the covenant idea had been developed in history. It contains an indication of the division of mankind into two parts, the seed of the woman and the seed of the serpent, and of the friendship of God established with the seed of the woman, involving enmity with the seed of the serpent. The covenant idea is therefore clearly present.

2. THE COVENANT OF NATURE WITH NOAH. The covenant with Noah is of a very general nature. God promises that He will not again destroy all flesh by

the waters of a flood, and that the regular succession of seedtime and harvest, cold and heat, summer and winter, day and night, will continue. The forces of nature are bridled, the powers of evil are put under great restraint, and man is protected against the violence of both man and beast. It is a covenant conferring only natural blessings, and is therefore often called the covenant of nature or of common grace. There is no objection to this designation, provided it does not convey the impression that this covenant has no connection whatever with the covenant of grace. Though the two differ, they are also most intimately connected. The covenant of nature also originated in the grace of God. It guarantees those earthly and temporal blessings which were absolutely necessary for the realization of the covenant of grace.

3. THE COVENANT WITH ABRAHAM. The covenant was formally established with Abraham. This transaction with Abraham marked the beginning of the particularistic Old Testament administration of the covenant. It is now limited to a single family, to Abraham and his descendants. In the establishment of the covenant with Abraham it becomes perfectly evident that man is a party in the covenant and must respond to the promises of God by faith. The great central fact in the attitude of Abraham is that he believed God and that this was reckoned unto him for righteousness. Moreover, the spiritual blessings of the covenant now become far more apparent than they were before, such as the forgiveness of sins and the gift of the Spirit. The

covenant with Abraham clearly had two sides. On the one hand it had reference to temporal blessings, such as the land of Canaan, a numerous offspring, and victory over the enemies; and on the other hand it referred to spiritual blessings. The temporal blessings served to symbolize and typify spiritual and heavenly things. The spiritual promises are not realized in the natural descendants of Abraham as such, but only in those who also follow in the footsteps of Abraham.

4. THE SINAITIC COVENANT. The covenant at Sinai was *essentially* the same as that established with Abraham, though the form differed somewhat. It was now established with the nation of Israel, and thus became a truly national covenant. In a large measure Church and State became one. The Sinaitic covenant included a service which contained a positive reminder of the strict demands of the covenant of works. It was not a renewed covenant of works, however; the law was made subservient to the covenant of grace. While the theocratic standing of the Israelite was made dependent on his keeping of the law, Lev. 18:5; Deut. 27:26; II Cor. 3: 7, 8, the law served a twofold purpose in connection with the covenant of grace, namely, (*a*) to increase the consciousness of sin, Rom. 3:20; 4:15; 5:13; Gal. 3:19; and (*b*) to be a tutor unto Christ, Gal. 3:24. There was a detailed ceremonial and typical service. A separate priesthood was instituted, and a continuous preaching of the gospel in symbols and types was introduced. These symbols and types appeared under two different aspects: as

the demands of God imposed on the people; and as a divine message of salvation to the people. The Jews largely lost sight of the latter aspect, and fixed their attention almost exclusively on the former. They regarded the covenant ever increasingly as a covenant of works, and saw in the symbols and types a mere appendage to this.

5. The New Testament Dispensation of the Covenant. The covenant of grace, as it is revealed in the New Testament, is essentially one with the covenant that stands out on the pages of the Old Testament. This is abundantly evident from Romans 4 and Galatians 3. It is true that it is sometimes called a new covenant, Jer. 31: 31; Heb. 8: 8, 13; but this finds a sufficient explanation in the fact that the New Testament administration of the covenant differs in several particulars from that of the Old Testament. While in the Old Testament form it was limited to a single nation, in its New Testament aspect it broke through the barriers of particularism and became universal in the sense that its blessings were extended to people of all nations. Through the finished work of Christ the middle wall of partition was broken down, all nations were given free access to God, and those that were afar off were brought near. Moreover, there is also a difference in the quality of its benefits, in the spiritual and gracious character of its blessings. The Holy Spirit is poured out upon the Church, and out of the fulness of the grace of God enriches believers with spiritual and eternal blessings. The present dispensation of the covenant will continue until the return of Jesus Christ, when the covenant

relation will be realized in the fullest sense of the word in a life of intimate communion with God. Rev. 21:3.

Questions for Review:

What distinction do we apply to the covenant of grace? What answer should be given to the question as to the second party in the covenant? What is the all-embracing promise of the covenant? What spiritual blessings does this include? What temporal blessings did it include in the Old Testament? What does God require of those with whom He enters into covenant relationship? Which are the characteristics of the covenant? In what sense is the covenant unbreakable, and in what sense is it sometimes broken? How can you prove the unity of the covenant in both dispensations? In what sense is it conditional and in what sense unconditional? Why can the covenant be called a testament? Where do we find the first revelation of the covenant? What is the nature of the covenant with Noah? Is it at all related to the covenant of grace? With whom was the covenant formally established? What characterizes the covenant with Abraham? How was the Sinaitic covenant related to the covenant with Abraham? How did the two differ? What characterizes the New Testament dispensation in the covenant? What is the position of Christ in the covenant of grace? In what twofold sense is He Mediator? How can adults become covenant members? How do children of believers enter the covenant? What is expected of them? In what sense can unregenerate persons be covenant members?

References for Further Study:

Berkhof, *Reformed Dogmatics*, I, pp. 256-294; Hodge, *Outlines of Theology*, pp. 367-377; Hodge, *Systematic Theology*, II, 354-377; Hendriksen, *The Covenant of Grace;* Dabney, *Theology*, pp. 440-463.

THE DOCTRINE OF THE PERSON AND WORK OF CHRIST

THE DOCTRINE OF THE PERSON AND WORK OF CHRIST

The discussion of the doctrine of man is followed in theology by that of the doctrine of Christ. The transition from the one to the other is not only logical, but also very natural and easy. Our study of the doctrine of man concluded with a discussion of the covenant of grace, and from this we now naturally pass on to a consideration of the Mediator of the covenant, Jesus Christ, and of the objective work of redemption wrought by Him for all His people. The subjective application of this work is discussed in a later section.

THE PERSON OF CHRIST

The Names of Christ

There is a great number of names that are applied to Christ in Scripture, of which some point to His essential being and others to His natures; some serve to designate His states and others His offices. He is called the Son of God, the Son of Man, the Man of Sorrows, the Lord of Glory, the Messiah, the Mediator, the Lord, Prophet, Priest, and King. Five of His names call for special discussion, namely, Jesus, Christ, Son of Man, Son of God, and Lord.

A. **The Name Jesus.** The name Jesus is simply the Greek form of the Hebrew name Jehoshua Jos. 1:1; Zech. 3:1, of which the regular form in the post-exilic historical books is Jeshua, Ezra. 2:2. The name is in all probability derived from the Hebrew word "to save." This is entirely in agreement with the interpretation of the name given by the angel of the Lord in Matt. 1:21. The name was borne by two well-known types of Jesus in the Old Testament, namely, by Joshua, the son of Nun, who prefigures Christ as the royal leader, giving His people the victory over their enemies and bringing them into the Holy Land; and by Joshua the son of Jehozadak, who typifies Christ as the great high priest bearing the sins of His people, Zech. 3:1 ff.

B. **The Name Christ.** The name Christ is the New Testament equivalent for the Old Testament name Messiah, which means "the anointed one." Kings and priests were regularly anointed during the old dispensation, Ex. 29:7; Lev. 4:3; Judg. 9:8; I Sam. 9:16; 10:1; II Sam. 19:10. The king is called "the anointed of Jehovah," I Sam. 24:6. Only a single instance of the anointing of a prophet is recorded, I Kings 19:16, but there were probably references to it in Ps. 105:15 and Isa. 61:1. The oil that was used in the anointing symbolized the Spirit of God, Isa. 61:1; Zech. 4:1-6, and the anointing itself represented a transfer of the Spirit to the consecrated person, I Sam. 10:1, 6, 10; 16:13, 14. It included three elements: (1) an appointment to office; (2) the establishment of a sacred relationship between the anointed one and God; and (3) a communication of the Spirit of God to the one inducted into office, I Sam. 16:13. The Old Testament refers to the anointing of the Lord in Ps. 2:2; 45:7, and the New Testament in Acts 4:27 and 10:38. Christ was set up or appointed to His offices from eternity, but historically His anointing took place when He was conceived by the Holy Spirit, Luke 1:35, and when He received the Spirit, especially at the time of His baptism, Matt. 3:16; Mark 1:10; Luke 3:22; John 1:32; 3:34. It served to qualify Him for His great task.

C. **The Name Son of Man.** The name "Son of Man" is found in Ps. 8:4; Dan. 7:13; Enoch 46 and 62; II Esdras 13, and is, moreover, a frequent designation of the prophet Ezekiel. It is now quite generally admitted that the name, as applied to Christ, is derived from Dan. 7:13, though in that passage it is merely a descriptive appellative, and not yet a title. It had already turned into a title, however, when the book of Enoch was written. The name "Son of Man" was the most common self-designation of Jesus. He used it on more than forty occasions, while others all but refrained from employing it, the only exceptions being those indicated in John 12:34; Acts 7:56; Rev. 1:13; 14:14. The name is, of course, expressive of the humanity of Christ, and is sometimes used in passages in which Jesus speaks of His sufferings and death; but it is also clearly suggestive of the uniqueness of Jesus, of His superhuman character and of His future coming with the clouds of heaven in celestial glory, Matt. 16:27, 28; Mark 8:38; John 3:13, 14; 6:27; 8:28. Some are of the opinion that Jesus preferred this name to others, because it was little understood and would excellently serve the purpose of veiling His Messiahship. It is more likely, however, that He gave it preference, because it contained no suggestion of the misinterpretations of the Messiahship that were current among the Jews.

D. **The Name Son of God.** The name "Son of God" is variously used in the Old Testament. It is applied to Israel as a nation, Ex. 4:22; Hos. 11:1, to the promised king of the house of David, II Sam. 7:14; Ps. 89:27, to angels, Job 1:6; 38:7; Ps. 29:1, and to pious people in general, Gen. 6:2; Ps. 73:15; Prov. 14:26. In the New Testament Jesus appropriated the name, and His disciples and even the demons occasionally ascribe it to Him or address Him by it. The name, as applied to Christ, does not always have exactly the same connotation. It is used:

1. In the Nativistic Sense, that is, to designate that the human nature of Christ owes its origin to the direct supernatural activity of God, more particularly, of the Holy Spirit. It is clearly expressive of that fact in Luke 1:35.

2. In the Official or Messianic Sense, as a description of the office rather than of the nature of Christ. The Messiah is frequently called the Son of God as God's heir and representative. The devils evidently so used the name, Matt. 8:29. The name seems to have this meaning also in Matt. 24:36; Mark 13:32. There are some passages in which it combines this meaning with the following one.

3. In the Trinitarian Sense, in which it serves to designate Christ as the second person in the Trinity. This is the most profound sense in which the name is used. In all probability Jesus Himself invariably employs the name in that particular sense. It is clearly so used in Matt. 11:27; 14:28-33; 16:16; 21:33-46; 22:41-46; 26:63, and in the parallel

places in the other gospels. In some of the passages indicated the idea of the Messianic sonship also enters more or less.

E. **The Name Lord.** The name Lord, as applied to Christ in the New Testament, also has several connotations.

1. In some cases it is simply used as a form of polite and respectful address, Matt. 8:2; 20:33. In such cases it means little more than the word "sir," which we frequently use in polite address.

2. In other passages it is expressive of ownership and authority, without implying anything as to the divine character of Christ and His authority in spiritual and eternal matters, Matt. 21:3; 24:42.

3. Finally, there are passages in which it is expressive of the exalted character of Christ, of His supreme spiritual authority, and is practically equivalent to the name of God, Mark 12:36, 37; Luke 2:11; 3:4; Acts 2:36; I Cor. 12:3; Phil. 2:11. It is particularly after the resurrection that the name is applied to Christ as an indication of the fact that He is the owner and the ruler of the Church, though there are instances which show that the name approached this specific meaning even before the resurrection, Matt. 7:22; Luke 5:8.

Questions for Review:

How does the doctrine of Christ connect up with the doctrine of man? What different kinds of names are applied to Christ in Scripture? What is the derivation and meaning of the name Jesus? Who are the Old Testament types of Jesus? What is the meaning of the name Christ? What did the oil used in anointing signify? What elements were included in the anointing? When was Christ anointed for His work? Whence is the name "Son of Man" derived? What does the name express? Why did Christ give preference to this name? Did others ever apply it to Him? In what sense is the name "Son of God" used in the Old Testament? What are its different connotations, as it is applied to Christ? What are the different meanings of the name "Lord," as it is applied to Christ in the New Testament?

References for Further Study:

Berkhof, *Reformed Dogmatics*, I, pp. 303-309; Dalman, *The Words of Jesus*, pp 234-331; Vos, *The Self-Disclosure of Jesus*, pp. 104-256; Warfield, *The Lord of Glory*.

THE NATURES OF CHRIST

A. **The Distinction of Natures in Christ.** While the Bible teaches that there is but a single Mediator between God and man, it represents this Mediator as having two distinct natures, the one divine and the other human. It is the great mystery of godliness, God manifested in the flesh, I Tim. 3:16. This is a mystery, not only in the Biblical sense of the word, as something that was not fully revealed in the Old Testament, but also in the sense that it is beyond the comprehension of man. The problem which it presents has given rise to many conflicting opinions, but has never yet received an adequate solution. Some of the suggested solutions failed to do justice to the two natures in Christ, while others failed to maintain the unity of the person. No solution can be regarded as satisfactory which does not safeguard both. Scripture demands that we recognize two distinct natures in Christ.

1. THE DIVINE NATURE OF CHRIST. There is today a widespread denial of the divinity or, more specically, the deity of Christ. And yet this is clearly taught in Scripture. Even the Old Testament affords proof for it in its predictions of the coming Messiah, Isa. 9:6; Jer. 23:6; Dan. 7:13; Micah 5:2; Zech. 13:7; Mal. 3:1. The New Testament proofs for it are even more abundant. It is a well known fact that the Gospel of John presents the most exalted view of Christ in such passages as John 1:1-3, 14, 18, 25-27; 11:41-44; 20:28. But it

is not generally recognized that the picture presented by the other Gospels is in full accord with that of John, and yet this is true. Notice particularly the following passages: Matt. 5:17; 9:6; 11:1-6, 27; 14:33; 16:16; 25:31 ff.; 28:18; Mark 8:38, and many others. Again, we have the very same representation of Christ in the Pauline Epistles and in the Epistle to the Hebrews, Rom. 1:7; 9:5; I Cor. 1:1-3; 2:8; II Cor. 5:10; Gal. 2:20; 4:4; Phil. 2:6; Col. 2:9; I Tim. 3:16; Heb. 1:1-3, 5, 8; 4:14; 5:8, and other passages.

2. THE HUMAN NATURE OF CHRIST. In the early Christian centuries some called the real humanity of Christ in question, but at the present time no one seriously questions this. For a long time there was a one-sided emphasis on the deity of Christ, and scant justice was done to His humanity, but today the opposite is true: an ever-growing humanitarianism places all the emphasis on the veritable humanity of Christ. The only divinity many still ascribe to Him is simply that of his *perfect* humanity. There is abundant Scriptural proof for the real humanity of Christ. He calls Himself "man" and is so called by others, John 8:40; Acts 2:22; Rom. 5:15; I Cor. 15:21. We are told repeatedly that He came or was manifested in the flesh, that is, in human nature, John 1:14; I Tim. 3:16; I John 4:2. He had the essential elements of human nature, a material body and a rational soul, Matt. 26:26, 28, 38; Luke 23:46; 24:39; John 11:33; Heb. 2:14. Moreover, He was subject to the ordinary laws of human development, and to human wants and sufferings, Matt. 4:2; 8:24; 9:36; Mark 3:5;

Luke 2:40, 52; 22:44; John 4:6; 11:35; 12:27; 19:28, 30; Heb. 2:10, 18; 5:7, 8. It should be noted however, that while Christ was a real man, He was without sin. He not only did no sin, but could not sin, because of the essential bond between the human and the divine natures in Him. In the present day some deny the sinlessness of Christ, but the Bible clearly testifies to it in the following passages: Luke 1:35; John 8:46; 14:30; II Cor. 5:21; Heb. 4:15; 9:14; I Pet. 2:22; I John 3:5.

3. The Necessity of the Two Natures in Christ. In the present day many consider Jesus as a mere man, and do not recognize the necessity of the two natures in Christ. But if Christ is not both man and God, He cannot be our Mediator. He had to be one of the human race, in order to be able to represent sinners in His redemptive work. It was necessary that He should assume human nature, not only with all its essential properties of body and soul, but also with all the infirmities to which it is liable after the fall. Only such a truly human Mediator, who had experimental knowledge of the woes of mankind and rose superior to all temptations, could enter sympathetically into all the experiences, the trials, and the temptations of man, Heb. 2:17, 18; 4:15—5:2, and be a perfect human example for His followers, Matt. 11:29; Mark 10:39; John 13:13-15; Phil. 2:5-8; Heb. 12:2-4; I Pet. 2:21. At the same time He had to be a sinless man, for one who had forfeited His own life surely could not atone for others, Heb. 7:26. Moreover, it was necessary that He should be very God,

in order that He might bring a perfect sacrifice of infinite value, might bear the wrath of God redemptively, that is, so as to deliver others from the curse of the law, and might be able to apply the fruits of His redemptive work, Ps. 49:7-10; 130:3.

B. **The Unity of the Person of Christ.** While the Church has maintained the doctrine of the two natures of Christ from the days of the Council of Chalcedon, it at the same time asserted the existence of these two natures in one person.

1. STATEMENT OF THE DOCTRINE OF THE TWO NATURES IN ONE PERSON. There is but one person in the Mediator, and that person is the unchangeable Son of God. In the incarnation He did not change into a human person, nor did He adopt a human person; He simply assumed a human nature, which did not develop into an independent personality, but became personal in the person of the Son of God. The one divine person, who possessed a divine nature from eternity, assumed a human nature and now has both. After this assumption of a human nature the person of the Mediator is not divine only but divine-human; He is now the God-man. He is a single individual, but possesses all the essential qualities of both the human and the divine nature. While He has but a single self-consciousness, He has both a divine and a human consciousness, as well as a divine and a human will.

2. SCRIPTURE PROOF FOR THE UNITY OF THE PERSON IN CHRIST. If there were a dual personality in Christ, we would naturally expect to find some

traces of it in the Bible; but there is not a single trace of it. It is always the same person who speaks, whether the consciousness that finds utterance be human or divine, cf. John 10:30; 17:5 as compared with Matt. 27:46, John 19:28. There is no interchange of "I" and "thou" between the human and divine natures, such as there is between the persons in the Trinity (cf. John 17:23). Human attributes and actions are sometimes ascribed to the person designated by a divine title, Acts 20:28; I Cor. 2:8; Col. 1:13, 14. On the other hand divine attributes and actions are ascribed to the person designated by a human title, John 3:13; 6:62; Rom. 9:5.

3. The Effects of the Union of the Two Natures in One Person. Since the divine nature is immutable, it naturally did not undergo any essential change in the incarnation. There is, however, a threefold communication, which results from the union of the two natures in Christ:

a. *A Communication of Attributes or Properties.* This means that, after the incarnation, the properties of both the human and the divine natures are the properties of the person and are therefore ascribed to the person. The person can be said to be almighty, omniscient, omnipresent, and so on, but can also be called a man of sorrows, of limited knowledge, and subject to human wants and miseries.

b. *A Communication of Operations.* In virtue of this it may be said that the redemptive work of Christ is the work of the one undivided personal subject in Christ; that it is brought about by the co-operation of both natures; that each one of these natures works with its own special power; and that the result of this, as the work of a single person, forms an undivided unity.

c. *A Communication of Graces.* From the very first moment of its existence the human nature of Christ was adorned with all kinds of rich and glorious gifts. It shares in the grace and glory of being united with the divine person, and even becomes the object of prayer and adoration. Moreover, it partakes of those gifts of the Holy Spirit, particularly of the intellect, of the will, and of power by which the human nature of Christ was exalted high above all other intelligent creatures.

C. Some of the Most Important Errors in the Doctrine of Christ.

1. DENIAL OF THE REALITY OF THE DIVINE NATURE. In the early Christian centuries the reality of the divine nature of Christ was denied by the Ebionites and the Alogi. In more recent times this denial was shared by the Socinians of the days of the Reformation, and by the Unitarians and modern liberal theologians of the present day.

2. DENIAL OF THE REALITY OF CHRIST'S HUMAN NATURE. Second century Gnosticism denied the real humanity of Christ. Some ascribed to Christ merely a refined or heavenly body, while others distinguished between a human Jesus and a divine Christ who was connected with the former temporarily. The Sabellians of the fourth century regarded Christ merely as a mode in which God manifested Himself.

3. DENIAL OF THE INTEGRITY OF THE TWO NATURES. The Arians regarded Christ as a created being, neither God nor man, a sort of demi-god, while Appolinaris, who conceived of man as consisting of three parts, body, soul, and spirit, maintained that the human nature of Christ consisted only of two, body and soul, while the divine Logos took the place of the spirit.

4. DENIAL OF THE UNITY OF THE PERSON OF CHRIST. The Nestorians virtually denied the real union of the two natures in Christ. They distinguished the two so sharply as to make them really two persons morally agreed in purpose and action.

5. DENIAL OF THE TWO NATURES OF CHRIST. The Eutichians represented the opposite extreme in speaking of the two natures of Christ as fused into some third nature neither human nor divine. Sometimes it was represented as if the human nature were absorbed in the divine. The Lutheran view of Christ is somewhat akin to the Eutichian.

Questions for Review:

What Bible proof is there for the deity and for the humanity of Christ? What Scripture proof is there for the sinlessness of Christ? What is the nature of the person of Christ, divine, human, or divine-human? How can the unity of the person of Christ be proved from Scripture? What are the effects of the union of the two natures in Christ? Is it proper to make Christ the object of our prayers? Which are the main errors relating to the doctrine of Christ?

References for Further Study:

Berkhof, *Reformed Dogmatics*, I, pp. 310-332; Hodge, *Outlines of Theology*, pp. 378-390; McPherson, *Christian Dogmatics*, pp. 288-321; Orr, *Side-Lights on Christian Doctrine*, pp. 115-122.

The doctrine of the states of Christ was developed in the seventeenth century. The states in question are the states of the person of the Mediator and not, as the Lutherans maintain, of the human nature of Christ. It should be borne in mind that a state is not exactly the same as a condition. The former is one's position in life and particularly the relation in which one stands to the law, while the latter is one's mode of existence, especially as this is determined by the circumstances of life. One who is found guilty in a court of justice is in a state of guilt or condemnation, and this is usually followed by a condition of incarceration with all its attendant deprivation and shame. The states of the Mediator are generally treated as including the resulting conditions. In fact, the usual enumeration of the stages of Christ's humiliation and exaltation makes the resulting conditions more prominent than the states themselves.

A. **The State of Humiliation.** The state of humiliation consists in this that Christ laid aside the divine majesty which was His as the sovereign Ruler of the universe, and assumed human nature in the form of a servant; and that He, who is Himself the supreme Lawgiver, became subject to the demands and the curse of the law. This doctrine is based on such passages as Matt. 3:15; Gal. 3:13; 4:4; Phil. 2:6-8. This state of Christ is reflected in the corresponding condition, in which we usually distinguish the following stages:

1. THE INCARNATION AND BIRTH OF CHRIST. In the incarnation the Son of God, sometimes called the

Word (John 1), became flesh. This does not mean that He ceased to be what He was and changed into a man. In His essential nature the Son of God is exactly the same before and after the incarnation. It merely means that He assumed, in addition to His divine nature, a complete human nature, consisting of body and soul, John 1:14; Rom. 8:3; I Tim. 3:16; I John 4:2; II John 7. Through the incarnation He really became one of the human race, since He derived His human nature from the substance of Mary. This should be maintained in opposition to the Anabaptists, who claim that He received it from heaven and that Mary was merely the conduit or channel through which it passed. Scripture teaches us that the incarnation was effected by a virgin birth, and in view of this our Confession states that the human nature of Christ was "conceived in the womb of the blessed virgin Mary by the power of the Holy Ghost, without the means of man." This doctrine is based on the following passages of Scripture, Isa. 7:14; Matt. 1:20; Luke 1:34, 35. The work of the Holy Spirit in connection with the birth of Christ was twofold: (*a*) He caused the conception of Christ's human nature in the womb of Mary; and (*b*) He sanctified this human nature in its very inception, and thus kept it free from the pollution of sin. The doctrine of the virgin birth was accepted by the Church from the earliest times, but is denied by modern liberal theologians, as contrary to the laws of nature. Some maintain that the incarnation is not a part of the humiliation of Christ, since He still has His human nature, and yet is no more in a state of humiliation. But we should carefully discriminate here. While an act of great condescension, it was not necessarily a humiliation that the Son of God assumed a human nature; but it was an act of humiliation that He assumed "flesh," that is, human nature as it is since the fall, weakened and subject to suffering and death, though in His case free from the taint of sin.

2. The Sufferings of Christ. We are often inclined to think of the sufferings of Christ as limited to His final agonies. Yet His whole life was a life of suffering. It was the servant-life of the Lord of Hosts, the life of the sinless One in a sin-cursed world. The way of obedience was for Him a way of suffering. He suffered from the repeated assaults of Satan, from the hatred and unbelief of His own people, and from the persecution of His enemies. His loneliness must have been oppressive, and His sense of responsibility crushing. The real essence of His sufferings should not be sought in His bodily discomfitures and pains as such, but in these accompanied with anguish of soul and a mediatorial consciousness of sin. Because of His ethical perfection and His passion for righteousness and holiness and truth, the causes of suffering were far more numerous for Him than they are for us. No one could feel the poignancy of pain and grief and moral evil as Jesus could. The temptations of Christ also formed a part of His sufferings, and a very essential part. It was only by entering into the very trials of men that Jesus could become a truly sympathetic High Priest, "able to succor them that are tempted," Matt. 4:1-11; Luke 22:28; John

12:27; Heb. 2:18; 4:15; 5:7-9. No fully satisfactory answer can be given to the question, how it was possible that Jesus, the sinless One, should be tempted. On the one hand we must maintain the reality of His temptations, and on the other hand the certainty that these temptations could never result in sin on His part.

3. THE DEATH OF CHRIST. When we speak of the death of Christ here, we have in mind His physical death. Christ did not die as the result of an accident, nor by the hand of an assassin, but under a judicial sentence. It was of importance that this should be so, because He had to be counted with the transgressors. Moreover, it was significant that He was tried and sentenced by a Roman judge, representing the highest judicial power in the world, functioning by the grace of God, and dispensing justice in God's name. Furthermore, it had special significance that He was not beheaded or stoned to death, but crucified. By suffering that Roman form of punishment He was reckoned with the meanest criminals and the scum of mankind, and thus met the extremest demands of the law. At the same time He suffered an accursed death, and thus gave evidence of the fact that He became a curse for us, Deut. 21:23; Gal. 3:13.

4. THE BURIAL OF CHRIST. It might seem that the death of Christ was the last stage of His humiliation, especially in view of the last words on the cross: "It is finished." But these words in all probability refer to His active sufferings. It is quite clear that His burial also formed a part of His

humiliation. Man's returning to the dust is part of the punishment of sin, Gen. 3:19. Moreover, several passages of Scripture clearly imply that the Saviour's abode in the grave was a humiliation, Ps. 16:10; Acts 2:27, 31; 13:34, 35. The sinner is represented as being buried with Christ, and this refers to the going down, the putting off, the destruction of the old man, Rom. 6:1-6. It clearly shows that the burial of Christ is regarded as a part of His humiliation. The burial of Christ served the purpose of removing the terrors of the grave for the redeemed and of sanctifying the grave for them.

5. THE DESCENT OF CHRIST INTO HADES. After speaking of the sufferings and death of the Saviour, the Apostolic Confession adds: "He descended into hell (hades)." These words are variously interpreted. Roman Catholics interpret them to mean that Christ after His death went down into the *Limbus Patrum,* where the Old Testament saints were confined, to release them and bring them to heaven. Lutherans regard the descent into hades as the first stage of Christ's exaltation, a triumphal march, perhaps between His death and resurrection, to celebrate His victory over the powers of darkness. The Church of England holds that, while Christ's body was in the grave, the soul went into that part of hades, called paradise, the abode of the righteous souls, and gave them a fuller exposition of the truth. Finally, the Reformed Churches usually interpret the phrase, "He descended into hell," figuratively as an expression of the idea that Christ suffered the pangs of hell both in Gethsemane and on the cross. On the

whole it seems best to combine two thoughts: (*a*) that Christ suffered the pangs of hell in the garden and on the cross; and (*b*) that He entered the deepest humiliation of the state of death. The Scripture passages on which the doctrine of the descent into hades is based are especially the following: Ps. 16:8:10; Eph. 4:9; I Pet. 3:18, 19; 4:6.

B. **The State of Exaltation.** In the state of exaltation Christ passed from under the law as a covenant obligation, having paid the penalty for sin and merited righteousness and eternal life for the sinner. As Mediator He now entered into the undivided favor and good pleasure of God, and was crowned with a corresponding honor and glory. It had to appear also in His condition that the penalty of sin was lifted. His exaltation was also His glorification. Roman Catholics and Lutherans teach that the exaltation of Christ began with the descent into hades. Reformed Churches, however, maintain that it began with the resurrection of Christ. Four stages must be taken into consideration here.

1. THE RESURRECTION OF CHRIST. The resurrection was the great turning-point in the states of Christ.

a. *The Nature of the Resurrection.* The resurrection of Christ did not consist in the mere fact that He came to life again and that body and soul were re-united. If this were all it involved, He could not be called "the firstfruits of them that slept," I Cor. 15:20, nor "the firstborn from the dead," Col. 1:18; Rev. 1:5. It rather consisted in this that in Him human nature, both body and soul, was restored to its pristine purity, strength, and perfection, and even raised to a higher level, while body and soul were re-united into a living organism. It was quite evident after the resurrection that His body had undergone a remarkable change. It was the same and yet so different that it was not easily recognized. It was a material and real body, and yet one that could suddenly appear and disappear in a surprising manner, a body transformed into a perfect organ of the spirit, and therefore "spiritual," Luke 24:31, 36, 39; John 20:19; 21:7; I Cor. 15:50. Evidently there was also a change in the soul life of Christ. This does not mean that He was changed religiously and ethically, but that His soul was endowed with new qualities, perfectly adjusted to His future heavenly environment. Through the resurrection He became the life-giving Spirit, I Cor. 15:45.

b. *The Significance of the Resurrection.* The resurrection of Christ has a threefold significance:

(*a*) It constitutes a declaration of the Father that Christ met all the demands of the law as a covenant obligation; (*b*) it symbolizes what will happen to believers in their justification, spiritual birth, and future resurrection, Rom. 6:4, 5, 9; 8:11; I Cor. 6:14; 15:20-22; II Cor. 4:10, 11, 14; Col. 2:12; I Thess. 4:14; and (*c*) it is the cause of our justification, regeneration, and final resurrection, Rom. 4:25 5:10; Eph. 1:20; Phil. 3:10; I Pet. 1:3.

c. The Denial of the Resurrection. The resurrection of Jesus Christ is a miracle which defies all natural explanation. For that very reason many at present deny the resurrection of Christ, declaring it to be a physical impossibility, since material particles in the course of time enter into the composition of many bodies, and can never be restored to all the bodies of which they once formed a part. But they who deny the resurrection must, of course, explain the undeniable fact that belief in the resurrection of Christ was general in the first Christian century. Various theories have been suggested in explanation, such as (*a*) that the apostles and other early witnesses palmed off a falsehood on a credulous people; (*b*) that Jesus did not really die, but merely swooned, while the apostles thought that He had actually died; (*c*) that the apostles and the women in their excited state of mind saw visions of Jesus and confused these with actual appearances; and (*d*) that the resurrection story was really imported from other oriental religions and derived from pagan myths. But these explanations fail to do justice to the facts in the case, as they are narrated in Scripture.

2. THE ASCENSION OF CHRIST. The ascension of Christ does not stand out as boldly on the pages of the Bible as the resurrection. The latter was the real turning-point in the life of Jesus, and the ascension may be called its necessary complement and completion. This does not mean that the ascension was devoid of independent significance. The Scriptural proof for it is quite sufficient. Jesus referred

to it time and again before His death, John 6:62; 14:2, 12; 16:5, 10, 17, 28; 17:5; 20:17. Luke gives us a double account of it, Luke 24:50-53; Acts 1:6-11. Paul refers to it repeatedly, Eph. 1: 20; 4:8-10; I Tim. 3:16, and the Epistle to the Hebrews calls attention to its significance, 1:3; 4: 14; 9:24.

a. *The Nature of the Ascension.* The ascension may be described as the visible ascent of the person of the Mediator from earth to heaven, according to His human nature. It was a local transition, a going from place to place. This implies, of course, that heaven is a place as well as earth. But the ascension of Jesus was not merely a transition from one place to another; it also included a further change in the human nature of Christ. That nature now passed into the fulness of heavenly glory, and was perfectly adapted to the life of heaven. Some Christian scholars of recent date consider heaven to be a condition rather than a place, and therefore do not conceive of the ascension locally. Scripture clearly represents heaven as a place, however. It is the dwelling-place of created beings, such as angels and saints, Matt. 18:10; II Cor. 5:1, and is often mentioned alongside of the earth, which is a place, I Chron. 16: 31; Eccl. 5:2; Isa. 66:1. Moreover, the Bible directs our thought upward to heaven and downward to hell, Deut. 30:12; Josh. 2:11; Ps. 139: 8; Rom. 10:6, 7.

b. *The Lutheran Conception of the Ascension.* The Lutheran view of the ascension differs from that of the Reformed. They do not regard it as a local transition but as a change of condition, whereby the human nature of Christ passes into the full enjoyment and exercise of the divine perfections, which were communicated to it at the incarnation, and thus became permanently omnipresent.

c. *The Significance of the Ascension.* In the ascension we see Christ as our great High Priest entering the inner sanctuary to present His completed sacrifice to the Father. It is prophetic of the ascension to all believers, who are even now set with Christ in heavenly places, Eph. 2:6, and are destined to be with Him forever, John 17:24. Finally, it is also instrumental in preparing a place for those that are of Christ. The Lord Himself points to the necessity of going to the Father. in order to prepare a place for His disciples, John 14:2, 3.

3. Christ's Session at the Right Hand of God. After His ascension Christ took His place on the throne at the right hand of the Father. He predicted that He would be seated at the right hand of power, Matt. 26:64. Peter makes mention of it in his sermons, Acts 2:33-36; 5:31, and several passages in the Epistles refer to it, Eph. 1:20-22; Heb. 10:12; I Pet. 3:22; Rev. 3:21; 22:1. Naturally, the expression "right hand of God" cannot be taken literally, but should be understood as a figurative indication of the place of power and glory. That Christ is seated at the right hand of the Father simply means that the reins of government over the

Church and the universe are entrusted to Him, and that He is made to share in the corresponding glory. It is His public inauguration as the God-man. During His session at the right hand of God, Christ rules and protects His Church and exercises authority over the universe in behalf of His people; presents His completed sacrifice to the Father, making it effective and securing its benefits by constant intercession for all believers; and continues to teach His people through the Holy Spirit and through the instrumentality of His servants.

4. THE PHYSICAL RETURN OF CHRIST. The highest stage in the exaltation of Christ is not reached until He returns in the capacity of Judge. He Himself refers to this as a special prerogative, John 5:22, 27, and so do the apostles, Acts 10:42; 17:31. Several other passages also refer to His judicial activity, Matt. 19:28; 25:31-34; Luke 3:17; Rom. 2:16; 14:9; II Cor. 5:10; II Tim. 4:1; Jas. 5:9. Some place the return of Christ in the past, claiming that the promise of His coming again was realized when He returned in the Holy Spirit on the day of Pentecost. But this was a spiritual and invisible return, while the Bible teaches us to look for a physical and visible return of Christ, Acts 1:11. Even after Pentecost we are taught to look forward to the coming of Christ, I Cor. 1:7; 4:5; 11:26; Phil. 3:20; Col. 3:4; I Thess. 4:15-17; II Thess. 1:7-10; Tit. 2:13; Rev. 1:7. The second coming of Jesus Christ will be for the purpose of judging the world and perfecting the salvation of His people. It will signalize the complete victory of His redemptive work.

Questions for Review:

What is meant by the states of the Mediator? What is the state of humiliation? In what did the incarnation consist? How did Christ receive His human nature? What Scripture proof have we for the virgin birth? What was the work of the Holy Spirit in connection with the birth of Christ? Was the incarnation a part of Christ's humiliation? Were the sufferings of Christ limited to the end of His life? What was the nature of His sufferings? What significance does it have that Christ died a judicial death, and that He died by crucifixion? What significance did the burial of Christ have? What different views are there of the descent into hades? What is the correct view? What is the state of exaltation? What was the nature of the resurrection of Christ? In what respect was the body of Christ changed after the resurrection? Did He undergo any other change? What was the significance of the resurrection? On what ground is it denied by some? What theories are suggested to explain the general belief in the resurrection of Christ? How is the ascension of Christ related to His resurrection? How does Scripture prove that the ascension was a change from place to place? How do the Lutherans conceive of the resurrection? What significance has the ascension? What is meant by the session of Christ at the right hand of God? What work does He accomplish during His session? Did Christ return in the Holy Spirit? Was this the predicted second coming of Christ? What is the purpose of His second coming?

References for Further Study:

Berkhof, *Reformed Dogmatics*, I, pp. 333-362; Hodge, *Systematic Theology*, II, pp. 610-638; Hodge, *Outlines of Theology*, pp. 438-44; McPherson, *Christian Theology*, pp. 321-330; Dick, *Lectures on Theology*, Lect. LX-LXIII.

THE WORK OF CHRIST

The Offices of Christ

Since the days of Calvin it is customary to speak of three offices of the Mediator. Man, as he was created by God, was intended to function as prophet, priest, and king. Hence he was endowed with knowledge and understanding, with righteousness and holiness, and with dominion over the lower creation. The entrance of sin into the world affected the whole man and made it impossible for him to function properly in his threefold capacity as prophet, priest, and king. He is subject to the power of error and deception, of unrighteousness and moral pollution, and of misery and death. Christ came as the ideal man and for the purpose of restoring man to his original condition, and as such necessarily functioned as prophet, priest, and king. In some circles there is a tendency to recognize only one of the offices of Christ. Rationalism stresses the prophetic, Mysticism the priestly, and Chiliasm the kingly office of Christ. Modern liberal theology is inclined to deny the offices altogether. It is so much in love with Christ as the ideal man, the loving helper, and the elder brother, that it dislikes to think of Him in any official capacity.

A. **The Prophetic Office.** The Old Testament predicts the coming of Christ as a prophet in Deut. 18:15, a passage that is applied to Christ in Act 3:22, 23. He speaks of Himself as a prophet in Luke 13:33. Moreover, He claims to bring a message from the Father, John 8:26-28; 12:49,, 50; 14:10, 24; 15:15; 17:8, 20, foretells future things, Matt. 24:3-35; Luke 19:41-44, and therefore speaks with singular authority, Matt.

7:29. In view of all this it is no wonder that the people recognized Him as a prophet, Matt. 21:11, 46; Luke 7:16; 24:19; John 3:2; 4:19; 6:14; 7:40; 9:17.

1. THE SCRIPTURAL IDEA OF A PROPHET. The classical passages, Ex. 7:1 and Deut. 18:18, indicate that there are two sides to the prophetic office, the one receptive and the other productive. The prophet receives divine revelations in dreams, visions, or verbal communications; and passes these on to the people, either orally, or visibly in prophetic actions, Num. 12:6-8; Isa. 6; Jer. 1:4-10; Ezek. 3:1-4, 17. The receptive side is the most important and controls the other. Without receiving the prophet cannot give, and he cannot give more than he receives. Yet the productive side is also essential. One who merely receives revelations is not yet a prophet. It was the duty of the prophets to reveal the will of God to the people, to interpret the law in its moral and spiritual aspects, to protest against formalism and sin, calling the people back to the path of duty, and to direct attention to the glorious promises of God for the future.

2. THE WAYS IN WHICH CHRIST FUNCTIONS AS PROPHET. The prophetic work of Christ should not be limited to the time of His earthly life or His public ministry. He functioned as prophet during the old dispensation as the Angel of the Lord, and also in and through the prophets, I Pet. 1:11; 3:18-20. He did it while He was on earth in His teachings and by means of the accompanying signs. And His prophetic work did not cease when He

ascended to heaven. He continued it by the operation of the Holy Spirit in and through the teaching of the apostles, John 14:26; 16:12-14; Acts 1:1; and still continues it through the ministry of the Word and in the spiritual illumination of believers. Even while He is seated at the right hand of the Father, He is ever active as our great Prophet.

3. MODERN EMPHASIS ON THE PROPHETIC WORK OF CHRIST. In so far as there is any recognition of the official work of Christ in modern liberal theology, the emphasis is altogether on the prophetic work of Christ. Christ stands out before the modern mind primarily as the great teacher of mankind. To believe in Christ is simply to accept His teachings and to submit to His guidance. By His word and example He is leading His followers to ever higher levels of moral and spiritual life.

B. **The Priestly Office.** The Old Testament predicts and prefigures the priesthood of the coming Redeemer. There are clear references to it in Ps. 110:4 and Zech. 6:13. In Isaiah 53 we see the Servant of the Lord especially in His priestly capacity. Moreover, the Old Testament priesthood, and particularly the high priest, clearly prefigured a priestly Messiah. In the New Testament there is only a single book in which He is called priest, namely, the Epistle to the Hebrews, but there the name is applied to Him repeatedly, 3:1; 4:14; 5:5; 6:20; 7:26; 8:1. However, other New Testament books also refer to His priestly work, Mark 10:45; John 1:29; Rom. 3:24, 25; I Cor. 5:7; Eph. 5:2; I John 2:2; 4:10; I Pet. 2:24; 3:18.

1. THE SCRIPTURAL IDEA OF A PRIEST. The Bible makes a broad but important distinction between a prophet and a priest. The prophet was appointed to be God's representative with the people, and was primarily a religious teacher. The priest, on the other hand, was man's representative with God. He had the special privilege of approach to God, and of speaking and acting in behalf of the people. The Old Testament priests were also teachers, but their teaching differed from that of the prophets. While the latter emphasized the moral and spiritual duties, responsibilities, and privileges, the former stressed the ritual observances involved in the proper approach to God. The characteristics of a priest are given rather fully in Heb. 5:1. The priest (*a*) is taken from among men to be their representative; (*b*) is appointed by God (vs. 3); (*c*) is active in the interest of men in things pertaining to God, that is, religious things; and (*d*) offers gifts and sacrifices for sins. In addition he also makes intercession for the people.

2. THE SACRIFICIAL WORK OF CHRIST.

a. The Nature of Christ's Sacrificial Work. The work of Christ was first of all to bring a sacrifice for sin. The peculiarity in His case was that the priest was also the sacrifice. In other words, the sacrifice of Christ was a self-sacrifice, a sacrifice in which He laid down His life for sinners. Moreover, this one sacrifice combined all the elements represented in the various sacrifices of the Old Testament. It was a sin- and trespass-offering to make atonement for sin; it was a burnt-offering of whole-hearted and complete consecration to God; and it was also a peace-offering through which the sinner enters into blessed communion with God. In view of this it may be said that the sacrifice of Christ was of a many-sided character.

b. *The Sacrificial Work of Christ Prefigured in the Old Testament.* The Old Testament sacrifices had spiritual aand typical significance. They were prophetical and prefigured the sacrifice of Christ. The paschal lamb is regarded as a type of Christ. There is a distant reference to it in John 1:29. Moreover, Christ is called "our passover" in I Cor. 5:7. There are clear indications and even express statements to the effect that the Old Testament sacrifices prefigured Christ and His work, Col. 2:17; Heb. 9:23, 24; 10:1; 13:11, 12. Besides, there are several passages which teach that Christ accomplished for sinners exactly what the Old Testament sacrifices were said to effect for those who brought them, and that He accomplished it in a similar manner, II Cor. 5:21; Gal. 3:13; I John 1:7.

c. *Scripture Proof for the Sacrificial Work of Christ.* The priestly work of Christ is most clearly represented in the Epistle to the Hebrews, where the Mediator is described as our only real, eternal, and perfect High Priest, appointed by God, who takes our place vicariously, and by His self-sacrifice obtains a real and perfect redemption, Heb. 5:1-10; 7:1-28; 9:11-15, 24-28; 10:11-14, 19-22; 12:24. While this is the only Epistle in which

Christ is called priest, His priestly work is also clearly represented in the Epistles of Paul, Rom. 3:24, 25; 5:6-8; I Cor. 5:7; 5:3; Eph. 5:2. The same representation is found in the writings of John, John 1:29; 3:14, 15; I John 2:2; 4·10, and in the First Epistle of Peter, 2:24; 3:18.

3. THE INTERCESSORY WORK OF CHRIST. The priestly work of Christ is not limited to the bringing of a sacrifice; He is also the intercessor of His people. He is called our "parakletos" by implication in John 14:16 and explicitly in I John 2:2. The term means *one who is called in to help, an advocate, one who pleads the cause of another.* Christ as the believer's advocate pleads His cause with the Father against Satan, Zech. 3:1; Heb. 7:25; I John 2:1; Rev. 12:10.

   a. *The Nature of Christ's Intercessory Work.* The intercessory work of Christ is based on His atoning sacrifice, is but a continuation of His priestly work, and carries this to completion. The nature of the work is indicated by Scripture in Rom. 8: 24; Heb. 7:25; 9:24. It is not limited to intercessory prayer, as is often mistakenly thought, but includes much more. As intercessor Christ continuously presents His sacrifice to God as the ground of all necessary blessings for His people, persistently claims these blessings for them according to their need, answers all accusations preferred against them by Satan, by the law, and by conscience, secures forgiveness for everything that is justly charged against them, and presents to God their worship and service, rendering it acceptable through His own righteousness.

b. *The Extent and Efficacy of His Intercession.* Christ intercedes for *all* those for whom He has made atonement and for those *only*. This may be inferred from the limited character of the atonement and from such passages as Rom. 8:29, cf. vss. 33, 34, and Heb. 7:25. Moreover, it is explicitly stated in John 17:9. It should be carefully noted, however, that Christ does not intercede for believers only, but for all the elect, whether they be already believers, or are still unbelievers, John 17:20. Furthermore, it should not be forgotten that He stands before God as an authorized intercessor, and therefore as one who can present legal claims. What He asks of the Father He asks as a matter of right, and therefore His prayers on behalf of His people never fail. They are based on His atoning work, and He has merited all that He asks.

C. **The Kingly Office.** Christ as the Son of God naturally shares in the dominion of God over all His creatures. This kingship is rooted in His divine nature and is His by original right. In this connection, however, we are concerned with a kingship with which He as Mediator was invested. We distinguish a twofold Mediatorial kingship of Christ, His spiritual kingship over the Church, and His kingship over the universe.

1. THE SPIRITUAL KINGSHIP OF CHRIST. The Bible speaks of this kingship in many places, Ps. 2:6; 45:6, 7 (cf. Heb. 1:8, 9); 132:11; Isa. 9:6, 7; Micah 5:2; Zech. 6:13; Luke 1:33; 19:27, 38; John 18:36, 37; Acts 2:30-36.

a. The Nature of This Kingship. The spiritual kingship of Christ is His royal rule over His people, or over the Church. It is called spiritual, because it relates to a spiritual realm, is established in the hearts and lives of believers, bears directly and immediately on a spiritual end, the salvation of sinners, and is administered, not by external, but by spiritual means, the Word and the Spirit. This kingship is exercised in the gathering, the government, the protection, and the perfection of the Church. The term "head" is sometimes applied to Christ as the king of the Church, I Cor. 11:3; Eph. 1:20-22; 5:23. It is just because Christ is the head of the Church that He can rule it in an organic and spiritual way.

b. The Realm Over Which it Extends. The spiritual kingdom of Christ is identical with what the New Testament calls the kingdom of God or the kingdom of heaven. This kingdom is first of all the kingship of God in Christ established and acknowledged in the hearts of man by the work of regeneration. In the second place it is also the realm over which the rule of God in Christ extends, a realm created by the Spirit of God and composed exclusively of those who share in the life of the Spirit. And, finally, it is also a new condition of things which results from the application of the principles of the kingdom of God and which often extends beyond the sphere of the kingdom in the strictest sense of the word. The citizenship of the kingdom is co-extensive with the membership of the invisible Church. Its field of operation, however, is wider than that of the Church and aims at the control of life in all its manifestations. The visible Church is the most important and the only divinely instituted external organization of the kingdom. The term "kingdom of God" is sometimes used in a sense which makes the kingdom practically equivalent to the visible Church, Matt. 8:12; 13:24-30, 47-50.

The spiritual kingdom of Christ is both present and future. It is on the one hand a present, ever-developing spiritual reality in the hearts and lives of men, and as such exercises influence in a constantly widening sphere, Matt. 12:28; Luke 17:21; Col. 1:13. But on the other hand it is also a future hope, which will not be realized until the return of Jesus Christ. This future aspect of it is the more prominent of the two in Scripture, Matt. 7:21; 19:23; Luke 22:29; I Cor. 6:9; 15:50; Gal. 5:21; Eph. 5:5; II Tim. 4:18; II Pet. 1:11. In essence the future kingdom will consist, like that of the present, simply in the rule of God established and acknowledged in the hearts of men. But at the glorious coming of Jesus Christ this establishment and acknowledgment will be perfected, the hidden forces of the kingdom will stand revealed, and the spiritual rule of Christ will find its consummation in a visible and majestic reign.

c. *The Duration of Christ's Spiritual Kingship.* Socinians claim that Christ did not become king until the time of His ascension, and Premillenarians, that He will not be seated upon the throne as Mediator until He establishes the millennium at the second advent. As a matter of fact, however, He was appointed as king from eternity, Prov. 8:23; Ps. 2:6, and began to function as such immediately after the fall. Yet He did not formally and publicly assume His throne until the time of His ascension and elevation to the right hand of God. Some opine that this kingship will cease at the return of Christ, but Scripture would seem to teach explicitly that it will endure forever, Ps. 45:6; 72:17; 89:36, 37; Isa. 9:7; Dan. 2:44; II Sam. 7:13, 16; Luke 1:33; II Pet. 1:11.

2. THE KINGSHIP OF CHRIST OVER THE UNIVERSE. Before His ascension Christ said to His disciples: "All authority hath been given unto me in heaven and on earth," Matt. 28:18. The same truth is also taught in Eph. 1:20-22; I Cor. 15:27.

   a. *The Nature of This Kingship.* This kingship should not be confused with the original kingship of Christ as the Son of God, though it extends to the same realm. It is the kingship of the universe entrusted to Christ as Mediator in behalf of His Church. As King of the universe He now guides the destinies of individuals, of social groups, and of nations, so as to promote the growth, the gradual purification, and the final perfection of the people which He has redeemed by His blood. Moreover, this kingship enables Him to protect His own against the dangers to which they are exposed in the world, and to vindicate His righteousness by the subjection and destruction of all His enemies.

b. The Duration of This Kingship. Christ was formally invested with this kingship over the universe when He was exalted at the right hand of God. It was a promised reward of His labours, Ps. 2:8, 9; Matt. 28:18; Eph. 1:20-22; Phil. 2:9-11. This investiture did not give Him any power or authority which He did not already possess as the Son of God; neither did it increase His territory. It simply gave this authority to Christ as the God-man, so that His human nature was now made to share in the glory of this royal dominion. The government of the world was made subservient to the interests of the Church of Jesus Christ. This kingship will last until the victory over the enemies of the kingdom is complete, I Cor. 15:24-28. When the end is accomplished, it will be returned to the Father.

Questions for Review:

Why has Christ a threefold office? What Scripture proof is there for the prophetic office of Christ? What is a prophet? What two sides are there to the prophetic office? What are the duties of a prophet? In what different ways does Christ function as prophet? How does modern liberal theology stress the prophetic office of Christ? How was Christ as priest prefigured? What Scripture proof is there for His priestly work? What is a priest in distinction from a prophet? How did their teaching differ among Israel? What are the characteristics of a priest? What was the nature of Christ's sacrificial work? How was this prefigured in the Old Testament? What Scripture proof is there for this work? What is a paraclete? In what does the work of Christ as intercessor consist? How far does His intercession extend and why is it always effective? What is the spiritual kingship of Christ? Over what realm does it extend? What does the term "kingdom of God" denote in the Gospels? Is the kingdom the same as the Church? How is the present kingdom related to the future kingdom? When did Christ become king? How long will His spiritual kingship last? What is the nature and purpose of Christ's kingship over the universe? How long will this kingship last?

References for Further Study:

Berkhof, *Reformed Dogmatics*, I, pp. 363-388; Hodge, *Outlines of Theology*, pp. 391-400; Hodge, *Systematic Theology*, II, pp. 459-479, 592-609; Stevenson, *The Office of Christ.*

A. The Moving Cause and Necessity of the Atonement.

1. THE MOVING CAUSE OF THE ATONEMENT. It is sometimes represented as if the moving cause of the atonement lay in the sympathetic love of Christ for sinners. In this representation the impression is often given that God is an angry God bent on the sinner's destruction, but that the loving Christ steps in between and at the cost of His life saves the transgressor. Christ receives the glory and God is forgotten, robbed of His honour. Scripture finds the moving cause of the atonement in the good pleasure of God to save sinners by a substitutionary atonement, Isa. 53:10; Luke 2:14; Col. 1:19, 20. This good pleasure of God should not be regarded as some arbitrary choice of God. It is more in harmony with Scripture to say that the good pleasure of God to save sinners by a substitutionary atonement was founded in the love and justice of God. It was the love of God that offered sinners a way of escape, John 3:16. And it was the justice of God which required that the demands of the law should be met, "that He might be just, and the justified of him which believeth in Jesus," Rom. 3:26; cf. vss. 24, 25.

2. THE NECESSITY OF THE ATONEMENT. Some, such as Duns Scotus, Socinus, and many modern liberal theologians, deny the necessity of the atonement. They do not believe that anything in God required

satisfaction for sin before He could pardon the sinner. It is quite evident, however, that atonement was necessary in view of the justice of God. This was violated by man's transgression, and therefore naturally called for satisfaction. The righteousness and holiness of God, which can brook no sin, certainly cannot simply overlook open defiance to His infinite majesty. God hates sin with a divine hatred, and His whole being reacts against it, Gen. 18:25; Ex. 20:5; 23:7; Ps. 5:6, 7; Nah. 1:2; Rom. 1:18, 32. Moreover, the veracity of God required that the sentence which He had pronounced on sin should be executed, Ezek. 18:4; Rom. 6:23.

B. The Nature of the Atonement.

1. It served to Render Satisfaction to God. The atonement has frequently been represented, and is now often regarded, as something that was primarily intended to influence the sinner, to awaken repentance, and thus to bring him back to God. But this is an entirely erroneous conception of it. If a man does wrong and renders satisfaction, this satisfaction is naturally intended to influence the person wronged, and not the offending party. In the case of the sinner the atonement served to propitiate God, and to regain His good favor by making amends for the sin committed. This means that the primary purpose of the atonement was to reconcile God to the sinner. This does not imply, however, that we cannot, in any sense of the word, speak of the sinner's being reconciled to God. The Bible does this in more than one place, Rom. 5:10;

II Cor. 5:19, 20. The reconciliation of the sinner to God may be regarded as the secondary purpose of the atonement. The reconciled God justifies the sinner and so operates in his heart by the Holy Spirit that the latter also lays aside his wicked alienation from God, and thus enters into the fruits of the perfect atonement of Christ.

3. It Was a Vicarious Atonement. There is a difference between personal and vicarious atonement. When man fell away from God, he became a transgressor and as such owed God satisfaction. But man could atone for his sin only by suffering the penalty of sin eternally; and this is what God might have required in strict justice, and would have required, if He had not been actuated by love and compassion for the sinner. Instead of insisting on such personal atonement, however, He appointed a vicar (substitute) in Jesus Christ to take man's place; and this vicar atoned for the sin of mankind and wrought an eternal redemption for man. In this case, therefore, the offended party himself made provision for atonement. While a personal atonement would have excluded the element of mercy, this vicarious atonement represents the highest form of mercy. And while a personal atonement by the sinner would have been forever in the making and could never have resulted in redemption, the vicarious atonement provided by God Himself leads to reconciliation and life everlasting. The vicarious atonement wrought by Christ was prefigured in the animal sacrifices of the Old Testament. Scripture repeatedly says that these sacrifices atoned for sin

and thus resulted in the pardoning of the transgressor, Lev. 1:4; 4:20, 31, 35; 5:10, 16; 6:7; 17:11. Several passages speak of our sins being "laid upon" Christ, and of His "bearing" sin or iniquity, Isa. 53:6; John 1:29; II Cor. 5:21; Gal. 3:13; Heb. 9:28; I Pet. 2:24. Others make mention of His dying or giving Himself for sin or for the sinner, Mark 10:45; Rom. 8:3; Gal. 1:4; I Pet. 3:18; I John 2:2.

3. It Included Christ's Active and Passive Obedience. It is customary to distinguish between the active and passive obedience of Christ. His active obedience consists in all that He did to observe the law in behalf of sinners, as a condition for obtaining eternal life; and His passive obedience in all that He suffered in paying the penalty of sin and thus discharging the debt of all His people. While it is necessary to discriminate between the two, it should be distinctly understood that they cannot be separated. The two accompany each other at every point in the Saviour's life. It was a part of Christ's active obedience that He subjected Himself voluntarily to suffering and death, John 10:18. On the other hand, it was also a part of Christ's passive obedience that He lived in subjection to the law and moved about in the form of a servant. In general it may be said that through His passive obedience He paid the penalty for sin and consequently removed the curse from man, Isa. 53:6; Rom. 4:25; I Pet. 3:18; I John 2:2; and that through His active obedience He merited eternal life for the sinner, bringing him to the goal which Adam failed

to reach, Rom. 8:4; 10:3, 4; II Cor. 5:21; Gal. 4:4, 5, 7.

C. **The Extent of the Atonement.** It is generally admitted that the satisfaction rendered by Christ was in itself sufficient for the salvation of all men, though they do not attain unto salvation. There is a difference of opinion, however, as to the question, whether Christ suffered and died *for the purpose* of saving all men or only the elect.

1. THE LIMITED EXTENT OF THE ATONEMENT. Roman Catholics, Lutherans, and Arminians of every description, maintain that the atonement wrought by Christ is universal. This does not mean that in their estimation all men will be saved, but simply that it was the intention of the Father in sending Christ, and of Christ in the accomplishment of His redemptive work, to save them all without any exception. They all admit that, as a matter of fact, the intended effect is not achieved. In distinction from them the Reformed Churches believe in a limited atonement. They maintain that it was the intention of both the Father and the Son to save only the elect, a purpose that is actually accomplished. The advocates of a universal atonement assert that Christ merely made salvation possible for all men, and that their actual redemption is dependent on their own free choice. The advocates of a limited atonement, on the other hand, maintain that Christ actually saves to the uttermost every one of those for whom He has laid down His life. Not one of those for whom the price is paid finally falls short of salvation. The Bible clearly teaches that the effect of the work of Christ is not merely to make

atonement possible, but to reconcile men to God and to put them in actual possession of eternal salvation, Luke 19:10; Rom. 5:10; II Cor. 5:21; Gal. 1:4; 3:13; Eph. 1:7. Moreover, it indicates in various ways that Christ laid down His life for a certain qualified number, for His people, Matt. 1:21, for His sheep, John 10:11, 15, for the Church, Acts 20:28; Eph. 5:25-27, or for the elect, Rom. 8:32-35. Moreover, if it was really the purpose of God to save all men, then we shall have to come to the conclusion that the divine purpose is frustrated by men, and this is an impossibility.

2. Objections to a Limited Atonement. Several objections have been raised to the doctrine of a particular atonement, of which the following are the most important.

   a. There are passages which teach that Christ died for the world, John 1:29; 3:16; I John 2:2; 4:14. The objectors proceed on the assumption that the word "world" in these passages always denotes all the individuals that constitute the world of humanity. But the word does not always have this meaning; its meaning is certainly more limited in Luke 2:1; 12:19. In the passages referred to it may simply serve to indicate that Christ died, not merely for the Jews, but for people of all the nations of the world.

   b. Again, there are passages in which Christ is said to have died for all men, Rom. 5:18; I Cor. 15:22; II Cor. 5:14; I Tim. 2:4, 6; Tit. 2:11; Heb. 2:9; II Pet. 3:9. But the word "all" sometimes has a restricted meaning in Scripture, denoting all of a particular class, I Cor. 15:22;

Eph. 1:23, or all kinds of classes, Tit. 2:11. If it were always taken in the absolute sense in the passages referred to by the objectors, some of these passages would teach that all men are actually saved, something which they themselves do not believe, cf. Rom. 5:18; I Cor. 15:22; Heb. 2:9, cf. v. 10.

c. Finally, it is said that the universal offer of salvation in the preaching of the word presupposes a universal atonement. If Christ did not die for all men, the offer of salvation cannot be extended to all in good faith. But the universal offer of salvation does not include the declaration that Christ made atonement for every individual; moreover, it is always conditioned by a faith and repentance that can only be wrought in the heart by the Holy Spirit. Only the elect comply with the requirements and thus receive the blessings of salvation.

D. **The Atonement in Present-Day Theology.** There is a wide-spread denial of the atonement in the proper sense of the word in present-day theology. Modern liberal theology really has no place for a doctrine of the atonement in any sense of the word. It regards sin simply as a weakness or as an imperfection which man has not yet overcome but will outgrow in the process of evolution; an imperfection for which man is not responsible, which constitutes no guilt, and therefore calls for no atonement. But even many modern evangelical Churches advocate a view of the atonement which is really equivalent to a denial of it. They ignore the idea that the atoning work of Christ served the purpose of appeasing the wrath of God against sin and of gaining His favor for the sinner. According to them the atonement did not effect a change in the attitude of God to the sinner, but only a change in the attitude of the sinner to God. What they call atonement is really reconciliation. Christ suffered and died to reveal to sinners the great love of God, and thus to awaken a responsive love in their hearts, which will induce them as lost sons to return to God in a penitent state of mind. This view of the atonement certainly does not do justice to the representations of Scripture respecting the work of Christ. It ignores the justice of God, which requires atonement, and fails to give any adequate reason for the death of Christ.

Questions for Review:

What was the moving cause of the atonement? Why was the atonement necessary? What erroneous conception do many have of the purpose of the atonement? What was the real purpose? How can this be proved from Scripture? What is the difference between personal and vicarious atonement? How was the vicarious sacrifice of Christ prefigured in the Old Testament? What Scripture proof is there for it? What is the difference between the active and the passive obedience of Christ? Can these two be separated? What did each one of these effect? What is the question in debate in connection with the extent of the atonement? What is meant by universal atonement, and who teach it? What is limited atonement, and what Scriptural proof is there for it? What objections are raised to the doctrine of a limited atonement, and what can be said in answer to these? What is the prevalent view of the atonement in present-day theology?

References for Further Study:

Berkhof, *Reformed Dogmatics*, I. pp. 389-427; Hodge, *Outlines of Theology*, pp. 401-425; Orr, *Side-Lights on Christian Doctrine*, pp. 125-139; McPherson, *Christian Dogmatics*, pp. 329-367. Hodge, *The Atonement.*

THE DOCTRINE OF THE APPLICATION OF THE WORK OF REDEMPTION

THE DOCTRINE OF THE APPLICATION OF THE WORK OF REDEMPTION

The Common Operations of the Holy Spirit

The immediately preceding division of this work was devoted to a discussion of the person and the work of Christ, by which the way of salvation was opened for sinners and all the blessings of salvation and of eternal life in communion with God were merited for all those whom Christ represented in the counsel of peace. This is naturally followed by a discussion of the way in which the work of redemption wrought by Christ is applied in the hearts and lives of sinners by the special operation of the Holy Spirit. In order that this work may be seen against the proper background, we shall briefly consider in an opening chapter the general operations of the Holy Spirit.

A. **The General Operations of the Holy Spirit in Nature.** It is of the highest importance that the special operations of the Holy Spirit in the work of redemption should be seen against the background of His general operations in the sphere of nature and in the life of man. There is a certain similarity between the two, but also a very essential difference. In the sphere of nature it is the Holy Spirit that gives birth to all life, organic, intellectual, and moral, that maintains it amid all changes, and that leads it to its development and destiny. And this is exactly what He also does in the sphere of grace or of redemption. He originates the new life in Christ Jesus, guides it in its development, makes it fruitful in good works, and leads it to its destiny. But there is also an essential difference between the two. The general operations of the Holy Spirit pertain to the established order of nature and of the life of man, as it is rooted in creation, and guarantee its development and completion. His special operation, on the other hand, bears directly only on the elect and introduces a new order of things that does not find its explanation in the work of creation, but only in the grace of God, revealed in Jesus Christ. Without the general operations of the Holy Spirit, however, there would be no proper sphere for His special operations.

B. **Common Grace.** Among the fruits of the general operations of the Holy Spirit common grace deserves special mention.

1. Description of Common Grace. The distinction between common and special grace does not apply to grace as an attribute of God, but only to the gracious operations of God and to the effects of these operations in nature and in the life of man. When we speak of common grace we have in mind either (*a*) those general operations of the Holy Spirit whereby He, without renewing the heart, exercises such a moral influence on man that sin is restrained, order is maintained in social life, and civil righteousness is promoted; or (*b*) those general blessings which God imparts to all men indiscriminately in whatever measure it seems good to Him. The Arminian believes that common grace enables man to perform a certain measure of spiritual good, and to turn to God with heartfelt repentance; and that it even incites man to accept

Jesus Christ by faith, and will accomplish its end, unless man obstinately resists its operations. But this is an un-Scriptural view of the matter. Common grace does not enable the sinner to perform any spiritual good, nor to turn to God in faith and repentance. It is not sufficient to remove the total depravity of man, nor to lead him in the way of spiritual renewal. The following points of distinction between common and special grace should be carefully noted: (*a*) The former effects no spiritual change in the heart of man, while the latter does; (*b*) the former works in a rational and moral way by making men receptive for the truth, presenting motives to the will, and appealing to the natural desires of man, while the latter works in a spiritual and creative way, renewing the whole nature of man and producing spiritual fruits; and (*c*) the former is resistible and is always more or less resisted, while the latter is irresistible, changing man so that he willingly yields to its operations.

2. Common Grace and the Atoning Work of Christ. By His atoning work Christ merited the blessings of special grace. Did He also by His sacrificial death merit the more common blessings of divine grace which are bestowed on all men, and therefore also on the impenitent and reprobate? If He did not merit them, then what is the legal basis on which God can extend grace and show favor to men who have forfeited everything and have no share in the righteousness of Christ? Now it is possible that no such basis is needed in view of the

fact (*a*) that common grace does not remove the guilt of sin and therefore does not carry pardon with it; and (*b*) that it does not lift the sentence of condemnation, but only postpones its execution. Perhaps the divine good pleasure to stay the manifestation of the wrath of God against sin offers a sufficient explanation for the blessings of common grace. It is not unlikely, however, that even these blessings must be connected in some way with the death of Christ. This does not necessarily mean that Christ merited these blessings for the impenitent and reprobate, but simply that important benefits accrue to the whole human race from the death of Christ, and that in these benefits the unbelieving, the impenitent, and the reprobate share. These general blessings indirectly resulting from the atoning work of Christ were, of course, not only foreseen by God, but also designed by Him as blessings for all mankind.

3. THE MEANS BY WHICH COMMON GRACE OPERATES. There are several means by which common grace operates, such as:

a. *The Light of God's Revelation.* This is fundamental, for without it all other means would be impossible and ineffective. We have in mind primarily the light of God's general revelation in nature, which lightens every man and serves to guide the conscience of the natural man. In a more restricted sense common grace also operates in connection with the light of God's special revelation.

b. *Governments.* Our Belgic Confession teaches that God instituted governments, in order to curb the evil tendencies, "the dissoluteness of men," and to promote among them "good order and decency."

c. *Public Opinion.* The light of God that shines in nature, especially when reinforced by the light of special revelation, results in the formation of a public opinion that is in harmony with the law of God; and this has a tremendous influence on the conduct of men who are very sensitive to the judgment of public opinion.

d. *Divine Punishment and Rewards.* God visits the iniquity of men upon them even in this life, and rewards deeds that are in outward conformity with the law. The punishments have a deterring effect, and the rewards serve as incentives. Thus whatever there is of moral goodness in the world is greatly encouraged.

4. THE EFFECTS OF COMMON GRACE.

a. *Execution of the Sentence Stayed.* It is due to common grace that God did not at once fully execute the sentence of death upon the sinner, and does not do so now, but maintains and prolongs the natural life of man and gives him time for repentance.

b. *Restraint of Sin.* Through the operation of common grace sin is restrained in the lives of individuals and society. The element of corruption that entered the life of the human race is not permitted, for the present, to accomplish its disintegrating work.

c. *Sense of Truth, Morality, and Religion.* In virtue of common grace man still has some sense of the true, the good, and the beautiful, appreciates these in a measure, and reveals a desire for truth, for external morality, and even for certain forms of religion.

d. *Civil Righteousness.* Common grace enables man to perform what is generally called civil righteousness or natural good, works that are outwardly in harmony with the law of God, though entirely destitute of any real spiritual quality.

e. *Natural Blessings.* To common grace man further owes all the natural blessings which he receives in the present life. Though he has forfeited all, he receives abundant tokens of the goodness of God from day to day.

5. Scripture Proof for Common Grace. Some passages of Scripture clearly intimate that there is a striving of the Spirit of God with men which does not lead to repentance and finally ceases, Gen. 6:3; Isa. 63:10; Acts 7:51; I Sam. 16:14; Heb. 6:4-6; Ps. 81:12; Rom. 1:24, 26, 28. Others point to the fact that God restrains sin in various ways, Gen. 20:6; 31:7; Job 1:12; 2:6; II Kings 19:27,28; Rom. 13:1-4. Still others represent unregenerate men as doing things which are good and right, II Kings 10:29, 30; 12:2; 14:3; Luke 6:33; Rom. 2:14. And, finally, there are some which point to God as showering undeserved blessings upon all men indiscriminately, Gen. 17:20; 39:5;

Ps. 145:9, 15, 16; Matt. 5:44, 45; Luke 6:35, 36; Acts 14:16, 17; I Tim. 4:10.

Questions for Review:

How does the present division link up with the preceding one? What is the nature of the general operations of the Holy Spirit in nature? How do His special operations compare with these? What is common grace? How does our view of it differ from that of the Arminian? What is the difference between special and common grace? Do the blessings of common grace in any sense result from the death of Christ? If so, in what sense? By what means does common grace work? What are the effects of common grace? What Scripture proof is there for common grace?

References for Further Study:

Berkhof, *Reformed Dogmatics*, II, pp. 11-31; Hodge, *Systematic Theology*, II, pp. 654-675; Boettner, *The Reformed Doctrine of Predestination*, pp. 179-181; Shedd, *Calvinism Pure and Mixed*, pp. 96-106; Bavinck, *Calvin and Common Grace* (in *Calvin and the Reformation*, pp. 99-130); H. Kuiper, *Calvin on Common Grace*.

CALLING AND REGENERATION

A. **General Remarks on the Order of Salvation.** We begin the discussion of the order of salvation, that is, of the order in which the Holy Spirit applies the work of redemption to the hearts and lives of man, with the study of calling and regeneration. This means that we take our starting-point in those redemptive acts of God in which man does not co-operate, and in which redemption stands out most prominently as a work of God. By doing this we clearly recognize the fact that God and not man begins the redemptive process, and that salvation is altogether a work of divine grace, a work of which we become partakers only in union with Jesus Christ, with whom we are united by the work of regeneration. Many others, such as the Lutherans and Arminians, take their starting-point in man and begin their treatment of the order of salvation with a discussion of saving faith, considered more particularly as an act of man, by which he takes unto himself the blessings of salvation wrought by Christ. They do not speak of the application of the work of redemption by the Holy Spirit, but of its appropriation by man. And in this appropriation everything is made dependent on man's act of faith. It is even by faith that man is regenerated. This representation clearly fits in with their conception of the free will of man. While we honour God as the author of our salvation, and as the primary cause of every redemptive act, we do not lose sight of the fact that, after regeneration, man appropriates the blessings of salvation by faith, and co-operates with the Spirit of God in some of the redemptive acts, such as conversion and sanctification.

B. **Calling.** When we speak of calling in general, we have reference to *that gracious act of God whereby He invites sinners to accept the salvation that is offered in Christ Jesus.* It is a work of the triune God, and is therefore ascribed to the Father, I Cor. 1:9; I Thess. 2:12; I Pet. 5:10, to the Son, Matt. 11:28; Luke 5:32; John 7:37; Rom. 1:6 (Auth. Ver.), and to the Holy Spirit, Matt. 10:20; John 15:26; Acts 5:31, 32. This calling may be either external or internal. God is the author of both; the Holy Spirit operates in both; and in both the Word of God is employed as an instrument. Yet there are important differences: the external calling comes to all those who hear the Word, while the internal calling comes only to the elect; the external calling as such, that is, without the special operation of the Holy Spirit, affects only the natural life, while the internal calling affects the internal or spiritual life. It is the external calling made effective unto salvation.

1. EXTERNAL CALLING. The Bible speaks of external calling in the great commission, Matt. 28:19; Mark 16:15; in passages showing that some who were called did not come, Matt. 22:2-14; Luke 14:16-24; in references to a rejection of the gospel, John 3:36; Acts 13:46; II Thess. 1:8; and, finally, in statements concerning the terrible sin of unbelief, Matt. 10:15; 11:21-24; John 5:40; 16:8, 9; I John 5:10. It consists *in the presentation and offering of*

salvation in Christ to sinners, together with an earnest exhortation to accept Christ by faith, in order to obtain the forgiveness of sins and eternal life.

a. *The Elements Comprised in it.* From the definition given it follows that the external calling comprises three elements: (1) A presentation of the gospel facts and ideas. The way of redemption revealed in Jesus Christ must be set forth clearly in all its relations. (2) An invitation to accept Christ in faith and repentance. The representation of the way of salvation must be supplemented by an earnest invitation, and even a solemn command to repent and believe, John 6:28, 29; Acts 19:4; II Cor. 5:11, 20. (3) A promise of forgiveness and salvation. This promise, however, is never absolute but always conditional. No one can expect its fulfilment, except in the way of true faith and repentance.

b. *Its Characteristics.* This external call has two characteristics: (1) It is general or universal. This does not mean that it actually comes or in the past has come to all men, but that it comes to all men indiscriminately to whom the gospel is preached. It is not limited to any age or nation or class of men. It comes to both the just and the wicked, the elect and the reprobate. The general nature of this calling appears from the following passages, Joel 2:32; Ps. 86:5; Isa. 55:1; Matt. 11:28; Rev. 22:17. That it is not confined to the elect, is quite evident from Prov. 1:24-26; Ezek. 3:19; Matt. 22:2-8, 14; Luke 14:16-24. (2) It is seriously meant. When God calls the sinner through the gospel, He calls him in good faith, and earnestly desires that the latter accept the invitation to believe in Jesus Christ; and when He promises those who repent and believe eternal life, His promise is dependable. This follows from the very nature, from the truthfulness and faithfulness of God, and also from such passages of Scripture as Num. 23:19; Ps. 81:13-16; Prov. 1:24; Isa. 1:18-20; Ezek. 18:23, 32; 33:11; Matt. 21:37; II Tim. 2:13.

c. *Its Significance.* By means of this external calling God maintains His claim on the sinner. He is entitled to the service of man, retained this right in spite of man's fall, and asserts His right in both the law and the gospel. Man is in duty bound to accept the call of the gospel. If he does not, he slights the claim of God and thus increases his guilt. This call is also the appointed means by which God gathers the elect out of all the nations of the world, Rom. 10:14-17. Moreover, it is a revelation of God's holiness, goodness, and compassion. In virtue of His holiness God dissuades sinners everywhere from sin, and in virtue of His goodness and mercy He warns them against self-destruction, postpones the execution of the sentence of death, and blesses them with the offer of salvation. This gracious call is represented as a blessing for sinners, Ps. 81:13; Prov. 1:24; Ezek. 3:18, 19; 18:23, 32; 33:11; Amos 8:11; Matt. 11:20-24; 23:37. Finally, this external calling also serves to justify God in the condemnation of sinners.

If sinners despise the forbearance of God and reject His gracious offer of salvation, the greatness of their corruption and guilt, and the justice of God in their condemnation, stands out in the clearest light.

2. INTERNAL OR EFFECTUAL CALLING. The calling which comes from God to the sinner is really one, though we speak of an external and an internal calling. Through the operation of the Holy Spirit the former issues in and is made effective in the latter. The fact that they are one does not mean, as the Lutherans maintain, that the inner call always accompanies the preaching of the Word. It does mean, however, that the inner call is always mediated by the word of preaching. The same word that is heard in the external call, is made effective in the heart of the sinner in the internal calling through the operation of the Holy Spirit. The internal call has certain distinctive marks: (*a*) It is a calling by the Word of God, *savingly applied by the operation of the Holy Spirit,* I Cor. 1:23, 24. (*b*) It is a powerful calling, that is, a calling that is effectual unto salvation, Acts 13:48; I Cor. 1:23, 24. (*c*) It is a calling *without repentance,* one that is not subject to change and is never withdrawn, Rom. 11:29. The person who is called will surely be saved. With respect to this calling the following particulars should be noted:

a. *It Works by Means of Moral Persuasion.* In the internal calling the Spirit of God does not work through the Word in a creative way but in a persuasive manner. God does sometimes work creatively through the word, Gen. 1:3; Ps. 33:6; Ps.

147:15, but in these cases the word referred to is the word of God's power, and not the word of preaching, which is instrumental in calling the sinner. The Spirit of God operates through the preaching of the Word by making its persuasions effective, so that man listens to the voice of his God.

b. *It Operates in the Conscious Life of Man.* If the word of preaching does not operate creatively but only in a moral and persuasive way, then it follows that it can only work in the conscious life of man. It addresses the understanding enlightened by the Holy Spirit, and through the understanding influences the will effectively, so that the sinner turns to God.

c. *It is Always Directed to an End.* Internal calling is always directed to a certain end, that is, to the salvation to which the Spirit of God is leading the elect, and consequently also to the intermediate stages on the way to this final destiny. It is a calling to the fellowship of Jesus Christ, I Cor. 1:9, to inherit blessing, I Pet. 3:9; to liberty, Gal. 5:13, to peace, I Cor. 7:15, to holiness, I Thess. 4:7, to one hope, Eph. 4:4, to eternal life, I Tim. 6:12, and to God's kingdom and glory, I Thess. 2:12.

C. **Regeneration.** The divine calling and regeneration stand in the closest possible relation to each other.

1. THE MEANING OF THE TERM "REGENERATION." The word "regeneration" is not always used in the same

sense. Calvin employed it in a very comprehensive sense, to denote the whole process of man's renewal, including even conversion and sanctification. In our confessional standards it serves to designate the beginning of man's renewal in the new birth plus conversion. At the present time it is used in a far more restricted sense, to denote the divine act by which the sinner is endowed with new spiritual life, and by which the principle of that new life is first called into action. Sometimes it is employed in an even more limited sense, as a designation of the implanting of the new life in the soul, apart from the first manifestations of this life. In this sense of the word regeneration may be defined as *that act of God by which the principle of the new life is implanted in man, and the governing disposition of the soul is made holy.*

2. The Essential Nature of Regeneration. The following particulars serve to indicate the essential nature of regeneration:

a. *It is a Fundamental Change.* Regeneration consists in the implanting of the *principle* of the new spiritual life in man, in a radical change of the *governing disposition* of the soul. In principle it affects the whole man: the intellect, I Cor. 2:14, 15; II Cor. 4:6; Eph. 1:18; Col. 3:10, -- the will, Phil. 2:13; II Thess. 3:5; Heb. 13:21; — and the emotions, Ps. 42:1, 2 Matt. 5:4; I Pet. 1:8.

b. *It is an Instantaneous Change.* The assertion that regeneration is an instantaneous change implies two things: (1) that it is not a work that is gradually prepared in the soul; there is no intermediate stage between life and death; and (2) that it is not a gradual process like sanctification, but is completed in a moment of time.

c. *It is a Change in the Sub-conscious Life.* Regeneration is a secret and inscrutable work of God that is never *directly* perceived by man, but can be perceived *only in its effects.* Naturally, man may be directly conscious of a change in cases where regeneration and conversion coincide.

3. The Relative Order of Calling and Regeneration. The order in which calling and regeneration stand to each other may best be indicated as follows: The external call in the preaching of the Word, except in the case of children, precedes or coincides with the operation of the Holy Spirit in the production of the new life. Then by a creative act God generates the new life, changing the inner disposition of the soul. This is regeneration in the restricted sense of the word. In it the spiritual ear is implanted which enables man to hear the call of God to the salvation of his soul. Having received the spiritual ear, the call of God is now brought home effectively to the heart, so that man hears and obeys. This effectual calling, finally, secures the first holy exercises of the new disposition that is born in the soul. The new life begins to manifest itself and issues in the new birth. This is regeneration in the broader sense and marks the point at which regeneration passes into conversion.

4. The Necessity of Regeneration. Scripture does not leave us in doubt about the necessity of regeneration, but asserts this in the clearest terms, John

3:3, 5, 7; I Cor. 2:14; Gal. 6:15. Cf. also Jer. 13:23; Rom. 3:11; Eph. 2:3. This necessity also follows from the sinful condition of man. Holiness or conformity to the divine law is the indispensable condition of securing the divine favour, attaining peace of conscience, and enjoying fellowship with God, Heb. 12:14. Now the natural condition of man is exactly the opposite of that holiness which is so indispensable. Consequently, a radical internal change is necessary by which the whole dispensation of the soul is altered.

5. THE USE OF THE WORD OF GOD AS AN INSTRUMENT IN REGENERATION. The question is often raised, whether the Word, that is, the word of preaching, is instrumental in the implanting of the new life, in regeneration in the most restricted sense of the word. Since regeneration is a creative act of God, and the word of the gospel can only work in a moral and persuasive way, it would seem that this cannot very well be instrumental in implanting the new life in man. Such an instrument has no spiritual effect on those who are still dead in sin. To assert its use would seem to imply a denial of the spiritual death of man, though this is not intended by those who make the assertion. Moreover, regeneration takes place in the sphere of the sub-conscious life, while the truth addresses itself to the consciousness of man. And, finally, the Bible clearly intimates that man is enabled to understand the truth only by a special operation of the Holy Spirit, Acts 16:14; I Cor. 2:12-15; Eph. 1:17-20. It is often said

that Jas. 1:18 and I Pet. 1:23 prove that the Word is used as an instrument in regeneration. But it is certain that James is speaking of regeneration in a broader sense, as including the new birth or the first manifestations of the new life, and in all probability this is also the case with Peter. And in that more inclusive sense regeneration is undoubtedly wrought through the instrumentality of the Word.

6. Regeneration Exclusively a Work of God. God is the author of regeneration. It is represented in Scripture as the work of the Holy Spirit directly and exclusively, Ezek. 11:19; John 1:13; Acts 16:14; Rom. 9:16; Phil. 2:13. This means that in regeneration God only works, and there is no co-operation of the sinner in this work whatever. The Arminians do not agree with this view. They speak of a co-operation of God and man in the work of regeneration. In their estimation the spiritual renewal of man is really the fruit of man's choice to co-operate with the divine influences exerted by means of the truth. Strictly speaking, they regard the work of man as prior to that of God. Man can resist, but he can also yield to the influences of the Holy Spirit.

7. Baptismal Regeneration. According to the Church of Rome regeneration includes not only spiritual renewal, but also justification or the forgiveness of sins, and is effected by means of baptism. An influential section of the Anglican Church is in agreement with the Church of Rome on this point. And even many Lutherans teach a certain kind of baptismal regeneration, though according to

some this does not include spiritual renewal, but only serves to place the baptized person in a new relation to the Church. All these groups agree in teaching that the blessing of regeneration can again be lost.

Questions for Review:

How does the Reformed order of salvation differ from the Arminian and Lutheran? What do we mean by calling? How do external and internal calling differ? What is external calling? What elements does it include? What are the two characteristics of the external call? What purpose does it serve? How is the internal calling related to the external? What are its distinctive marks? How does it operate? In what sphere does it operate? To what end is it directed? What different meanings has the word "regeneration"? What is regeneration in the restricted sense? What is the nature of the change wrought in regeneration? What is the relative order of calling and regeneration? How can we prove the absolute necessity of regeneration? Why is it unlikely that the Word is used as an instrument in regeneration? Do Jas. 1:18 and I Pet. 1:23 teach the contrary? Is regeneration a work of God only or of God and man together? Who teach baptismal regeneration?

References for Further Study:

Berkhof, *Reformed Dogmatics*, II, pp. 33-71; Hodge, *Outlines of Theology*, pp. 445-464; McPherson, *Christian Dogmatics*, pp. 377-378, 397-401; Orr, *Side-Lights on Christian Doctrine*, pp. 143-152; Candlish, *The Work of the Holy Spirit*, pp. 49-76.

Conversion

A. **The Scriptural Terms for Conversion.** The Bible uses several terms to denote conversion.

1. In the Old Testament. The Old Testament employs two words, each one of which indicates a specific element of conversion. The one (*nicham*) means *to repent* with a repentance which is often accompanied with a change of plan and of action. And the other (*shubh*) signifies *to turn about,* and especially *to return* after a departure. In the prophets it usually refers to Israel's return to the Lord, after it has departed from Him. This is a very important aspect of conversion.

2. In the New Testament. The New Testament contains three important words for conversion. The word that occurs most frequently (*metanoeo, metanoia*) denotes primarily *a change of mind.* However, this change is not to be conceived exclusively as an intellectual, but also as a moral change. Both the mind and the conscience are defiled, Tit. 1:15, and when a person's mind is changed, he not only receives new knowledge, but the direction of his conscious life, its moral quality is also changed. The word that is next in importance (*epistrepho, epistrophe*) means *to turn about,* or *to turn back.* It really stresses the fact that the active life is made to move in another direction, and thus indicates the final act in conversion. While the first word stresses the element of repentance, though not always to the exclusion of the element of faith, the second always

contains both elements. The third word (*metamelomai*) occurs only five times, and literally means *to become a care to one afterwards*. It stresses the element of repentance; but that this is not always true repentance is evident from the fact that it is also used of the repentance of Judas, Matt. 27:3. The emotional element is uppermost in this word.

B. **The Biblical Idea for Conversion.** The Scriptural doctrine of conversion is based not merely on the passages in which the terms referred to are found, but also on many others in which conversion is described or concretely represented in living examples. The Bible does not always speak of conversion in the same sense.

1. NATIONAL CONVERSION. It makes mention repeatedly of national conversions, as, for instance, of Israel in the days of the judges, of Judah in the time of the kings, and of the Ninevites, Jonah 3:10.

2. TEMPORARY CONVERSION. It also speaks of conversions that represent no change of heart, and are of only passing significance, Matt. 13:20, 21; Acts 8:9 ff.; I Tim. 1:19, 20; II Tim. 2:18; 4:10; Heb. 6:4, 5. These may for a time have all the appearance of true conversion.

3. TRUE CONVERSION. The Bible contains several examples of true conversion, such as Naaman, II Kings 5:15; Manasseh, II Chron. 33:12, 13; Zaccheus, Luke 19:8, 9; the man born blind, John 9:38; the Samaritan woman, John 4:29, 39; the eunuch, Acts 8:30 ff.; Cornelius, Acts 10:44 ff., Paul Acts 9:5 ff.; Lydia, Acts 16:14, etc. This conversion is but the outward expression of the

work of regeneration, or the accompanying change wrought in the conscious life of the sinner. There are two sides to this conversion, the one active and the other passive. In the former conversion is contemplated as the change wrought by God in which He changes the conscious course of man's life. And in the latter it is regarded as the result of this divine action as seen in man's changing his course of life and turning to God. From the former point of view it may be defined as *that act of God whereby He causes the regenerated, in their conscious life, to turn to Him for faith and repentance.*

4. Repeated Conversion. Regeneration as the implanting of the new life cannot possibly be repeated. Neither can conversion in the strict sense of the word, for this is but the initial outward manifestation, in the conscious life of man, of the change wrought in regeneration. At the same time it is possible to speak of a repeated conversion. The activity of the new life may suffer eclipse through worldliness, carelessness, and indifference, and then may be called forth and renewed again and again. Scripture refers to such repeated conversion in Luke 22:32; Rev. 2:5, 16, 21, 22; 3:3, 19.

C. **The Elements of Conversion.** From the preceding it already appears that conversion comprises two elements, namely, repentance and faith. Of these the former has reference to the past, and the latter to the future, the former is directly connected with sanctification, and the latter more particularly, though not exclusively, with justification. In view of the fact that faith will be discussed in a separate chapter, we limit ourselves to repentance here.

1. The Elements of Repentance. Repentance includes three elements: (*a*) An intellectual element, namely, a change of view in which the past life is recognized as a life of sin, involving personal guilt, defilement, and helplessness. This is the knowledge of sin of which the Bible speaks, Rom. 3:20. (*b*) An emotional element, which is really a change of feeling, a sense of sorrow for sin as committed against a holy and just God. If this issues in a real change of life, it is called a godly sorrow, II Cor. 7:9, 10. (*c*) A volitional element, which consists in a change of purpose, an inward turning from sin, and a disposition to seek pardon and cleansing, Acts 2:38; Rom. 2:4. This is the crowning element of repentance.

2. The Roman Catholic Conception of Repentance. The Church of Rome has externalized the idea of repentance entirely in its *sacrament of penance.* This contains especially three elements· (*a*) *Contrition,* that is, real sorrow for sin, not for inborn sin, but for personal transgressions. In lieu of this, however, *attrition,* may also suffice. This is really nothing more than fear for the punishment of sin. (*b*) *Confession,* which in the sacrament of penance is confession to the priest who, on a satisfactory confession, not merely declares that God forgives the sin of the penitent, but actually pardons it himself. (*c*) *Satisfaction,* consisting in the sinner's doing penance, that is, enduring something painful, or performing some difficult or distasteful task.

3. The Scriptural View of Repentance. The Scriptural view of repentance is quite different from the external view of the Roman Catholics. It views repentance wholly as an inward act, an act of contrition or sorrow on account of sin. It does not confound this with the change of life in which it results, but regards confession of sin and reparation of wrongs as *fruits* of repentance. Moreover, it conceives of real repentance as always accompanied with true faith. The two go hand in hand, and are but different aspects of the same change in man.

D. **The Characteristics of Conversion.** The following characteristics should be noted:

1. Conversion is not a legal act of God like justification, but a moral or re-creative act like regeneration. It does not alter the state but the condition of man.

2. Conversion does not, like regeneration, take place in the subconscious, but in the conscious life of man. It may be said to begin in regeneration, and therefore in the region below consciousness, but as a completed act it certainly falls within the range of the conscious life.

3. It includes in principle not only the putting away of the old man, but also the putting on of the new man. The sinner consciously forsakes the old sinful life and turns to a life in communion with and devoted to God.

4. If we take the word "conversion" in its specific sense, it denotes a momentary change and not a process like sanctification. It is a change that takes

place but once and cannot be repeated. In a slightly different sense, however, it is possible to speak of repeated conversion.

E. **The Author of Conversion.** God only can be called the author of conversion. This is the clear teaching of Scripture, Acts 11:18; II Tim. 2:25. There is an immediate action of the Holy Spirit in conversion. The new life of the regenerate man does not issue in conscious action by its own inherent power, but only through the illuminating and fructifying influence of the Holy Spirit, John 6:44; Phil. 2:13. There is also a mediate operation through the Word of God, however. In general it may be said that God works repentance by means of the law, Ps. 19:7; Rom. 3:20, and faith by means of the gospel, Rom. 10:17; II Cor. 5:11. But while God works alone in regeneration and man is entirely passive, man co-operates with God in conversion. That man is active in conversion is quite evident from such passages as Isa. 55:7; Jer. 18:11; Ezek. 18:23, 32; 33:11; Acts 2:38; 17:30, and others. But this activity of man always results from a previous work of God in man. Man works only with the power which God imparts to him.

F. **The Necessity of Conversion.** Scripture speaks in the most absolute terms of the necessity of regeneration, John 3:3, 5. No such absolute expression can be found respecting conversion. This may be due to the fact that in the case of children which die in infancy we cannot speak of conversion, but only of regeneration. The Bible does teach the necessity of conversion in the case of adults in such passages as Ezek.

33:11; Matt. 18:3, though it is true that these statements are not absolute but refer to specific groups. It may be said that in the case of all adults conversion is necessary. This does not mean, however, that conversion must appear in the life of each one as a strongly marked crisis. This can be expected, as a rule, only in the case of those who are regenerated after they have come to years of discretion. In them the life of conscious enmity to God is at once transformed into a life of friendship with God. It can hardly be expected as such, however, in the life of those who, like Jeremiah and John the Baptist, were regenerated from early youth. Yet the elements of conversion, that is, real repentance and true faith, must be present in the lives of all.

Questions for Review:

What do the Old Testament words for conversion mean? What is the meaning of the New Testament words? In how many different senses does the Bible speak of conversion? What is temporary conversion? What is true conversion? What is repeated conversion, and where does Scripture speak of it? What elements are included in conversion? How do they differ? What elements are included in repentance? What elements are included in the Roman Catholic sacrament of penance? What is the Scriptural view of repentance? What are the characteristics of conversion? Who is the author of conversion? How can it be proved from Scripture that man is also active in conversion? Is conversion necessary in all cases? In what sense is it necessary?

References for Further Study:

Berkhof, *Reformed Dogmatics*, II, pp. 72-84; McPherson, *Christian Dogmatics*, pp. 393-397; Candlish, *The Work of the Holy Spirit*, pp. 67-84; Walden, *The Great Meaning of Metanoia*.

A. **The Scriptural Words for Faith.** The Old Testament really has no word for faith, though there are especially three words which denote various aspects of the activity of faith. The most common word for "to believe" (*he'emin*) stresses the intellectual element and signifies the acceptance of something as true on the testimony of another. The other two words (*batach* and *chasah*) emphasize rather the element of confident reliance on or of trust in someone else. The New Testament has one very important word for faith (*pistis*), which denotes (1) general confidence in a person, (2) the ready acceptance of his testimony on the basis of this confidence, and (3) the trust reposed in him for the future. As a designation of saving faith it denotes a conviction respecting the veracity of God, a believing acceptance of His Word, and a heartfelt trust in Him for the salvation of the soul. The corresponding word for "to believe" is used with various shades of meaning, in some cases stressing the element of knowledge, and in others the element of trust.

B. **Different Kinds of Faith Mentioned in the Bible.** Scripture does not always speak of faith in the same sense, and this has given occasion for the following distinctions:

1. HISTORICAL FAITH. Historical faith is a purely intellectual acceptance of the truth of Scripture without any real moral or spiritual response. The name does not imply that it embraces only historical

facts and events to the exclusion of moral and spiritual truths; nor that it is based only on the testimony of history, for it may have reference to present facts, John 3:2. It is rather expressive of the idea that this faith accepts the truths of Scripture as one might accept a history in which one is not personally interested. This means that, while the truth is accepted intellectually, it is not taken seriously and awakens no real interest. The Bible refers to it in Matt. 7:26; Acts 26:27, 28; Jas. 2:19.

2. Faith of Miracles. Faith of miracles consists in a person's conviction that a miracle will be wrought by him or in his behalf. If he is persuaded that he himself can or will work a miracle, he has this faith in the active sense, Matt. 17:20; Mark 16:17, 18, while he has it in the passive sense, if he is satisfied that a miracle will be performed on him or in his behalf, Matt. 8:11-13; John 11:22 (comp. 25-27), 40; Acts 14:9. This faith may or may not be accompanied with saving faith. Roman Catholics claim that we are still warranted in exercising this faith, while Protestants generally deny this, since there is no basis for it, though they do not deny that miracles may still occur.

3. Temporal Faith. Temporal faith is a persuasion of the truths of religion which is accompanied with some promptings of conscience and a stirring of the affections, but is not rooted in a regenerated heart. The name is derived from Matt. 13:20, 21. It is called temporary faith, because it has no abiding character and fails to maintain itself in days of trial and persecution. It cannot be regarded as a hypocritical faith, for they who possess it really believe

that they have true faith, but it may be called an imaginary faith, seemingly genuine but of an evanescent character. Great difficulty may be experienced in distinguishing it from true saving faith. Christ says of the one who so believes: "he hath no root in himself," Matt. 13:21. In general it may be said that temporal faith is grounded in the emotional life and seeks personal enjoyment rather than the glory of God.

4. TRUE SAVING FAITH. True saving faith is a faith that has its seat in the heart and is rooted in the regenerate life. The seed of the faith is implanted by God in the heart in regeneration, and it is only after God has implanted this seed in the heart that man can actively exercise faith. The conscious exercise of it gradually forms a habit, and this becomes a powerful aid in the further exercise of faith. When the Bible speaks of this faith it generally, though not always, refers to it as an activity of man. It may be defined *as a certain conviction, wrought in the heart by the Holy Spirit, as to the truth of the gospel, and a hearty reliance on the promises of God in Christ.*

C. **The Elements of Faith.** Faith is an activity of man as a whole. As an activity of the soul it appears simple, and yet on closer scrutiny it is found to be rather intricate and complex. Several elements should be distinguished.

1. AN INTELLECTUAL ELEMENT (KNOWLEDGE). While saving faith does not consist in a mere intellectual

acceptance of the truth, it does include a positive recognition of the truth revealed in the Word of God. This knowledge of faith should not be regarded as a complete comprehension of the truth; neither should it be considered as a mere taking notice of the things believed, without the conviction that they are true. It is a spiritual insight into the truths of the Christian religion, so that these find response in the heart of the sinner. It is an absolutely certain knowledge, based on the promises of God, and therefore having its divine warrant in God Himself. It need not be very comprehensive, though it should be sufficient to give the believer some idea of the fundamental truths of the gospel. In general it may be said that, if all other things are equal, one's faith will become richer and fuller in the measure in which one's knowledge increases in fulness and clarity.

2. An Emotional Element (Assent). The Heidelberg Catechism does not mention this element of faith separately. This is due to the fact that what is called "assent" is really included in the knowledge of saving faith. It is characteristic of the knowledge included in saving faith that it carries with it a conviction of the great importance of its object, and this is assent. While the man who has a merely historical faith does not react on the truth, because it does not grip his soul, this is quite different with the person who possesses and exercises saving faith. He is conscious of a personal interest in the truth, and responds to it with a hearty assent.

3. A Volitional Element (Trust). This is the crowning element of faith. Faith is not merely a matter of the intellect, nor of the intellect and the emotions combined; it is also a matter of the will which determines the direction of life, an act of the soul by which it goes out to its object and embraces this. This third element consists in a personal trust in Christ as Saviour and Lord, which includes a surrender of the soul as guilty and defiled to Christ, and a reception and appropriation of Him as the source of pardon and spiritual life. It naturally carries with it a certain feeling of safety and security, of gratitude and joy. Faith, which is in itself certainty, tends to awaken a sense of security and a feeling of assurance in the soul.

D. **The Object of Saving Faith**. In connection with the object of faith it is necessary to distinguish between faith in a general and faith in a specific sense.

1. Saving Faith in General. The object of saving faith in the more general sense of the word is the whole of divine revelation as contained in the Word of God. Everything that is explicitly taught in Scripture or can be deduced from it by good and necessary inference, belongs to the object of faith in this general sense.

2. Saving Faith in the More Specific Sense. While it is necessary to accept the Bible as the Word of God, this is not the specific act of faith which justifies and therefore saves directly. It must, and as a matter of fact does, lead on to a more special faith. There are certain doctrines

concerning Christ and His work, and certain promises made in Him to sinful men, which the believer accepts believingly and which induce him to put his trust in Jesus Christ. Briefly stated, the object of saving faith is Jesus Christ and the promise of salvation in Him. The special act of saving faith consists in receiving Christ and resting on Him as He is presented in the gospel, John 3:15, 16, 18; 6:40.

E. **The Roman Catholic View of Faith.** The Roman Catholic Church conceives of faith as a mere assent to the truth, though it does not regard this as a full-fledged and therefore saving faith. It virtually denies the absolute necessity of the element of knowledge in faith. If one is only ready to assent to the teachings of the Church, without really knowing what these are, one can be considered as a true believer. Faith will be fuller and richer, however, if it includes the element of knowledge. But this assent to the truth, with or without knowledge, becomes real saving faith only when it becomes operative through love in the performance of good works.

F. **Faith and Assurance.** The question arises, whether faith always carries with it the assurance of salvation. Opinions differ very much as to the relation of assurance to faith. Roman Catholics and the Arminians of the seventeenth century teach that believers cannot, except in very rare cases, be sure of their salvation. Moreover, they hold that such assurance is on the whole undesirable. Wesleyan Arminians or Methodists maintain that conversion carries immediate certainty with it. He who believes is at once sure that he is redeemed. This does not mean, however, that he is also certain of ultimate salvation. This is a certainty to which the consistent Methodist cannot attain, since he is always liable to fall from grace. The correct view would seem to be that true faith, including, as it does, trust in God, naturally carries with it a sense of safety and security, though this may vary in degree. The assurance which is included in faith is not always a conscious possession, however, since the Christian does not always live the full-orbed life of faith and consequently is not at all times aware of the riches of the life of faith. He is often swayed by doubts and uncertainties, and is therefore urged to cultivate assurance, Eph. 3:12; II Tim. 1:12; Heb. 10:22; — Heb. 6:11; II Pet. 1:10; I John 2:9-11; 3:9, 10, 18, 19; 4:7, 20. Assurance can be cultivated by prayer, by meditating on the promises of God and by the development of a truly Christian life in which the fruits of the Spirit become evident.

Questions for Review:

What is the meaning of the Old Testament words for faith? What is the meaning of the New Testament word? Of how many different kinds of faith does the Bible speak? What is characteristic of historical faith? What is the faith of miracles? Is there any warrant for it at the present time? How does temporal faith differ from true saving faith? What is the characteristic of true saving faith? What elements are included in faith? How much knowledge is needed in faith? How is the assent of faith related to its knowledge? What is the nature of the trust included in faith? What is the object of saving faith? What conception does the Roman Catholic Church have of faith? What different views are there respecting the assurance of faith? What is the true view? How can assurance be cultivated?

References for Further Study:

Gerkhof, *Reformed Dogmatics*, II, pp. 85-106; Hodge, *Outlines of Theology*, pp. 465-481; McPherson, *Christian Dogmatics*, pp. 388-393; Candlish, *The Work of the Holy Spirit*, pp. 76-84; Machen, *What is Faith;* Berkhof, *The Assurance of Faith.*

JUSTIFICATION

A. **The Scriptural Terms for "to justify."** The Old Testament employs two different forms of the same word (*hidsdik* and *tsiddek*) to express this idea. These words do not, except in a couple of passages, denote a moral change wrought by God in man, but regularly designate a divine declaration respecting man. They convey the idea that God in the capacity of Judge declares man righteous. Hence the thought which they express is often placed in opposition to that of condemnation, Deut. 25:1; Prov. 17:15; Isa. 5:23, and is represented as the equivalent of not entering into judgment with the sinner, Ps. 143:2, and of forgiving his sins, Ps. 32:1. The New Testament word (*dikaio-o*) has the same meaning, namely, to declare righteous, as appears from the following facts: (1) In many instances it can bear no other sense, Rom. 3: 20-28; 4:5-7; 5:1; Gal. 2:16; 3:11; 5:4. (2) It is placed in opposition to condemnation, Rom. 8:33, 34. (3) Other terms which are sometimes used instead of it also convey a legal idea, John 3:18; 5:24; Rom. 4: 6, 7; II Cor. 5:19. From the study of these words it is quite evident that in Scripture "to justify" does not mean to *make* but to *declare* righteous.

B. **The Nature and Characteristics of Justification.** Justification may be defined as *that legal act of God by which He declares the sinner righteous on the basis of the perfect righteousness of Jesus Christ.* It is not an act or process of renewal, such as regeneration, conversion, and sanctification, and does not affect the condition but the state of the sinner. The following points of difference between justification and sanctification should be noted particularly:

1. Justification removes the guilt of sin and restores the sinner to all the rights of a child of God, including an eternal inheritance. Sanctification removes the pollution of sin and renews the sinner in conformity with the image of God.
2. Justification takes place outside of the sinner in the tribunal of God, though it is appropriated by faith. Sanctification takes place in the inner life of man and gradually affects his whole being.
3. Justification takes place once for all: it is not repeated, nor is it a process; it is complete at once and for all time. Sanctification, on the other hand, is a continuous process which is not completed in the present life.
4. While both are fruits of the merits of Christ, the work of justification is ascribed more particularly to the Father, and that of sanctification to the Holy Spirit.

C. **The Elements of Justification.** There are especially two elements in justification, of which the one is negative, and the other positive.

1. THE NEGATIVE ELEMENT. The negative element of justification is the forgiveness of sins on the basis of the imputed righteousness of Jesus Christ. The pardon granted in justification applies to all sins, past, present, and future, and therefore includes the removal of all guilt and of every penalty.

This follows from the fact that justification does not admit of repetition, and from such passages as Rom. 5:21; 8:1, 32-34; Heb. 10:14; Ps. 103:12; Isa. 44:22, and is also implied in the answer to the 60th question of the Heidelberg Catechism. It may seem to be contradicted by the fact that Christ taught His disciples to pray for the forgiveness of sins, and that Bible saints are often found pleading for pardon and obtaining it, Matt. 6:12; Ps. 32:5; 51:1-4; 130:3, 4. The explanation for this lies in the fact that the sins of believers in themselves still constitute guilt (though it is guilt already covered), and as such call for confession; that the consciousness of guilt still remains and naturally urges the believer to confess his sin and to seek the comforting assurance of forgiveness; and that the consciousness of pardon, which is repeatedly obscured by sin, is again quickened and strengthened by confession and prayer, and by a renewed exercise of faith.

2. THE POSITIVE ELEMENT. There is also a positive element in justification, in which two parts may be distinguished:

a. *The Adoption of Children.* In justification God adopts the believer as His child, that is, places him in the position of a child and gives him all the rights of a child. This sonship by adoption must be distinguished from the moral sonship of believers, which results from regeneration and sanctification. Believers are not only children of God by adoption and therefore in a legal sense, but also by virtue of the new birth and therefore in a spiritual sense. This twofold sonship is mentioned together in John 1:12, 13; Rom. 8:15, 16; Gal. 4:5, 6.

b. *The Title to Eternal Life.* This privilege is virtually included in the preceding one. When sinners are adopted to be children of God, they are invested with all the legal rights of children, and become heirs of God and co-heirs with Christ, Rom. 8:17. They are constituted heirs of all the blessings of salvation in the present life, and in addition to that receive a title to "an inheritance incorruptible, and undefiled, and that fadeth not away," reserved in heaven for them. I Pet. 1:4.

D. **The Sphere in Which Justification Takes Place.** In answering the question as to the sphere in which justification takes place, we must distinguish between active and passive justification.

1. Active Justification. Active justification takes place in the tribunal of God, Rom. 3:20; Gal. 3:11. In the sphere of heaven God, appearing as a righteous Judge, declares the sinner righteous, not in himself, but in view of the fact that the righteousness of Christ is imputed to him. The Judge is also the gracious Father freely forgiving and accepting the sinner.

2. Passive Justification. Passive justification takes place in the heart or conscience of the sinner. A justification that is not brought home to the sinner would not answer the purpose. Pardon means nothing to a prisoner unless the glad tidings are

communicated to him and the doors of the prison are opened. The sentence of acquittal, pronounced in the tribunal of God, is communicated to the sinner and accepted by faith. When the Bible speaks of justification by faith, it usually refers to this aspect of it.

E. **The Time of Justification.** Opinions differ somewhat as to the time of justification. In some cases, however, the differences are due to the fact that the term "justification" is not always used in the same sense. In such cases the different opinions are not necessarily mutally exclusive, but may exist alongside of each other.

1. Justification from Eternity. Many Antinomians confuse the divine decree respecting the redemption of men with the application of the work of redemption by the Holy Spirit. They believe that the grace of God to sinners in the eternal decree is all that is necessary for the redemption of man. There is no further need that Christ should merit this grace, nor that the Holy Spirit should apply it. Everything is accomplished in the decree; this means among other things that man is justified from eternity. But there are also others who believe in justification from eternity. Some Reformed theologians advocate this doctrine, though without subscribing to the peculiar tenets of the Antinomians. They are of the opinion that the elect were justified in the counsel of redemption, when the righteousness of Christ was imputed to them; but they believe at the same time that this justification from

eternity is followed in time by another justification. Some even speak of a four-fold justification: a justification from eternity, a justification in the resurrection of Christ, a justification by faith, and a public justification in the final judgment. Now there is no doubt about it that there was a certain imputation of the righteousness of Christ to the elect in the counsel of redemption, but it may well be doubted that this is what the Bible means, when it speaks of the justification of the sinner. We must distinguish between what was merely ideal in the counsel of God, and what is realized in the course of history.

2. Justification in the Resurrection of Christ. Some Antinomians do not go to the extent of maintaining that everything was accomplished in the decree, and that even the work of Christ was, strictly speaking, unnecessary; but they do hold that, after Christ has accomplished His work, nothing further is required, and thus ignore the application of the work of redemption by the Holy Spirit. The elect were justified in the resurrection of Jesus Christ. Those Reformed scholars who also speak of a justification in the resurrection of Christ, naturally do not regard this as the whole of the justification of the sinner. They also believe in justification by faith. It may be said that, while we can speak of a justification of the body of Christ as a whole in the resurrection of Christ, this is something purely objective and should not be confused with the personal justification of the sinner.

3. Justification by Faith. When the Bible speaks of the justification of the sinner, it usually refers to the subjective application and appropriation of the justifying grace of God. It speaks of this as justification by faith, because it is by faith that we appropriate the merits of Christ as the basis of our justification and thus come into possession of the justifying grace of God. The relation of faith to justification is not always represented in the same way. There are especially two significant representations of it. (*a*) In the Protestant Confessions it is usually called *the instrument* or *the instrumental cause* of justification. Faith is on the one hand the gift of God wrought in the sinner unto justification, the means by which He carries the declaration of pardon into the heart. But it is also on the other hand the instrument by which man appropriates Christ and all His precious gifts, Rom. 4:5; Gal. 2:16. (*b*) It is also frequently called *the appropriating organ.* This name expresses the idea that by faith the sinner appropriates the righteousness of Christ, on the basis of which he is justified before God. Faith justifies in so far as it takes possession of Christ.

F. **The Ground of Justification.** There was a very important difference of opinion between the Church of Rome and the Reformer's respecting the ground of justification. The Roman Catholic Church teaches that the sinner is justified on the basis of his own inherent righteousness, which is infused into his heart in regeneration. But it is impossible that the intrinsic righteousness of the believer or his good works should ever constitute the ground of his justification, since it is itself the fruit of the renewing grace of God, and always remains imperfect in the present life. Moreover, Scripture teaches that man is justified freely by the grace of God, Rom. 3:24, and cannot possibly be justified by the works of the law, Rom. 3:28; Gal. 2:16; 3:11. The real ground of justification can be found only in the perfect righteousness of Jesus Christ, which is imputed to the sinner in justification. This is plainly taught in several passages of Scripture, Rom. 3:24; 5:9, 19; 8:1; 10:4; I Cor. 1:30; 6:11; II Cor. 5:21; Phil. 3:9.

G. **Objections to the Doctrine of Justification.** Three objections are frequently raised against the doctrine of justification:

1. It is said that justification is a legal transaction, and therefore excludes grace, while Scripture teaches that the sinner is saved by grace. But justification, with all that it includes, is a gracious work of God. The gift of Christ, the imputation of His righteousness, and God's dealing with believers as righteous, — it is all grace from start to finish.

2. Some speak of justification as a procedure unworthy of God, because it declares sinners righteous, while as a matter of fact they are not righteous. The objection does not hold, however, because it does not declare that they are righteous in themselves, but that they are clothed with the righteousness of Jesus Christ.

3. It is often said that this doctrine leads to licentiousness, since they who are justified are apt to think that their personal piety is a matter of little importance. However, in justification the sure foundation is laid for that vital and spiritual union with Christ, which is the surest guarantee of a truly godly life.

Questions for Review:

What is the meaning of the Scriptural terms for "to justify"? What is justification? How does it differ from santification? What elements are included in justification? In how far are sins forgiven in justification? Proof. Why is it necessary to pray for the forgiveness of sins? What is included in the adoption of children? In what sphere does justification take place? How do active and passive justification differ? What is the Antinomian position respecting the time of justification? Does Scripture teach justification from eternity? In what sense can we speak of a justification in the resurrection of Christ? How is faith related to justification? What is the ground of justification? What objections are raised to the doctrine of justification, and how can they be answered?

References for Further Study:

Berkhof, *Reformed Dogmatics*, II pp. 107-125; Hodge, *Outlines of Theology*, pp. 496-514; McPherson, *Christian Dogmatics*, pp. 379-386; Orr, *Side-Lights on Christian Doctrine*, pp. 154-159; Buchanan, *The Doctrine of Justification.*

SANCTIFICATION

A. **The Scriptural Terms for Sanctification.** The Hebrew word for "to sanctify" (*qadash*) is in all probability derived from a root which means "to cut," and therefore emphasizes the idea of separation. This is also the primary idea of the New Testament word (*hagiazo*). In dealing with the subject of sanctification it is necessary to bear this point in mind. To the minds of the great majority of Christians it conveys first of all the idea of spiritual renewal, of the endowment of man with moral and spiritual qualities. And yet this is not the original idea. The Biblical words express the idea of a position or relationship between God and man rather than that of spiritual qualities wrought in the heart. The man who is sanctified is in principle lifted out of the sinful relations of life and placed in a new relation to God, in which he is consecrated to Him and to His service. The Old Testament speaks repeatedly of holy persons and holy things, referring to persons and things which are externally set aside or consecrated to the service of God. This external consecration to the service of God symbolized the deeper and inner devotion of the heart. But while the Scriptural words are first of all indicative of a relationship, they also denote that operation of God by which He, through the Holy Spirit, works in man the subjective quality of holiness, John 17:17; Acts 20:32; 26:18; I Cor. 1:2; I Thess. 5:23.

B. **The Biblical Idea of Holiness and Sanctification.** In Scripture the idea of holiness is applied first of all to God. It denotes primarily that God is absolutely distinct from the creature, is exalted far above it in heavenly majesty, and is therefore the unapproachable One. Out of this first idea a second gradually developed. Since sinful man is more keenly conscious of the majesty of God than a sinless being, he becomes aware of his impurity as over against the majestic purity of God, cf. Isa. 6. Thus the idea of God's separation from the creature passed into that of His separation from all impurity and particularly from sin. Only the clean in heart can stand in His presence, Ps. 24:3 f. But even this is not all. Positively, the idea of the divine holiness shades right into and becomes almost identical with that of the light of the divine glory.

In the second place the idea of holiness is also applied to persons and things that are placed in special relationship to God. Israel had its holy places, such as Jerusalem and the temple, its holy persons in the priests and levites, and its holy rites in sacrifices and purifications. These persons and things were separated unto the service of God. But this external consecration of certain persons merely served to symbolize the inner consecration of the heart, and did not necessarily carry this with it. One might be a sacred person, and yet be entirely devoid of the grace of God in the heart. And yet only they who possessed the latter were truly holy unto the Lord. Through the influence of the Holy Spirit ethical qualities are wrought in their heart. This Old Testament idea of holiness passed right over into the New Testament. It is of great importance to observe that this Biblical idea of holiness is never that of mere moral goodness, considered in itself, but always that of ethical goodness seen in relation to God.

A man may boast of great moral improvement, and yet be an utter stranger to the work of sanctification. The Bible does not urge moral improvement pure and simple, but moral improvement in relation to God, for God's sake, and with a view to the service of God.

Sanctification may be defined as *that gracious and continuous operation of the Holy Spirit by which He purifies the sinner from the pollution of sin, renews his whole nature in the image of God, and enables him to perform good works.*

C. The Characteristics of Sanctification.

1. God and not man is the author of sanctification. This does not mean, however, that man is entirely passive in the process. He can and should co-operate with God in the work of sanctification by a diligent use of the means which God has placed at his disposal, II Cor. 7:1; Col. 3:5-14; I Pet. 1:22.
2. Sanctification is not, like justification, a legal act of God, but a moral and re-creative activity, by which the sinner is renewed in his inner being and made to conform ever-increasingly to the image of God.
3. It is usually a lengthy process and never reaches perfection in this life. In cases in which regeneration and conversion are soon followed by death, the process may, of course, be very short.
4. The process of sanctification is either completed at death or immediately after it as far as the soul is concerned, and at the resurrection in so far as it pertains to the body, Phil. 3:21; Heb. 12:23; Rev. 14:5; 21:27.

D. **The Nature of Sanctification.**

1. Sanctification Is A Supernatural Work of God. Some have the mistaken notion that sanctification consists merely in the drawing out of the new life which is implanted in regeneration by presenting motives to the will and thus persuading man to increase in holiness. In reality it is a divine operation in the soul whereby the holy disposition imparted in regeneration is strengthened and its holy exercises are increased. It is essentially a work of God, partly immediate and partly mediate In so far as God uses means man is expected to co-operate by the proper use of the means at his disposal, I Thess. 5:23; Heb. 13:20, 21; II Cor. 7:1; Heb. 12:14.

2. It Consists of Two Parts:

a. *The Mortification of the Old Man.* The negative side of sanctification consists in this that the pollution and corruption of human nature which results from sin is gradually removed. The old man, that is, human nature in so far as it is controlled by sin, is gradually crucified, Rom. 6:6; Gal. 5:24.

b. *The Quickening of the New Man.* The positive side of sanctification lies in this that the holy disposition of the soul is strengthened, its holy exercises are increased, and thus a new course of life is engendered, Rom. 6:4, 5; Col. 2:12; 3:1, 3. The new life to which it leads is called "a life unto God," Rom. 6:11; Gal. 2:19.

3. It Affects the Whole Man. Since sanctification takes place in the heart, it naturally affects

the whole organism. The change in the inner man is bound to carry with it a change in the outer life, Rom. 6:12; I Cor. 6:15, 20; II Cor. 5:17; I Thess 5:23. It is completed especially in the crisis of death and in the resurrection of the dead. Scripture teaches that it affects the understanding, Jer. 31:34; John 6:45, the will, Ezek. 36:25-27; Phil. 3:13; the passions, Gal. 5:24, and the conscience, Tit. 1:15; Heb. 9:14.

4. It Is A Work in Which Believers Co-operate. That man must co-operate in the work of sanctification follows from the repeated warnings against evils and temptations, Rom. 12:9, 16, 17; I Cor. 6:9, 10; Gal. 5:16-23; and from the constant exhortations to holy living, Micah 6:8; John 15:2, 8, 16; Rom. 8:12, 13; 12:1, 2, 17; Gal. 6:7, 8, 15.

E. **The Imperfect Character of Sanctification in This Life.** While sanctification affects every part of man, yet the spiritual development of believers in this life remains imperfect in degree. Believers must contend with sin as long as they live, I Kings 8:46; Prov. 20:9; Eccl. 7:20; Jas. 3:2; I John 1:8. According to Scripture there is a constant warfare between the flesh and the spirit in the lives of God's children, and even the best of them are still striving for perfection, Rom. 7:7-26; Gal. 2:20; 5:17; Phil. 3:12-14. Confession of sin and prayer for forgiveness are represented as a necessity, Job. 9:3, 20; Ps. 32:5; 130:3; Prov. 20:9; Isa. 64:6; Dan. 9:16; Rom. 7:14; Matt. 6:12, 13; I John 1:9. This truth is denied by the Perfectionists, who believe that man can attain to perfection in this life. They appeal to the fact that the Bible commands believers to be perfect, I Pet. 1:16; Matt. 5:48; Jas. 1:4; that holiness and perfection are often ascribed to believers, I Cor. 2:6; II Cor. 5:17; Eph. 5:27; Heb. 5:14; Phil. 3:15; Col. 2:10; that some Biblical saints led perfect lives, as Noah, Gen. 6:9; Job, Job 1:8; and Asa, I Kings 15:14; and that John declares explicitly that they who are born of God do not sin, I John 3:6, 8, 9; 5:18. But all this does not prove the point. God demands holiness of the unregenerate as well as of the regenerate, but this certainly does not prove that the unregenerate can lead a holy life. If the Bible occasionally speaks of believers as perfect, this does not necessarily mean that they are without sin. They can be called perfect in Christ, or perfect in principle, or perfect in the sense of fullgrown, I Cor. 2:6; 3:1, 2; Heb. 5:14; II Tim. 3:17. The Bible contains no examples of believers who led sinless lives. Even the men mentioned as examples fell into grievous sins, Gen. 9:21; Job 3:1; II Chron. 16:7 ff. And the statement found in the Epistle of John that he who is born of God does not sin evidently means either that the new man as such does not sin, or that the believer does not *live* in sin. Moreover, this statement of John would prove too much for the Perfectionist, namely, that the believer actually never sins. Even the Perfectionist does not maintain that. Consequently it proves nothing to the point.

F. **Sanctification and Good Works.** Sanctification naturally issues in a life of good works. These may be called the fruits of sanctification, and as such come into consideration here.

1. The Nature of Good Works. When we speak of good works, we do not mean perfect works, but works which, at least in principle, answer to the divine requirements and which are good in the spiritual sense of the word. Such good works spring from the principle of love to God and the desire to do His will, Deut. 6:2; I Sam. 15:22; Isa. 1:12; Matt. 7:17, 18; 12:33; they are not only in external conformity to the law of God, but are also done in conscious obedience to the revealed will of God; and whatever their proximate aim may be, their final aim is the glory of God, Rom. 12:1; I Cor. 10:31; Col. 3:17, 23. Only they who are regenerated by the Spirit of God can perform such good works. This does not mean, however, that the unregenerate cannot do good in any sense of the word. To say this would be to contradict the plain teachings of Scripture, II Kings 10:29, 30; 12:2; 14:3; Luke 6:33; Rom. 2:14. They can perform works that are in external conformity with the law, that spring from noble motives respecting their fellowmen, and that answer to a proximate aim which meets the approval of God. These works find their explanation only in the common grace of God. While they can be called good in a general sense, they are yet radically defective, because they are divorced from the spiritual root of love to God, represent no real inner obedience to the law of God, and do not aim at the glory of God.

2. The Meritorious Character of Good Works. The good works of believers are not meritorious in the strict sense of the word, that is, they do not

have the inherent value which naturally carries with it a just claim to a reward. If God does reward their good works, it is not because He is under obligation to them, but only because He has graciously promised to attach a reward to works that meet with His approval. It is a reward like parents occasionally bestow upon their children. Scripture clearly teaches that the good works of believers are not meritorious, Luke 17:9, 10; Rom. 5:15-18; 6:23; Eph. 2:8-10; II Tim. 1:9; Tit. 3:5. There are several reasons why they cannot be: (*a*) Believers owe their whole life to God, and cannot merit anything by giving God simply what is His due, Luke 17:9, 10. (*b*) They cannot perform good works except with the strength which God imparts to them from day to day, and therefore cannot claim credit for them, I Cor. 15:10; Phil. 2:13. (*c*) Even their best works are imperfect, while God can be satisfied with nothing less than perfect obedience, Isa. 64:6; Jas. 3:2. (*d*) Their good works are out of all proportion to the eternal reward of glory. The Roman Catholic Church holds that, after the sinner has received the grace of God in his heart, he can perform meritorious works, that is, works which give him a just claim to salvation and glory.

3. The Necessity of Good Works. There can be no doubt about the necessity of good works, but this necessity should be properly understood. They are not necessary to merit salvation, nor even as a necessary condition of salvation. Infants enter heaven without having done any good works. The Bible

does not teach that no one can be saved apart from good works. Yet they are necessary in the lives of adult believers as required by God, Rom. 7:4; 8: 12, 13; Gal. 6:2, as the fruits of faith, Jas. 2:14, 17, 20-22, as an expression of gratitude, I Cor. 6:20, unto the assurance of faith, II Pet. 1:5-10, and to the glory of God, John 15:8; I Cor. 10:31. Their necessity must be maintained over against the Antinomians, who assert that believers are free from the obligation to keep the law as a rule of life, since Christ did this for them. This is a thoroughly false position. Christ fulfilled the law as a covenant obligation and bore its penalty in behalf of His people, but He kept the law as a rule of life for Himself and for Himself only. By the operation of His Spirit He enables believers to keep the law in principle for themselves, and they, without any constraint, willingly obey it from the heart.

PERSEVERANCE OF THE SAINTS

A. **Nature of the Perseverance of the Saints.** The Reformed Churches stand practically alone in maintaining that a Christian cannot fall from the state of grace. Roman Catholics, Socinians, Arminians, and even Lutherans maintain that he can, and therefore do not believe in the perseverance of the saints. This doctrine can easily be misunderstood. The name naturally suggests a continuous activity of believers whereby they persevere in the way of salvation. As a matter of fact, however, this perseverance is not thought of primarily as an activity of believers, though it is certainly regarded as a work in which they co-operate. Believers would fall away, if they were left to themselves. Strictly speaking, it is not man but God that perseveres. Perseverance is *that continuous operation of the Holy Spirit in the believer, by which the work of divine grace that is begun in the heart, is continued and brought to completion.*

B. **Proof for the Doctrine of Perseverance.** The doctrine of perseverance may be proved by direct statements of Scripture, such as John 10:28, 29; Rom. 11:29; Phil. 1:6; II Thess. 3:3; II Tim. 1:12; 4:18. It follows also from the doctrine of election, which is never merely election to certain means of salvation or to a way in which man may be saved, but to the end of a perfect salvation. It may be inferred from the efficacy of the merits and the intercession of Christ. They for whom He has paid the price can never again fall under condemnation. Moreover, His constant intercession for them is always effective, John 11:42; Heb. 7:25. It is also a natural inference from the mystical union of believers with Christ. How can they who are once implanted in Christ and therefore in possession of eternal life again be severed from the body of Christ and lose this life? Can we proceed on the assumption that eternal life will not be everlasting? Finally, it follows from the fact that believers can in this life attain to the assurance of salvation, Heb. 3:14; 6:11; 10:22; II Pet. 1:10. This would be quite impossible, if believers could fall from grace at any moment.

C. **Objections to the Doctrine of Perseverance.** It is often said that the doctrine of perseverance leads to false security and to indolence, license, and immorality. But this is not true. While the Bible tells us that we are kept by the grace of God, it does not encourage the idea that God keeps us without constant watchfulness, diligence, and prayer on our part. Moreover, there are three classes of passages in Scripture which are declared to be contrary to this doctrine. These are: (1) Passages containing warnings against apostasy which would be unnecessary, if the believer could not fall away, Matt. 24:12; Col. 1:23; Heb. 2:1; 3:14; 6:11; I John 2:6. But these only prove that the believer must co-operate in the work of perseverance. Compare Acts 27:22-25 with verse 31 for an illustration of this point. (2) Passages in which believers are exhorted to continue in the way of sanctification. Such exhortations would seem unnecessary, if there is no doubt about their continuance. But these only go to show that God uses moral means to attain His end. (3) Passages which record cases of actual apostasy, I Tim. 1:19, 20; II Tim. 2:17, 18; 4:10; II Pet. 2:1, 2. But there is no proof that the persons mentioned were true believers. The Bible itself teaches that there are persons who profess the faith and yet are not of the faith, Rom. 9:6; I John 2:9; Rev. 3:1. John says of some: "They went out from us, but they were not of us; for if they had been of us, they would have continued with us," I John 2:19.

Questions for Review:

What is the primary meaning of the Scriptural words for "to sanctify"? What is the original idea of sanctification? What are the different meanings of holiness as applied to God? What does it mean, when it is applied to persons and things? What is the difference between sanctification and moral improvement? What are the characteristics of sanctification? Is sanctification a work of God or of man? What is the negative and the positive side of sanctification? How far does sanctification extend? What proof is there that it is incomplete in this life? Who deny this and on what grounds? How can their arguments be met? What are good works in the strict sense of the word? In how far can the unregenerate perform good works? What is meant when it is said that good works are not meritorious? How can we prove that they are not? Why is it impossible that they should be meritorious? Are they not represented as meritorious when we are taught that they are rewarded? In what sense are good works not necessary, and in what sense are they necessary? What is meant by the perserverance of the saints? Who deny this doctrine? How can this doctrine be proved? What objections are there to it, and how can these be met?

References for Further Study:

Berkhof, *Reformed Dogmatics*, II, pp. 126-151; Hodge, *Outlines of Theology*, pp. 520-547; McPherson, *Christian Dogmatics*, pp. 404-408; Candlish, *The Work of the Holy Spirit*, pp. 89-96; Orr, *Side-Lights on Christian Doctrine*, pp. 159-162.

THE DOCTRINE OF THE CHURCH AND THE MEANS OF GRACE

THE DOCTRINE OF THE CHURCH AND THE MEANS OF GRACE

THE DOCTRINE OF THE CHURCH AND THE MEANS OF GRACE

THE CHURCH

Nature of the Church

A. **Different Uses of the Word "Church" in Scripture.** The principal designation of the Church in the Old Testament is derived from a root which means "to call." It was applied especially to the assembly of Israel as it met for worship. The most common word for "church" in the New Testament, which is also the most important, comes from a verb meaning, "to call out." Both words contemplate the Church as an assembly called by God. In the New Testament the word "church" is first used by Jesus. He applied it to the company that gathered round about Him, recognized Him publicly as their Lord, and accepted the principles of the kingdom of heaven. Later on the word acquired several different connotations.

1. Most frequently it denotes a circle of believers in some definite locality, a local church, irrespective of the question, whether it is assembled for worship or not. Some passages regard it as assembled, Acts 5:11; 11:26; I Cor. 11:18; 14:19, 28, 35, and others do not, Rom. 16:4; I Cor. 16:1; Gal. 1:2; I Thess. 2:14, etc.

2. In some passages it denotes a domestic church, or "the church in the house" of some individual. The wealthy, it would seem, often provided a

meeting-place in their homes, Rom. 16:5, 23 I Cor. 16:19; Col. 4:15; Philemon 2.

3. In its most comprehensive sense the word serves as a designation of the whole body of believers, whether in heaven or on earth, who have been or shall be spiritually united to Christ as their Saviour, Eph. 1:22; 3:10, 21; 5:23, 24, 25, 27, 29, 32; Col. 1:18, 24.

There are several figurative designations of the Church in Scripture. It is called "the body of Christ," I Cor. 12:27; Eph. 1:23; Col. 1:18, "the temple of the Holy Spirit," I Cor. 3:16; I Pet. 2:5, "the Jerusalem that is above," Gal. 4:26, "the heavenly," Heb. 12:22, or "the new Jerusalem," Rev. 21:2 (cf. verses 9 and 10), and "the pillar and ground of the truth," I Tim. 3:15. It should be noted that our word "church" is derived from a word which means "belonging to the Lord," and thus stresses the fact that the Church is the property of God.

B. **The Essence of the Church.** There is quite a difference of opinion between Roman Catholics and Protestants as to the essential nature of the Church. The former find its essence in the Church as an external and visible organization. And this organization, strictly speaking, does not consist of the whole body of the faithful that constitute their Church, but of the hierarchy, consisting of the priests together with the higher orders of bishops, archbishops, cardinals, and the Pope. They distinguish this body as the "teaching church" from the common body of believers as the "learning" or "hearing church." This hierarchical body shares directly in the glorious attributes of the Church, such as its unity, holiness, catholicity, and apostolicity, while the general body of believers is adorned with these only indirectly. Theoretically Roman Catholics still hold to the principle that there is no salvation outside of their external organization, though the facts often constrain them to modify it in various ways. The Reformation reacted against this external conception of the Church and sought the essence of the Church in the invisible and spiritual communion of the saints. This Church includes the believers of all ages and no one else, and outside of it there is no salvation. It is the spiritual body of Jesus Christ, destined to reflect the glory of God as this is manifested in the work of redemption.

C. **The Many-sided Character of the Church.** In speaking of the Church several distinctions come into consideration.

1. THE CHURCH MILITANT AND THE CHURCH TRIUMPHANT. The Church as she now exists on earth is a militant Church, that is, she is called unto and is actually engaged in a holy war. She must carry on an incessant warfare against the hostile world in every form in which it reveals itself, and against the spiritual powers of darkness. The Church in heaven, on the other hand, is the triumphant Church, in which the sword is exchanged for the palm of victory, the battle-cries are turned into songs of triumph, and the cross is replaced by the crown.

2. THE VISIBLE AND THE INVISIBLE CHURCH. The one Church of Jesus Christ is on the one hand visible

and on the other invisible. This is a distinction applied to the Church as it exists on earth. She is called invisible, because she is essentially spiritual and cannot, as far as her essential nature is concerned, be discerned by the physical eye, and because it is impossible to determine precisely who do and who do not belong to her. This same Church, however, becomes visible in the profession and conduct of its members, in the ministry of the Word and the Sacraments, and in her external organization and government.

3. THE CHURCH AS AN ORGANISM AND THE CHURCH AS AN INSTITUTION OR ORGANIZATION. This distinction applies only to the visible Church. The Church as an institution or organization becomes visible in the offices, in the administration of the Word and the sacraments, and in a certain form of Church government. But even if these were absent, the Church would still be visible as an organism, as a communion of believers, in their communal life and profession, and in their joint opposition to the world.

D. **Definition of the Church.** In defining the Church it will be necessary to bear in mind the distinction between the visible and the invisible Church. (1) The former may be defined as *the company of the elect who are called by the Spirit of God,* or briefer still, as *the communion of believers.* (2) The latter is a broader concept, and may be defined as *the community of those who profess the true religion together with their children.* It is important to bear in mind that these two are not entirely parallel. Some who are members of the invisible Church may never become members of the visible organization or may be shut out from it; and some who belong to the visible Church may be unbelievers and hypocrites and as such form no part of the body of Christ.

E. **The Church in the Different Dispensations.** The Church existed from the moment that God set enmity between the seed of the woman and the seed of the serpent, but it did not always assume the same form.

1. In the Patriarchal Period. In the patriarchal period the Church was best represented in the pious households, where the fathers served as priests. There was at first no collective worship, though Gen. 4:26 seems to imply a public calling upon the name of the Lord. At the time of the flood the Church was saved in the family of Noah. And when true religion was again on the point of dying out God separated unto Himself the family of Abraham. Up to the time of Moses the fear of God was kept alive in the families.

2. In the Mosaic Period. After the exodus the people of Israel were organized into a nation and also constituted the Church of God. They were enriched with a ceremonial cultus in which the religion of the nation could find expression. The Church had no independent organization, but had its organized existence in the State. Israel was a Church-State. Foreigners could enter the Church only by joining the nation. Religious worship was regulated down to the minutest details, was largely

ritual and ceremonial, and found its highest expression in the services at the central sanctuary at Jerusalem.

3. In the New Testament Period. On the day of Pentecost the Church was divorced from the national life of Israel and obtained an independent organization. What had up to this time been a national Church now assumed a universal character. And in order to realize the ideal of a world-wide extension, it had to become a missionary Church, carrying the gospel of salvation to all the nations of the world. Moreover, the ritual worship of the past made place for a more spiritual worship in harmony with the greater privileges of the New Testament.

F. **The Attributes of the Church.** The attributes of the Church belong primarily to the invisible Church, though Roman Catholics ascribe them almost exclusively to the visible Church.

1. The Unity of the Church. According to Roman Catholics the unity of the Church consists in its imposing world-wide organization, which aims at the inclusion of all nations. It centers especially in the hierarchy. Protestants maintain that the unity of the Church is primarily of a spiritual character. It is the unity of a body, the mystical body of Jesus Christ, of which all believers are members. This unity expresses itself to a certain extent in Christian profession and conduct, in public worship, and in the external organization of the Church.

2. THE HOLINESS OF THE CHURCH. Roman Catholics also conceive of the holiness of the Church in an external fashion. Instead of the inner holiness of its members, it stresses the ceremonial holiness of its dogmas, its moral precepts, its worship, and its discipline. Protestants apply the idea of holiness to the members of the Church. They regard these as objectively holy in Christ, as subjectively holy in principle, since they are in possession of the new life, and as destined for perfect holiness. This holiness finds external expression in a life devoted to God.

3. THE CATHOLICITY OF THE CHURCH. The Church of Rome lays special claim to the attitude of catholicity in view of the fact that she is spread over the whole earth, has existed from the beginning and continues to exist, while sects come and go, and has a greater number of members than all the sects taken together. Protestants stress the fact that the invisible Church is the real catholic Church, because it includes all believers of all ages, has its members among all the nations of the world, and exercises a controlling influence on the entire life of man.

Besides these three attributes the Church of Rome also claims the attitude of apostolicity, since she traces her origen back to the apostles, bases her doctrine on an apostolic tradition, and has in her bishops and the Pope the lawful successors of the apostles.

G. **The Notes or Characteristic Marks of the Church.** The marks of the Church belong to the visible Church and serve to distinguish the true from the false.

Reformed Churches usually mention three marks, but the three can be reduced to one, namely, faithful adherence in teaching and practice to the standard of God's Word. The three notes of the Church are the following:

1. THE TRUE PREACHING OF THE WORD OF GOD. This is the most important mark of the Church, John 8:31, 32, 47; 14:23; I John 4:1-3; II John 9. This does not mean that a Church's preaching of the Word must be perfect and absolutely pure, if it is to be recognized as a true Church. Such an ideal is not attainable on earth. It does mean, however, that its preaching must be true to the fundamentals and must have a controlling influence on faith and practice. Naturally, the Church that excels in its adherence to the Word of God is the best Church.

2. THE RIGHT ADMINISTRATION OF THE SACRAMENTS. The sacraments should never be divorced from the Word of God, as they are in the Church of Rome, since they are in fact but a visible preaching of the Word. They should be administered by lawful ministers of the Word, in accordance with the divine institution, and only to believers and their seed. Their administration stands out prominently as a mark of the early Church, Matt. 28:19; Mark 16:16; Acts 2:42; I Cor. 11:23-30.

3. THE FAITHFUL EXERCISE OF DISCIPLINE. The faithful exercise of discipline is quite essential for maintaining purity of doctrine and safeguarding the holiness of the sacraments. Churches that are lax in discipline soon find the light of the truth eclipsed,

and that which is holy abused. The Word of God insists on proper discipline in the Church of Christ, Matt. 18:18; I Cor. 5:1-5, 13; 14:33, 40; Rev. 2: 14, 15, 20.

Questions for Review:

What is the meaning of the Scripture words for "church"? What different meanings has the word in the New Testament? How is the Church described figuratively? How do Roman Catholics and Protestants differ as to the essence of the Church? What is the difference between the militant and the triumphant Church? To what Church does the distinction between the visible and invisible Church apply? In what respects is the Church called invisible? How do the Church as an organism and the Church as an institution differ? How can we define the invisible Church? How the visible Church? What form did the Church assume in the patriarchal period? In what respect did it change in the Mosiac period? What is the characteristic of the New Testament Church? Which are the attributes of the Church? Do they belong to the visible or to the invisible Church? How do we, in distinction from the Catholics, conceive of the unity, the holiness, and the catholicity of the Church? Which are the notes of the Church? Do they belong to the visible or to the invisible Church? How must we conceive of the true preaching of the Word? What belongs to the right administration of the sacraments? Why is discipline necessary?

References for Further Study:

Berkhof, *Reformed Dogmatics*, II, pp. 157-179; McPherson, *Christian Dogmatics*, pp. 414-419; Binnie, *The Church*, pp. 1-18; Morris, *Ecclesiology*, pp. 13-33; Bannerman, *The Church of Christ*, I, pp. 5-67.

A. Different Theories Respecting the Government of the Church.

1. QUAKERS AND DARBYITES. Quakers and Darbyites reject all Church government as a matter of principle. They believe that every external church organization necessarily degenerates and leads to results that are contrary to the spirit of Christianity. For the Word of God they substitute special revelations, for what they call the humanly instituted offices, the divinely given charisms, and for public preaching, words of exhortation prompted by the Spirit.

2. THE ERASTIAN SYSTEM. Erastians regard the Church as a society which owes its existence and form to regulations enacted by the State. The officers in the Church are merely instructors or preachers of the Word, without any right or power to rule, except that which they derive from the civil magistrate. The State governs the Church, exercises discipline, and excommunicates, if necessary. This system ignores the independence of the Church and the headship of Jesus Christ.

3. THE EPISCOPALIAN SYSTEM. The Episcopalians hold that Christ, as the Head of the Church, has entrusted the government of the Church directly and exclusively to an independent order of bishops, as the successors of the apostles. The community of

believers has absolutely no share in the government of the Church. This was at one time the system of the Roman Catholic Church, and is now the system in vogue in the Church of England.

4. THE PRESENT ROMAN CATHOLIC SYSTEM. This is the Episcopal system carried to its logical conclusion. It recognizes not only successors of the apostles in the bishops, but also a successor of Peter, who had the primacy among the apostles. The Pope is honored as the infallible head of the Church. As the representative of Christ he has the right to determine and regulate the doctrine, the worship, and the government of the Church.

5. THE CONGREGATIONAL SYSTEM. This is also called the system of independency. In this system each local church or congregation is regarded as a complete church, independent of every other. The governing power rests exclusively with the members of the Church. The officers are simple functionaries of the local church, having no other power than that which is delegated to them by the members of the church. This is the theory of popular government in the Church.

6. THE NATIONAL CHURCH SYSTEM. This proceeds on the assumption that the Church is a voluntary association just as the State. The separate churches or congregations are merely subdivisions of the one national Church. The State has the right to reform public worship, to decide disputes respecting doctrine and practice, and to convene synods. The rights of the local church are disregarded altogether

B. **The Fundamental Principles of the Reformed or Presbyterian System.** The general principles of the Reformed system are derived from Scripture, while many of its details are determined by human wisdom or expediency. Its fundamental principles are as follows:

1. CHRIST THE HEAD OF THE CHURCH AND THE SOURCE OF ALL ITS AUTHORITY. Christ is the Head of the Church in a twofold sense. He is the Head of the Church in an organic sense. The Church is the body to which He stands in vital and organic relationship, which He fills with His life and controls by His Spirit, John 15:1-8; Eph. 1:10, 22, 23; 2:20-22; 4:15; 5:30; Col. 1:18; 2:19; 3-11. He is also the Head of the Church in the sense that He is its King who has authority and rule over it, Matt. 16:18, 19; 23:8, 10; John 13:13; I Cor. 12:5; Eph. 1:20-23; 4:4, 5, 11, 12; 5:23, 24. This is the Headship which comes into consideration here. In this capacity Christ established the Church, made provision for its ordinances, instituted its offices and clothed its officers with authority, and is ever present in the Church, speaking and acting through its officers.

2. CHRIST EXERCISES HIS AUTHORTY BY MEANS OF THE WORD. Christ does not rule the Church by force, but by His Spirit and by the Word of God as its standard of authority. All believers are unconditionally bound to obey the word of the King. As Christ is the only King of the Church, so His word is the only word that is law in the absolute

sense, and that must be obeyed by all. It is the word of the King and is therefore binding on the conscience. All those who have rule in the Church are clothed with the authority of Christ and must submit to the control of His Word.

3. Christ as King Endowed His Church with Power. Christ endowed the Church with the power that is necessary for carrying on the work which He entrusted to it. He invests all the members of the Church with a certain measure of power, but bestows a special measure of it upon the officers of the Church. Their authority is not delegated to them by the people, though the people choose them for office. While they share in the original power, they receive directly from Christ that additional measure of power which is required for their work as officers in the Church of Christ.

4. The Ruling Power Resides Primarily in the Local Church. The ruling power of the Church resides primarily in the local consistories and is by these passed on to classes and synods. Every local church has a certain measure of autonomy or independence, but this is naturally restricted in various ways as soon as it is affiliated with other local churches. The interests of the Church in general may not be sacrificed to those of any local church.

C. **The Officers of the Church.** Different kinds of officers may be distinguished in the Church. A very common distinction is that between extraordinary and ordinary officers.

1. Extraordinary Officers. Of these the New Testament mentions three classes:

a. *Apostles.* Strictly speaking, the name apostle applies only to the Twelve chosen by Jesus and Paul; but it is also given to some apostolic men, Acts 14:4, 14; I Cor. 9:5, 6; II Cor. 8:23; Gal. 1:19. The apostles had certain special qualifications. They: (1) received their commission directly from God or from Jesus Christ, Mark 3:14; Gal. 1:1; (2) were witnesses of the resurrection of Christ, I Cor. 9:1; (3) were conscious of being inspired, I Cor. 2:13; I Thess. 4:8 (4) confirmed their message by miracles, II Cor. 12:12; Heb. 2:4; and (5) were richly blessed as a sign of the divine approval of their labors, I Cor. 9:1; II Cor. 3:2, 3; Gal. 2:8.

b. *Prophets.* The New Testament also speaks of prophets, Acts 11:28; 13:1, 2; 15:32; I Cor. 12:10; 13:2; 14:3; Eph. 2:20; 4:11. These were men who were specially gifted to speak for the edification of the Church, and were occasionally instrumental in revealing mysteries and predicting future events.

c. *Evangelists.* Some New Testament passages make mention of evangelists, Acts 21:8; Eph. 4:11; II Tim. 4:5. Philip, Mark, Titus, and Timothy belonged to this class. They frequently accompanied and assisted the apostles in their work, preaching, appointing officers, and also exercising discipline, Tit. 1:5; 3:10; I Tim. 5:22.

2. Ordinary Officers. The following classes of ordinary officers should be mentioned.

a. Elders. The term "elders" is sometimes used to denote the older men of the community, and sometimes to designate a class of officers somewhat similar to those who functioned in the synagogue. Frequent mention is made of them in the book of Acts, 11:30; 14:23; 15:2, 6, 22; 16:5; 20:17; 21:18. As a designation of office the name was gradually eclipsed and even superseded by the name "bishop." The terms are used interchangeably in several passages, Acts 20:17, 28; I Tim. 3:1; 5:17, 19; Tit. 1:5, 7; I Pet. 5: 1, 2. While both were applied to the same class of officers, the name "elder" stressed their age, and the name "bishop" their work as overseers.

b. Teachers. It is clear that the elders were not originally teachers. There was no need of separate teachers at first, since there were apostles, prophets, and evangelists. Gradually, however, the teaching function was connected with the office of elder or bishop, Eph. 4:11; I Tim. 5:17; II Tim. 2:2. Finally, ever increasing heresies made the task of those whose duty it was to teach more exacting, so that it required special preparation, II Tim. 2:2; Tit. 1:9. Those who prepared for this work were set free from other labours and were supported by the churches. In all probability the "angels" of the seven churches of Asia Minor were such teachers, Rev. 2:1, 8, 12, 18; 3:1, 7, 14.

c. *Deacons.* The New Testament repeatedly speaks of deacons, Phil. 1:1; I Tim. 3:8, 10, 12. According to the prevailing opinion Acts 6:1-6 records the institution of the diaconate. Some are of the opinion, however, that the seven men mentioned there were appointed to be elders; and others that they were simply appointed temporarily for a special function. In all probability, however, they were the first deacons, though their work assumed a special form which was demanded by the occasion of their appointment.

3. The Officers' Calling and Induction Into Office. In the discussion of these points we limit ourselves to the ordinary officers.

a. *Their Calling.* The calling of the officers is twofold:

(1) *Internal calling.* This internal calling should not be regarded as a supernatural call by means of special revelation. It consists in certain providential indications, such as a strong desire, prompted by love to God, the special work in the kingdom of God, the conviction that the necessary gifts are in some measure present, and the experience that God is paving the way.

(2) *External calling.* The internal calling finds its necessary complement in the external calling by the Church. This external call serves to confirm the internal, and thus gives the recipient the assurance that he is called of God. The officers of the church have a guiding hand in the extension of this call, but do

not ignore the voice of the people, Acts 1:15-26; 6:2-6; 14:23.

b. *Their Induction Into Office.* There are two rites connected with this:

1) *Ordination.* This presupposes the calling and examination of the candidate for office. It is an act of the classes or presbytery, and may be called a public acknowledgement and confirmation of the candidate's calling to the ministerial office.

2) *Laying on of hands.* Ordination is accompanied with the laying on of hands. The two went hand in hand in apostolic times, Acts 6:6; 13:3; I Tim. 4:14; 5:22. It signified that a person was set aside for a certain office, and that some special spiritual gift was conferred upon him. Today it is regarded merely as a symbolical indication of the fact that one is set aside for the ministerial office.

D. The Ecclesiastical Assemblies.

1. THE VARIOUS ECCLESIASTICAL ASSEMBLIES. The Reformed Churches have a number of governing bodies. Their relation to each other is marked by a careful judicial gradation. These are known as consistory (session), classis (presbytery), and synod. Some Churches have an intervening link, known as particular synods, between classes and what is called the general synod or the general assembly. The consistory consists of the minister (ministers) and the elders of the local church. The classis is composed of one minister and one elder of each

local church within a certain district. And the synod consists of an equal number of ministers and elders from each one of the classes.

2. THE GOVERNMENT OF THE LOCAL CHURCH. In Reformed Churches the government of the local church is of a representative character. The people choose ruling elders as their representatives, and these together with the minister(s) form a council or consistory for the government of the church. In doing this they follow the example of the early apostolic church, Acts 11:30; 14:23; 20:17; Phil. 1:1; I Tim. 3:1; Tit. 1:5, 7. While the elders are chosen by the people, they do not receive their authority from the people, but directly from Jesus Christ, the Lord of the Church. They exercise their rule in name of the King and are responsible only to Him. Every local church is a complete church, fully equipped with all that is required for the government of the church, and is therefore relatively independent. It cannot and may not submit to any kind of government which is imposed upon it from without. At the same time such a local church can and should affiliate with other churches on the basis of a common agreement, and every affiliation of that kind naturally involves certain limitations of the original rights of the local church. In such cases a Church Order is usually drawn up, which on the one hand guards the rights and interests of the local church, but on the other hand also the collective rights and interests of the affiliated churches. Matters of mutual agreement may not be ignored. The local church may occasionally be called upon to

deny itself for the greater good of the Church in general.

3. THE MAJOR ASSEMBLIES. The major assemblies are classes and synods, and these call for a few remarks.

a. *Scripture Warrant for Major Assemblies.* Scripture contains no explicit command to the effect that local churches must affiiliate and form an organic union. The duty of such affiliation would seem to follow, however, from the spiritual unity of the Church, which certainly ought to find some sort of external expression. Moreover, there are reasons to think that the church of Jerusalem and that of Antioch consisted of several local congregations. And, finally, Acts 15 acquaints us with the council of Jerusalem, which certainly partook of the nature of a major assembly.

b. *The Representative Character of Major Assemblies.* The immediate representatives of the people, who form the consistory, are themselves represented by a limited number in classes, and these, in turn, are represented in synods or general as semblies. The more general the assembly is, the more remote it is from the people; yet none of them is too remote for the expression of the unity of the Church, for the maintenance of good order, and for the general effectiveness of its work.

c. *The Matters Falling Under Their Jurisdiction.* Ecclesiastical assemblies should naturally deal only with church matters, matters of doctrine and morals, of church government and discipline, and whatever pertains to the preservation of unity and good order in the Church of Jesus Christ. More particularly, they deal with matters which (*a*) as to their nature belong to the province of a minor assembly, but for some reason cannot be settled there; and (*b*) as to their nature belong to the province of a major assembly, because they pertain to the churches in general.

d. *The Power and Authority of These Assemblies.* The major assemblies do not represent a higher kind of power than is vested in the consistories. It is the same kind of power, but represented in a greater measure. Since several churches are represented, there is naturally an accumulation of power. Moreover, the decisions of these assemblies are not merely advisory but authoritative, except in cases in which they are explicitly declared to be only advisory. They are binding on the churches, unless they can be shown to be contrary to the Word of God.

Questions for Review:

What is the view of Quakers and Darbyites respecting church government? What is the Erastian system? The Episcopal system? The present Roman Catholic system? The congregational system? The national church system? In what sense is Christ the Head of the Church? What is the standard by which He rules? Whom does He endow with power in the Church? Does original church power reside in the consistories or in the major assemblies? What extraordinary officers were there in the early Church? What were the characteristics of the apostles? What characterizes the New Testament prophets? What were the evangelists mentioned in the Bible? Which were the ordinary officers? What other name was used for the elders? How did the office of teachers gradually arise? Does Acts 6 record the institution of the office of deacon? What constitutes internal calling? How is the external call related to the internal? What is the significance of ordination? Of the laying on of hands?

What ecclesiastical assemblies do we distinguish? What is representative church government? How are the elders chosen? In how far is the local church independent? What Scripture warrant is there for major assemblies? How are they constituted? What matters fall under their jurisdiction? Are their decisions merely advisory or binding?

References for Further Study:

Berkhof, *Reformed Dogmatics*, II, pp. 180-200; McPherson, *Presbyterianism*, pp. 37-151; Morris, *Ecclesiology*, pp. 98-151; Binnie, *The Church*, pp. 111-146.

The Power of the Church

A. **The Source of Church Power.** Jesus Christ not only founded the Church, but also endowed it with the necessary power or authority. He did this in His capacity as King of the Church as a spiritual commonwealth. He gave unto His disciples power to bind and to loose, that is, to determine what is forbidden and what is permitted in the sphere of the kingdom or of the Church, Matt. 16:18, and also to forgive sins and to retain them declaratively, or to admit to the kingdom and exclude from it, John 20:23. The power, extended to the apostles in the fullest degree, is also given to the Church in general, though in a less absolute sense. In exercising this power the Church is bound by the standard of right living and proper conduct transmitted to it in the apostolic Word. While a certain measure of power is given to the people as a whole, I Cor. 5:7, 13; 6:2-4; 12:28, a special measure of it is bestowed upon the officers, through whom the Church mainly exercises its power. These officers receive their authority directly from Christ, though the Church is instrumental in putting them in office.

B. **The Nature of This Power.** The power with which Christ endows His Church is:

1. A Spiritual Power. That the power of the Church is spiritual does not mean that it is altogether internal and invisible, since Christ rules both body and soul. The ministry of the deacons has special reference to the needs of the body. It is spiritual because

it is given by the Holy Spirit, Acts 20:28, is a manifestation of the power of the Spirit, John 20: 22, 23; I Cor. 5:4, pertains exclusively to men as believers, I Cor. 5:12, and can only be exercised in a moral or spiritual way, II Cor. 10:4. And because the power of the Church is exclusively spiritual, it does not resort to force in the maintenance of good order.

2. A MINISTERIAL POWER. It is clear from Scripture that the power of the Church is no independent and sovereign power, Matt. 20:25, 26; 23:8, 10; II Cor. 10:4, 5; I Pet. 5:3, but a ministerial power, Acts 4:29, 30; 20:24; Rom. 1:1, etc., which is derived from Christ and is subordinate to His sovereign authority over the Church, Matt. 28:18. It must be exercised in harmony with the Word of God, under the direction of the Holy Spirit, and in the name of Jesus Christ, the King of the Church, Rom. 10:14, 15; Eph. 5:23; I Cor. 5:4.

C. **Different Kinds of Church Power.** From the threefold office of Christ it also follows that there is a threefold power of the Church.

1. A DOGMATIC OR TEACHING POWER. The Church has a task in connection with the truth. The Word of God was given to the Church as a precious deposit of the truth, and the Church is commissioned to guard the truth, to hand it on faithfully from generation to generation, and to defend it against all the forces of unbelief, I Tim. 1:3, 4; II Tim. 1:13; Tit. 1:9-11. It has the further duty of preaching the Word for the conversion of sinners and for the edification of the saints, and to provide translations

of it, so that the work of preaching may be carried on among all the nations of the world, Isa. 3:10, 11; II Cor. 5:20; I Tim. 4:13; II Tim. 2:15; 4:2; Tit. 2:1-10. Furthermore, it must draw up creeds and confessions, in which it formulates its faith, so that the world may know exactly what it believes. The need of such creeds is felt especially in times of defection, when many depart from the historic faith of the Church. Finally, it is also the duty of the Church to develop the truth by theological study. It owes this to the truth itself as a revelation of God, but also to the training of its future ministers. According to Scripture the Church is in duty bound to provide for and to supervise the training of successive generations of teachers and pastors, II Tim. 2:2.

2. A GOVERNING POWER. The governing power of the Church includes two elements:

   a. *A Regulating Power.* "God is not a God of confusion, but of peace," I Cor. 14:33. He desires that in the Church "all things be done decently and in order," vs. 40. For that reason He has made provision for the proper regulation of the affairs of the Church. In virtue of this the Church has the right to carry into effect the laws which Christ has ordained for the Church. All the members of the Church possess this power in a measure, Rom. 15:14; Col. 3:16; I Thess. 5:11, but it is vested in a special sense in the officers, John 21:15-17; Acts 20:28; I Pet. 5:2. This power also includes the right to draw up regulations for the proper application of the law, such as canons or Church Orders. These serve to stipulate who can be recognized as members in good standing, on what terms persons are permitted to bear office in the Church, how public worship should be conducted, and how discipline should be exercised. While these regulations must be based on general principles found in the Word of God, their details will always be dictated in part by considerations respecting the special needs, the well-being, and the edification of the Church.

b. A Judicial Power. The Church is in duty bound to guard its holiness by the exercise of proper discipline. The power of discipline is based on such passages as Matt. 16:19; 18:18; John 20: 23; I Cor. 5:2, 7, 13; II Cor. 2:5-7; II Thess. 3: 14, 15; I Tim. 1:20; Tit. 3:10. The purpose of discipline in the Church is twofold. In the first place it seeks to carry into effect the law of Christ concerning the admission and exclusion of members; and in the second place it aims at promoting the spiritual edification of the members of the Church by securing their obedience to the laws of Christ. Both of these aims are subservient to a higher end, the maintenance of the holiness of the Church of Jesus Christ. If there are diseased members, the Church will first of all seek to effect a cure, but if this proves impossible, it will put away the diseased member for the protection of the other members. While all the members of the Church are in duty bound to warn and admonish the wayward, only the officers of the Church can apply Church censures. The latter can deal with private sins only when these are brought to their attention according to the rule given in Matt. 18:15-17, but are in duty bound to deal with public sins even when no formal accusation is brought. The disciplinary action of the consistory has three stages: (1) The sinner is restrained from celebrating the Lord's Supper. This initial action is not published and is followed by several private admonitions to bring the sinner to repentance. (2) Three public announcements and admonitions. In the first of these the sin is mentioned but the sinner is not named. In the second the name is made known in accordance with the advice of the classis. And in the third the imminent excommunication is announced. (3) Finally, this is followed by the excommunication proper, by which one is cut off from the fellowship of the Church, Matt. 18:17; I Cor. 5:13; Tit. 3:10.

3. A Power or Ministry of Mercy. When Christ sent out His apostles and the seventy disciples, He not only instructed them to preach, but also gave them power to cast out devils and to cure all manner of diseases, Matt. 10:1, 8; Luke 9:1, 2; 10:9. 17. And among the early Christians there were some who had the gift of healing and could perform miracles, I Cor. 12:9, 10, 28, 30; Mark 16: 17, 18. The special gifts with which the apostles and some of the early believers were endowed, ceased when the period of revelation had come to an end. From that time on the ministry of mercy was largely limited to the Church's care for the poor. The Lord hinted at this as the task of the

Church in Matt. 26:11; Mark 14:7. The early Church practiced a sort of communion of goods, and thus saw to it that no one wanted the necessities of life, Acts 4:34. Later on seven men were appointed to "serve the tables," that is, to provide for an equitable division of that which was placed on the tables for the needy, Acts 6:1-6. The Epistles repeatedly make mention of a class of deacons as officers in the Church, Rom. 16:1; Phil. 1:1; I Tim. 3:8-12. Moreover, the New Testament places great emphasis on the necessity of giving or collecting for the poor, Acts 11:29; 20:35; I Cor. 16:1, 2; II Cor. 9:1, 6, 7, 12-14; Gal. 2:10; 6:10; Eph. 4:28; I Tim. 5:10, 16; Jas. 1:27; 2:15, 16; I John 3:17.

Questions for Review:

What is the source of Church power? What power was given to the apostles? Do later officers have this power in the same degree? Is this power given to the officers only or also to the people? What is the nature of the power given to the Church? Why is it called spiritual? Why ministerial? What is included in the dogmatic power of the Church? Why are creeds necessary? What elements are included in the Church's governing power? Must all Church regulations be based directly on the Word of God? What is the general purpose of Church discipline? What two specific purposes does it serve? What three stages are included in the disciplinary action of the consistory? How are matters of discipline brought to its attention? What was the nature of the ministry of mercy in the apostolic Church? What is its main function at present?

References for Further Study:

Berkhof, *Reformed Dogmatics*, II, pp. 201-213; McPherson, *Christian Dogmatics*, pp. 419-422; Bannerman, *The Church*, I. pp. 187-275; Morris, *Ecclesiology*, pp. 143-151.

THE MEANS OF GRACE

The Word as a Means of Grace

A. **The Word of God the Most Important Means of Grace.** The term "means of grace" is sometimes used in a very general sense to denote whatsoever may minister to the spiritual welfare of believers, such as the Church, the preaching of the Word, the sacraments, the sabbath prayer, etc. It is generally employed in a more restricted sense, however, as a designation of the Word of God and the sacraments. Strictly speaking, only these two can be regarded as means of grace. When we speak of the Word as a means of grace, we do not think of the personal Word (the second person in the Trinity, John 1:1 ff), nor of the word of power by which all things were created and are maintained, Ps. 33:6; Heb. 1:3, nor of any kind of revelation such as the prophets received; but very specifically of the Word of God as it is contained in Scripture and as it is preached to the Church. It is the word of God's grace, and as such the most important means of grace. While the emphasis falls on the Word as it is *preached* in the name of God, it may also be brought to men in other ways: in the home and in the school, by means of conversation and literature. While the sacraments can only be administered in the Church by a lawful minister, the Word of God can be carried out into the world by all believers and operate in many different ways.

B. **The Relation of the Word to the Spirit.** There has always been a difference of opinion as to the relation between the operation of the Word and that of the Holy Spirit. Pelagians and Rationalists regard the intellectual and moral operation of the Word as quite sufficient for the production of the new life, and feel no need of an additional operation of the Holy Spirit. Antinomians, on the other hand, expect everything from the operation of the Holy Spirit. They stress the importance of the inner word or the inner light, and do not regard the external Word as necessary at all. As a matter of fact, however, the Word alone is not sufficient to work faith and conversion, and while the Holy Spirit can, He does not ordinarily work without the Word. In the application of the work of redemption the two work together, the Spirit using the Word as His instrument. The preaching of the Word does not yield the desired fruit until it is made effective by the Holy Spirit.

C. **The Two Parts of the Word as a Means of Grace.** We distinguish two parts in the Word of God as a means of grace, namely, the law and the gospel.

1. THE DISTINCTION BETWEEN THE LAW AND THE GOSPEL. The law and the gospel should not be represented as absolute opposites, as is sometimes done in the present day. They who do this contemplate the law as the condition of the covenant of works and usually fail to recognize its other aspects. And if the law is regarded *merely* as the condition of the covenant of works — a broken covenant — it naturally cannot now be a means of grace. When we speak of the law as a means of grace, we think of

it as the necessary expression of God's character and will, and more particularly of it as it is made subservient to the covenant of grace. As such it is closely linked up and is even permeated with the promises of God. It is possible to speak of the gospel in the law. In the gospel the promises of God are naturally in the foreground, but this does not mean that there are no demands in connection with the gospel, nor that they who live in the gospel dispensation are in every respect free from the law. The law requires that we shall believe the gospel, and the gospel aims at the fulfillment of the law in our lives. Clearly the law is held high also in the New Testament, Matt. 5:17-19; Rom. 13:10; Eph. 6:2; Jas. 2:8-11; I John 3:4; 5:3.

2. The Function of the Law. The law serves the purpose of common grace in the world at large by restraining sin and promoting righteousness. However, this is not its specfic use as a means of grace, for the "means of grace" are means of special grace. In this capacity the law first of all serves the purpose of bringing man under conviction of sin, Rom. 3:20, making him conscious of his inability to meet the demands of the law, and becoming his tutor to lead him to Christ, Gal. 3:24. In the second place it is also a rule of life for believers, reminding them of their duties and leading them in the way of life and salvation. This use of the law is denied by the Antinomians.

3. The Function of the Gospel. The law, conceived purely as law, can only point away from itself, and in connection with the promises of the

Old Testament points to the coming Redeemer as the way of salvation. The gospel is a clear representation of the way of salvation revealed in Jesus Christ. It exhorts the sinner to come to Christ in faith and repentance, and promises those who truly repent and believe all the blessings of salvation in the present and in the future. It is the power of God unto salvation for every one that believeth.

Questions for Review:

What is the meaning of the term "means of grace"? What do we mean by "the Word of God" as a means of grace? Why is the Word the most important means? How do Pelagians and Rationalists conceive of the relation between the Word and the Spirit? What position do the Antinomians take on this point? What is the proper conception of this relation? Are the law and the gospel absolute opposites? Are believers free from the law in every respect? What is the function of the law as a means of grace? What is the function of the gospel?

References for Further Study:

Berkhof, *Reformed Dogmatics,* II, pp. 214-223; McPherson, *Christian Dogmatics,* pp. 422-427; Binnie, *The Church,* pp. 61-67.

The Sacraments in General

A. **Relation Between the Word and the Sacraments.** The Word of God can exist and is also complete as a means of grace without the sacraments, but the sacraments cannot exist and are not complete without the Word. This must be maintained over against the Roman Catholics, who proceed on the assumption that the sacraments contain all that is necessary for the salvation of sinners. The sacraments are a special aid for man, since they address the eye which is more sensuous than the ear and therefore deepen the impression made. The Word and the sacraments agree in that both have God for their author and Christ as their central content, and in their appropriation by faith. At the same time they differ in some important points: (1) the Word is absolutely necessary, while the sacraments are not; (2) the Word is intended to beget and to strengthen faith, while the sacraments can only strengthen it; and (3) the Word goes out into all the world, while the sacraments are administered only to those who are in the covenant.

B. **Origin and Meaning of the Word "Sacraments."** The word "sacrament" is not found in the Bible. It is derived from the Latin *sacramentum,* which originally denoted a sum of money deposited by two parties in a lawsuit. After the decision of the court the winner's money was returned, while that of the loser was forfeited as a sort of offering to the gods. The transition to the Christian use of the term is probably to be sought

(1) in its military use to denote the oath by which a soldier solemnly pledged obedience to his commander; and (2) in the Vulgate's use of it to translate the Greek word for mystery. The sacraments were regarded as both pledges of obedience and mysteries. The following definition may be given of a sacrament: *A sacrament is a holy ordinance instituted by Christ, in which by sensible signs the grace of God in Christ is represented, sealed, and applied to believers, and they, in turn, express their faith and obedience to God.*

C. **The Component Parts of the Sacraments.** Three parts must be distinguished in the sacraments:

1. THE OUTWARD AND VISIBLE SIGN. Each one of the sacraments contains an external element, namely, the water in baptism, and the bread and wine in the Lord's Supper. Where these elements are administered and appropriated, there we have the entire external matter of the sacrament. This is sometimes called *the sacrament* as, for instance, when unbelievers are said to receive the sacrament; but it is not the whole of the sacrament, nor even the most important part of it.

2. THE INWARD SPIRITUAL GRACE SIGNIFIED. A sign naturally points to something that is signified, and this constitutes the internal matter of the sacrament. This is variously indicated in Scripture, as the covenant of grace, Gen. 17:11, the righteousness of faith, Rom. 4:11, the forgiveness of sins, Mark 1:4; Matt. 26:28, faith and repentance, Mark 1:4; 16:16, communion with Christ in His death and resurrection, Rom. 6:3, 4; Col. 2:11, 12.

3. The Union Between the Sign and the Thing Signified. It is this union between the sign and the thing signified that really constitutes the essence of the sacrament. This should not be conceived as physical, as if the external matter naturally included the internal (Roman Catholic), nor local, as if both were present in the same space (Lutheran), but spiritual, so that, where the sacrament is received in faith, the grace of God accompanies it.

D. **The Necessity of the Sacraments.** Roman Catholics hold that baptism is absolutely necessary unto salvation, and that the sacrament of penance is equally necessary for those who have committed a mortal sin after baptism; but that confirmation, the eucharist, and extreme unction are necessary only in the sense that they have been commanded and are very helpful. Protestants, however, do not regard the sacraments as absolutely necessary unto salvation, but yet as binding in virtue of the divine precept. Wilful neglect of their use results in the destruction of the soul, just as all wilful and persistent disobedience to God does.

E. **The Old and New Testament Sacraments Compared.** The Church of Rome claims that there is an essential difference between the sacraments of the Old and those of the New Testament. It maintains that the Old Testament sacraments were merely typical, did not affect the spiritual condition, but only the legal standing of the recipient, and were dependent for their operation on the faith of those who received them; and that the New Testament sacraments merely in virtue of the sacramental action (*ex opere operato*) work spiritual grace in the hearts of the recipients. As a matter of fact, however, there is no essential difference between the two sets of sacraments. This may be inferred from such passages as Rom. 4:11; I Cor. 5:7; 10:1-4; Col. 2:11. At the same time there are certain points of difference: (1) The Old Testament sacraments had a national aspect in addition to their spiritual significance. (2) They pointed forward to Christ and were seals of a grace that still had to be merited, while the New Testament sacraments point back to Christ and His completed sacrifice of redemption. (3) In harmony with the whole Old Testament dispensation they did not convey to the recipient as rich a measure of spiritual grace as do the sacraments of the New Testament.

F. **The Number of the Sacraments.** During the old dispensation there were just two sacraments, namely, circumcision and passover. Circumcision was practiced among other nations as a measure of health, but among Israel it became a sacrament of the covenant of grace, symbolizing the cutting away of sin. In the time of Moses the passover was added to it, which symbolized and typified the deliverance of the people of God. Both were bloody sacraments and thus harmonized with the sacrificial system of the Old Testament. The Church of the New Testament also has two sacraments, namely, baptism and the Lord's Supper. In harmony with the new dispensation as a whole, they are unbloody sacraments. After Christ has brought His perfect sacrifice on the cross no more shedding of blood is needed. The Church of Rome has enlarged the number of sacraments to seven in an entirely unwarranted manner by adding confirmation, penance, orders, matrimony, and extreme unction.

Questions for Review:

How are the sacraments related to the Word? In what respects do they differ as means of grace? What is the original meaning of the word "sacrament"? How did it acquire its present meaning? What is a sacrament? What are the component parts of a sacrament? What is the sign in each one of the sacraments? What is signified in each? How should we conceive of the relation between the sign and the thing signified? How do Roman Catholics and Protestants differ as to the necessity of the sacraments? In what respect did the Old Testament sacraments differ from those of the New? Which are the seven sacraments of the Church of Rome?

References for Further Study:

Berkhof, *Reformed Dogmatics*, II, pp. 224-231; McPherson, *Christian Dogmatics*, pp. 427-431; Binnie, *The Church*, pp. 68-71; Hodge, *Outlines of Theology*, pp. 588-602; Candlish, *The Sacraments*, pp. 11-44.

Christian Baptism

A. **The Institution of Christian Baptism.** Christ instituted baptism after the resurrection, that is, after He had finished His atoning work. He did it with the fulness of His mediatorial authority and made it binding for all following ages. All those who were made disciples were to be baptized as a sign that they had entered a new relationship. The apostles were instructed to baptize "in (into) the name of the Father and of the Son and of the Holy Spirit." This does not mean that they were to baptize the new converts on the authority of the triune God, but rather that they had to baptize them in relation to Him. Baptism was to be expressive of the fact that they had entered into a new relationship to God through faith. While Christ did not intend to prescribe a formula for baptism, in later times, when the Church felt the need of a formula, it could find no better one than that contained in the words of the institution. It was already in use in the beginning of the second century.

B. **The Proper Mode of Baptism.** Baptists maintain that dipping or immersion, followed by emersion, is the only proper mode of baptism, since this rite must symbolize the spiritual death and resurrection of the believer. Two questions arise at this point: (1) What is the essential thing in the symbolism of baptism? and (2) Is immersion the only proper mode of baptism?

1. What is the Essential Thing in the Symbolism of Baptism? According to Baptists the essential

thing in baptism is immersion. Baptism in any other form is not baptism at all, for the real baptismal idea is expressed in the going down into and the coming up out of the water. It is admitted that such an immersion also involves a certain purification, but this is regarded as purely accidental. Their opinion is based on Mark 10:38, 39; Luke 12:50; Rom. 6: 3, 4; Col. 2:12, but these passages do not prove the point. Scripture clearly represents the idea of purification as the essential thing in the symbolism of baptism. This was the pertinent thing in all the Old Testament washings, Ps. 51:7; Ezek. 36:25, and also in the baptism of John and Jesus, John 3: 25, 26. It is perfectly evident from several passages that baptism symbolizes spiritual cleansing or purification, Acts 2:38; 22:16; I Cor. 6:11; Tit. 3:5; Heb. 10:22; I Pet. 3:21. This is the point on which all the emphasis is placed.

2. Is Immersion the Only Proper Mode of Baptism? In opposition to the Baptists, who regard immersion as the only proper mode of baptism, we maintain that the mode is quite immaterial, as long as the fundamental idea of purification finds expression in the rite. Jesus did not prescribe a certain mode of baptism, and the Bible never stresses any particular mode. The word employed by Jesus does not necessarily mean "to immerse," but may also mean "to purify by washing." It is possible and even probable that some of the cases mentioned in the Bible were cases of baptism by immersion, though this is not absolutely certain in a single case. From the earliest times it was customary to baptize

by sprinkling and pouring as well as by immersion. Purification was frequently, if not generally effected by sprinkling during Old Testament times, Num. 8:7; 19:13, 18, 19, 20; Ps. 51:7; Ezek. 36:25; Heb. 9:10, 13. The baptism with the Spirit certainly did not take place by immersion, Matt. 3:11; I Cor. 3:11; nor did the baptisms mentioned in Luke 11:37, 38; 12:50; I Cor. 10:1, 2. It is not likely that the multitudes that flocked to John the Baptist, nor that the three thousand converts of the day of Pentecost were baptized by immersion. Neither does it seem that this mode was followed in the cases mentioned in Acts 9:18; 10:47; 16:33. 34. Spiritual renewal is sometimes said to have been effected by sprinkling, Ezek. 36:25; Heb. 10:22.

C. **The Lawful Administrators of Baptism.** Protestants generally proceed on the assumption that the administration of the Word and that of the sacraments belong together, and that therefore only the minister of the gospel is the lawful administrator of baptism. Moreover, they hold that it should be administered in the public gathering of believers. Usually they regard a baptism legitimate which is administered by a duly accredited minister and in the name of the triune God. Roman Catholics consider baptism absolutely necessary unto salvation; and because they regard it as cruel to make the salvation of anyone dependent on the accidental presence or absence of a priest, they also permit baptism by others, particularly by midwives, in cases of necessity.

D. **The Proper Subjects of Baptism.** There are two classes to whom baptism is applied, namely, adults and infants.

1. Adult Baptism. Baptism is intended for believers and their seed. When Jesus gave His disciples the great commission, instructing them to make disciples of all nations and to baptize them in the name of the triune God, He undoubtedly had in mind primarily the baptism of adults, for it was only with these that they could begin in their missionary labours. His instruction also implies, though it does not explicitly state, that in the case of adults baptism had to be preceded by a profession of faith, Mark 16:16. On the day of Pentecost those that received the word of Peter were baptized, Acts 2:41. In the case of the eunuch, Acts 8:37 (not found in some MSS.), and of the jailor at Philippi baptism was preceded by faith. Hence it is entirely proper that the Church should require a profession of faith of all adults seeking baptism. When such a profession is made, this is accepted by the Church at its face value, unless there are good reasons to doubt its veracity. It does not belong to her province to pry into the secrets of the heart and thus to pass on the genuineness of such a profession. The responsibility rests on the person who makes it.

2. Infant Baptism. While there is general agreement as to the legitimacy of the baptism of adult believers, there is no such unanimity respecting the lawfulness of baptizing their children. The Baptists deny that these are entitled to baptism. In

connection with the baptism of infants several points deserve consideration.

a. *The Scriptural Basis for Infant Baptism.* There is no explicit command in Scripture to baptize children; nor is there a single instance in which we are plainly told that children were baptized. But this does not necessarily make infant baptism un-Biblical. The Scriptural basis for it is found in the following:

1) The covenant made with Abraham was primarily a spiritual covenant, though it also had a national aspect, and of this spiritual covenant circumcision was a sign and seal. The spiritual nature of the covenant is proved by the interpretation of its promises in the New Testament, Rom. 4:16-18; II Cor. 6:16-18; Gal. 3: 8, 9, 14, 16; Heb. 8:10; 11:9, 10, 13, and by the spiritual significance ascribed to circumcision Deut. 10:16; 30:6; Jer. 4:4; 9:25, 26; Acts 15:1; Rom. 2:26-29; 4:11; Phil. 3:2; Gal. 3:8.

2) This covenant is still in force and is essentially the same as the "new covenant" of the present dispensation. Paul argues in Rom. 4: 13-18 and Gal. 3:15-18 that the covenant was not changed nor abrogated by the giving of the law, that Christ and those who are of Christ constitute the seed to which the promise applies, and that therefore New Testament believers are heirs according to promise. And the writer of Hebrews speaks of the covenant as immutable, Heb. 6:13-18.

3) Children shared in the blessings of the covenant, and therefore received circumcision as its sign and seal. Infants were present whenever the covenant was renewed, Deut. 29:10-13; Josh. 8:35; II Chron. 20:13, and were reckoned as part of the congregation of Israel, II Chron. 20:13; Joel 2:16. And in view of the rich promises in the Old Testament, Isa. 54:13; Jer. 31:34; Joel 2:28, it is inconceivable that they would be excluded in the New Testament.

4) In the New Testament baptism is substituted as the sign and seal of entrance into the covenant of grace. Circumcision was done away, Acts 15:1, 2; 21:21; Gal. 2:3-5; 5:2-6; 6:12, 13, 15, and if baptism did not take its place, then there is no initiatory rite at present. But Christ clearly instituted it as such, Matt. 28:19, 20; Mark 16:15, 16. It agrees with circumcision in spiritual meaning as denoting the removal of sin, Acts 2:38; I Pet. 3:21; Tit. 3:5. Moreover, it is linked up with the promise in Acts 2:39. Finally, Col. 2:11, 12 clearly proceeds on the assumption that baptism has taken the place of circumcision. The exclusion of New Testament children would require an unequivocal statement to that effect, but quite the contrary is found, Acts 2:39; Matt. 19:14; I Cor. 7:14.

5) There are reasons to believe that even in the apostolic age children were sometimes baptized along with their parents. The language

of the New Testament is perfectly consistent with a continuation of the former state of things, Matt. 19:14; Acts 2:39; I Cor. 7:14. Whole households were repeatedly baptized, and this is represented as something perfectly normal. It is but natural to assume that there were children in some of these households. We know that in the second century children were baptized.

6) It is true that there is no explicit command to baptize children, nor any clear example of infant baptism in the New Testament; but neither is there any explicit warrant for the practice of the Baptists. We are not taught, either by word or example, that persons born and reared in Christian families may not be baptized until they have come to years of discretion and have professed their faith in Christ.

b. *The Ground for Infant Baptism.* The question is raised on what ground children of believers are baptized. A twofold answer has been given to this question in Reformed circles. Some have said that they are baptized on the basis of a presumptive regeneration. They who take this position do not pretend to know that the infants offered for baptism are regenerated, but proceed on the assumption that they are, and baptize them on the strength of that assumption. They regard these children as regenerated until they give evidence of an unregenerated heart. Others have taken the position that children are baptized on the ground of the all-comprehensive promise of God in the covenant, which also includes the promise of regeneration. This would seem to be the only tenable position. The covenant and the covenant promise afford the only certain and objective ground for the baptism of infants. Children of believers are baptized, because they are in the covenant, irrespective of the question, whether they are already regenerated or not.

c. *Infant Baptism as a Means of Grace.* If the sacraments serve only to strengthen the grace of God that is present in the heart, then the question naturally arises, how must we conceive of the operation of baptism as a means of grace in the case of infants. Here the doctrine of presumptive regeneration affords an answer. If children are supposed to be regenerated, when they are baptized, then it may be assumed that the beginnings of grace present in the heart are strengthened in some mystical way. But it is not necessary to assume that the operation of baptism as a means of grace is limited to the very moment of its administration. It may be instrumental in strengthening faith later on, when the significance of baptism is clearly understood.

Questions for Review:

When did Christ institute baptism? What is the meaning of the words, "in (into) the name of the Father and of the Son and of the Holy Spirit"? Were the words of Christ intended as a formula? What do Baptists regard as the essential thing in the symbolism of baptism? What is the essential thing in it? Did Christ prescribe a certain mode of baptism? Can the necessity of immersion be proved from Scripture? Who are the proper administrators of baptism? What position does Rome take on this point and why? What is the condition of adult baptism? How can infant baptism be proved from Scripture? What different views are there as to the ground of infant baptism? Which should be preferred and why? How does baptism work as a means of grace?

References for Further Study:

Berkhof, *Reformed Dogmatics*, II, pp. 232-251; Hodge, *Outlines of Theology*, pp. 601-630; McPherson, *Christian Dogmatics*, pp. 431-436; Binnie, *The Church*, pp. 71-76; Candlish, *The Sacraments*, pp. 47-83.

A. **Institution of the Lord's Supper.** There are four different accounts of the institution of the Lord's Supper, namely, in Matt. 26:26-29; Mark 14:22-25; Luke 22:19, 20; I Cor. 11:23-25. The new sacrament was linked up with the central element in the paschal meal. The bread that was eaten with the lamb was consecrated to a new use, and so was the wine of the third cup or "the cup of blessing." When the real Lamb of God was slain, the bloody sacrament made place for an unbloody one which, like it, had nourishing properties. The passover, which was a symbol with a national flavor, was replaced by one that carried with it no implications of nationalism. The broken bread and the wine symbolize the Lord's broken body and shed blood. The physical eating and drinking of these elements are indicative of a spiritual appropriation of the body and blood of the Lord, that is, of the fruits of the sacrifice of Jesus Christ on the cross, and are a constant memorial of the redemptive work of the Lord until the great day of His return.

B. **The Things Signified and Sealed in the Lord's Supper.**

1. THE THINGS SIGNIFIED. Sacraments always represent one or more spiritual truths by means of outward signs. The sign in the Lord's Supper includes not only the visible elements of bread and wine, but also the appropriation of these by eating and drinking. Several things are signified in the Lord's Supper: (*a*) It is a symbolical representation of the

Lord's death, I Cor. 11:26. (*b*) It symbolizes the believer's participation in the crucified Christ. (*c*) It represents the effect of this spiritual eating and drinking as giving life, strength, and joy to the soul. And (*d*) It is a symbol of the union of believers with one another as members of the mystical body of Jesus Christ.

2. THE THINGS SEALED. The Lord's Supper is not only a sign but also a seal. These two aspects of the sacrament are closely related. The sacrament as a sign or with all that it signifies constitutes a seal. The seal is attached to the thing signified and is a pledge of its realization. (*a*) It seals to the participant the great love of Christ revealed in His self-surrender to a bitter and shameful death. (*b*) It gives the believing partaker of the sacrament the assurance that all the promises of the covenant and all the riches of the gospel offer are his. (*c*) It even assures the believing participant that the blessings of salvation are his in actual possession. And (*d*) it is a badge of profession on the part of those who partake of the sacrament in faith. They profess their faith in Christ as their Saviour, and their allegiance to Him as their King, and solemnly pledge a life of obedience to His divine commandments.

C. **The Question of the Real Presence in the Lord's Supper.** The question as to the nature of the presence of Christ in the Lord's Supper is one that has long been debated, and one on which there is still considerable difference of opinion. There are four views that come into consideration here.

1. THE VIEW OF ROME. The Church of Rome conceives of the presence of Christ in the sacrament in a *physical* sense. It maintains that, when the priest utters the formula, "this is my body," bread and wine change into the body and blood of Christ. This view is based primarily on a literal interpretation of the words of the institution, "this *is* my body." In answer to the objection that even after the pronunciation of the formula the elements still taste like bread and wine, Rome avers that, while the substance of bread and wine are changed, their attributes remain. This view is open to several objections: (*a*) Jesus stood before the disciples in the body and therefore could not very well say that He had His body in His hand. (*b*) Scripture speaks of the bread as bread even after the supposed change has taken place, I Cor. 10:17; 11:26-28. (*c*) A change of the substance of a thing without a corresponding change of attributes is an impossibility. (*d*) It is contrary to common sense to believe that what looks and smells and tastes like bread and wine is indeed flesh and blood.

2. THE LUTHERAN VIEW. Luther rejected the Roman Catholic doctrine of *transsubstantiation* and substituted for it the doctrine of *consubstantiation.* This avers that, while bread and wine remain what they are, the whole person of Christ, body and blood, is present *in, under,* and *along with* the elements. When Christ had the bread in His hand, He held His body along with it, and therefore could say,

"this is my body." On this view everyone who receives the bread also receives the body, whether he be a believer or not. This is no great improvement on the Roman Catholic doctrine. It really makes the words of Jesus mean, *this accompanies my body,* which is a very unnatural interpretation. Moreover, it is burdened with the impossible notion of the ubiquity of the Lord's glorified human nature, for it represents Christ as locally present wherever the Lord's Supper is administered.

3. THE ZWINGLIAN VIEW. Zwingli denied the bodily presence of Christ in the Lord's Supper, but at the same time believed that the true communicant conceived of Him as present in a spiritual manner. He stressed the significance of the Lord's Supper as a memorial of what Christ did for sinners and as an act of profession on the part of the participant. It is hardly correct, however, to say that this is all it meant for the Swiss reformer. Some of his statements point to a deeper significance of the sacrament and regard it as a seal or pledge of what God does for the believer in Christ. Yet he does not do justice to this idea. The impression remains that for him the Lord's Supper is mainly a mere sign or symbol, a memorial of the death of Christ, and an act of profession on the part of the believer. There is an evident tendency to exclude the mystical element from the sacrament altogether.

4. THE REFORMED VIEW. Calvin took exception to Zwingli's view as well as to the Roman Catholic and Lutheran views. His conception represents a mean between the two. Instead of the physical and local he taught the spiritual presence of Christ in the

Lord's Supper. In distinction from Zwingli he stressed the deeper significance of the sacrament and the mystical communion which the believer enjoys in it. Moreover, he saw in it a seal and pledge of what God did for the believing participant rather than a pledge of the believer's consecration to God. The virtues and effects of the sacrifice of Christ on the cross are present and actually conveyed to the worthy received by the power of the Holy Spirit.

D. **The Efficacy of the Lord's Supper as a Means of Grace.** The Lord's Supper was instituted for believers only, and therefore does not serve the purpose of beginning the work of grace in the heart, but only of strengthening it. The grace that is received in the sacrament does not differ in kind from that which is received through the instrumentality of the Word. The sacrament merely adds to the effectiveness of the Word and to the measure of the grace received. It is the grace of an ever closer fellowship with Christ, of spiritual nourishment and quickening, and of an ever increasing assurance of salvation. According to the Roman Catholics, and also many Anglicans and Lutherans, all those who partake of the Lord's Supper by that very act also receive the grace signified, except when they put an obstacle in the way. The gracious operation of the sacrament does not depend in any way on the faith of the recipient. According to the Reformed conception, however, only those who partake of the sacrament in faith receive the grace that is signified by the external elements.

E. **The Person for whom the Lord's Supper is Designed.** The Lord's Supper was not instituted for all indiscriminately, but only for those who can actively exercise faith, and who are able to prove themselves as to a correct estimation of the spiritual significance of the Lord's Supper. This means that children who have not yet come to years of discretion are not fit to partake of this sacrament. And even true believers are entitled to participation in it only when their conduct is not in flagrant opposition to their profession. Hence the apostle Paul insists on the necessity of self-examination, I Cor. 11:28-32. Unbelievers are naturally excluded from the table of the Lord, and professing Christians cannot be admitted, if they consciously and persistently depart from the truth or lead offensive lives.

Questions for Review:

Where do we find accounts of the institution of the Lord's Supper? How does the Lord's Supper differ from the passover? What belongs to the sign in the Lord's Supper? What does this sacrament signify? What does it seal? What is the Roman Catholic view of the presence of Christ in the Lord's Supper? How do the Lutherans conceive of it? What objections are there to these views? What is the Zwinglian conception of the Lord's Supper? What objections are there to this view? How does Calvin's conception differ from it? How does he conceive of the presence of the Lord in the sacrament? Does the grace received through the sacrament differ from that received through the Word? Does the reception of this grace depend in any way on the faith of the recipent? For whom was the Lord's Supper instituted? Who should be excluded from the table of the Lord?

References for Further Study:

Berkhof, *Reformed Dogmatics,* II, pp. 252-267; Hodge, *Outlines of Theology,* pp. 631-650; McPherson, *Christian Dogmatics,* pp. 436-441; Binnie, *The Church,* pp. 76-82; Candlish, *The Sacraments,* pp. 87-129.

THE DOCTRINE OF THE LAST THINGS

THE DOCTRINE OF THE LAST THINGS

INDIVIDUAL ESCHATOLOGY

Physical Death

A. **The Nature of Physical Death.** Physical death is variously represented in Scripture. It is spoken of as the death of the body, as distinguished from that of the soul, Matt. 10:28; Luke 12:4, as the termination or loss of animal life, Luke 6:9; John 12:25, and as a separation of body and soul, Eccl. 12:7; Jas. 2:26. On the basis of these Scripture representations it may be described as *a termination of physical life by the separation of body and soul.* It is never an annihilation, though some sects represent the death of the wicked as such. Death is not a cessation of existence, but a severance of the natural relations of life.

B. **The Connection Between Sin and Death.** Pelagians and Socinians teach that man was created mortal, not merely in the sense that he could fall a prey to death, but in the sense that he was subject to the law of dissolution, and was therefore destined to die. But this is certainly not in harmony with the teachings of Scripture, for these positively point to death as something introduced into the world of humanity by sin and as a punishment for sin, Gen. 2:17; 3:19; Rom. 5:12, 17; 6:23; I Cor. 15:21; Jas. 1:15. Death is not represented as something natural in the life of man, but very decidedly as something foreign and hostile to human life. It is an expression of divine anger, Ps. 90:7, 11, a judgment, Rom. 1:32, a condemnation, Rom. 5:16, and a curse, Gal. 3:13, and it fills the hearts of men with dread and fear. The entrance of sin into the world brought with it the reign of death. In strict justice God might have imposed death on man in the fullest sense of the word immediately after his transgression, Gen. 2:17. But by His common grace He restrained the operation of sin and death, and by His special grace in Christ Jesus He conquered these hostile forces, Rom. 5:17; I Cor. 15:45; II Tim. 1:10; Heb. 2:14; Rev. 1:18; 20:14.

C. **The Significance of the Death of Believers.** The Bible speaks of physical death as a punishment, as "the wages of sin." Since believers are set free from the guilt of sin, the question naturally arises, Why must they die? It is evident that death cannot be a punishment for them, since they are no more under condemnation. Why then does God cause them to pass through the harrowing experience of death? In their case death must evidently be regarded as the culmination of the chastisements which God has ordained for the sanctification of His people. The very thought of death, bereavement through death, the feeling that sicknesses and sufferings are harbingers of death, and the consciousness of the approach of death, — these all have a very beneficial effect on the people of God. They serve to humble the proud, to mortify the flesh, to check worldliness, and to foster spiritual-mindedness.

Questions for Review:

How is physical death represented in Scripture? How may it be described? Who teach that man was created mortal, that is, subject to the law of death? How can it be proved that death is not something natural in the life of man? What is the connection between sin and death? Is physical death a punishment for believers? What purpose does it serve in their case?

References for Further Study:

Berkhof, *Reformed Dogmatics*, II, pp. 276-280; Dahle, *Life After Death*, pp. 24-58; Mackintosh, *Immortality and the Future*, pp. 149-152.

The Intermediate State

There is a great deal of difference of opinion respecting the condition of man in the period between the death of the individual and the general resurrection. The most important theories call for a brief discussion.

A. **The Modern Idea of Man's Existence in Sheol-Hades.** The idea is very prevalent at present that at death both the pious and the wicked descend into an intermediate place, which the Old Testament calls *sheol* and the New Testament *hades*. This underworld is not a place of punishment nor of reward, but a place where all share the same fate. It is a dreary abode, where the dead are doomed to an existence that is merely a dreamy reflection of life on earth. It is a place of weakened consciousness, of slumbrous inactivity, where life has lost its interests and the joys of living are turned into sadness. But the idea of such a separate locality, which is neither heaven nor hell, in which all the dead are gathered and where they remain, either permanently or until some general resurrection, is an idea that may have been more or less current in popular thought and may have given rise to some figurative descriptions of the state of the dead, but certainly is not a part of the positive teachings of Scripture. The terms *sheol* and *hades* are evidently not always used in the same sense in Scripture. If it always denotes the place to which both the pious and the wicked descend, how can the descent of the wicked into *sheol* be held up as a warning, as it is in several places, Job 21:13;

Ps. 9:17; Prov. 5:5; 7:27; 9:18; 15:24; 23:14? And how can Scripture speak of God's anger as burning there, Deut. 32:22? In view of such passages as these we may proceed on the assumption that these terms sometimes serve to designate the place of punishment for the wicked. It is perfectly evident, however, that they do not always have this meaning, since the Bible also speaks of the pious as going down into or as being in *sheol*. In several instances they do not denote a place at all, but simply serve to designate the state or condition of death, the state of the separation of body and soul. This state is sometimes figuratively represented as the place whither all the dead go, be they great or small, rich or poor, pious or wicked. They are all alike in the state of death. The following are some of the passages in which *sheol* and *hades* refer to the condition or the state of death rather than to a place: Job 14:13, 14; 17:13, 14; Ps. 89:48; Hos. 13:14; I Cor. 15:55; Rev. 1:18; 6:8. Finally, there are also passages in which *sheol* and *hades* designate the grave, though it is not always easy to determine, whether in any particular place the words refer to the grave or to the state of death, Gen. 42:38; 44:29, 31; Num. 16:30, 33; John 17:13; Ps. 16:10; 49:14, 15.

B. The Doctrine of Purgatory, of the Limbus Patrum and of the Limbus Infantum.

1. Purgatory. According to the Church of Rome the souls of those who are perfect at death are at once admitted to heaven or the beatific vision of God, Matt. 25:46; Phil. 1:23, but those who are not perfectly cleansed, but are still burdened with

the guilt of venial sins — and this is the condition of most believers at death — must undergo a process of cleansing before they can enter into the supreme blessedness and joys of heaven. This purification takes place in purgatory, where the souls are oppressed with a sense of deprivation, but also suffer positive pains. The length of their stay in purgatory as well as the intensity of their sufferings varies according to the need of individual cases. The time can be shortened and the suffering alleviated by the prayers and the good works of the faithful and especially by the sacrifice of the Mass. The main support for this doctrine is found in II Macc. 12:42-45, though it is supposed to be favored also by Isa. 4:4; Mic. 7:8; Zech. 9:11; Mal. 3:2; Matt. 12:32; I Cor. 3:13-15; 15:29. However, these passages do not support it at all.

2. LIMBUS PATRUM. The Limbus Patrum is the place where, according to the Roman Catholic Church, the souls of the Old Testament saints were detained in a state of expectation until the Lord's resurrection from the dead. After His death Christ went down into this part of hades, released these saints, and carried them in triumph to heaven.

3. LIMBUS INFANTUM. Roman Catholics speak of the Limbus Infantum as the abode of the souls of unbaptized children, irrespective of their descent from heathen or from Christian parents. These children cannot be admitted to heaven, cannot enter the kingdom of God, John 3:5. They remain in the Limbus Infantum without any hope of deliverance.

There is no unanimous opinion as to their exact condition. The prevailing opinion is that they suffer no positive punishment, but are simply excluded from the blessings of heaven. They know and love God by the use of their natural powers, and have full *natural* happiness.

C. **The Doctrine of the Sleep of the Soul.** Certain sects in the early Christian centuries, in the Middle Ages, and also at the time of the Reformation, advocated the notion that, after death, the soul indeed continues to exist, but in a state of unconscious repose or sleep. This view is also held by the Irvingites in England and by the Russellites of our own country. It has a peculiar fascination for those who find it hard to believe in a continuance of consciousness apart from the brain. Scripture support for it is found especially in passages that represent death as a sleep, Matt. 9:24; Acts 7:60; I Cor. 15:51; I Thess. 4:13, and in those that seem to assert that the dead are unconscious, Ps. 6:5; 30:9; 115:17; 146:4; Eccl. 9:10; Isa. 38:18, 19. It should be noted, however, that the Bible never says that the soul falls asleep, nor that the body does so, but only the dying person. And this Scriptural representation is simply based on the similarity between a dead body and a body asleep. Moreover, the passages which seem to teach that the dead are unconscious clearly intend to stress only the fact that in the state of death man can no more take notice of nor share in the activities of this present world. The Bible represents believers as enjoying a conscious life in communion with God and with Jesus Christ immediately after death, Luke 16:19-31; 23:43; Acts 7:59; II Cor. 5:8; Phil. 1:23; Rev. 6:9; 7:9; 20:4.

D. **The Doctrine of Annihilation and of Conditional Immortality.** According to these doctrines there is no conscious existence, if any existence at all, of the wicked after death. These two views agree in their conception of the ultimate condition of the wicked, but differ in a couple of fundamental points. Annihilationism teaches that man was created immortal, but that they who continue in sin are by a positive act of God deprived of the gift of immortality and ultimately destroyed or — what amounts to practically the same thing — bereft forever of consciousness. According to the doctrine of conditional immortality, however, immortality is not a natural endowment of man, but a gift of God in Christ to those that believe. The person that does not accept Christ is ultimately annihilated or loses all consciousness. Some of the advocates of these doctrines teach a limited duration of conscious suffering for the wicked after death. These doctrines are based primarily on the fact that the Bible represents eternal life as a gift of God to those who are in Christ Jesus, John 10:27, 28; 17:3; Rom. 2:7; 6:22; Gal. 6:8, and threatens sinners with "death" and "destruction," asserting that they will "perish," terms which are taken to mean that they will be reduced to non-existence. These arguments are not conclusive. Eternal life is indeed a gift of God in Jesus Christ, but this is something far greater and richer than bare immortality. Moreover, it is arbitrary to assume that the terms "death," "destruction," and "perish" denote annihilation. The Bible teaches that sinners as well as saints will continue to exist forever, Eccl. 12:7; Matt. 25:46; Rom. 2:8-10; Rev. 14:11; 20:10, and that there will be degrees in the punishment of the wicked,

Luke 12:47, 48; Rom. 2:12. Extinction of either being or consciousness precludes the possibility of such degrees. Moreover, annihilation can hardly be called a punishment, for this implies a consciousness of ill desert and pain. People who have grown tired of life often consider extinction of being as a very desirable thing

E. **The Doctrine of a Second Probation.** Several scholars adopt the theory that in the intermediate state those who died in their sins will have another opportunity to accept Christ in repentance and faith unto salvation. According to them the eternal state of man will not be irrevocably fixed until the day of judgment. The salvation of many will depend on their decision between death and the resurrection. No man will perish without having been offered a favorable opportunity to know and to accept Jesus. One is condemned only for the obstinate refusal to accept the salvation that is offered in Christ Jesus. The advocates of this theory appeal to such passages as Eph. 4:8, 9; I Cor. 15:24-28; Phil. 2:9-11; Col. 1:19, 20; Matt. 12:31, 32; and I Pet. 3:19; 4:6. But these passages fail to carry conviction. Moreover, Scripture represents the state of unbelievers after death as a fixed state, Eccl. 11:3; Luke 16:19-31; John 8:21, 24; II Pet. 2:4, 9; Jude 7, 13. It also invariably speaks of the final judgment as determined by the things that are done in the flesh, and never represents this as dependent in any way on what transpires in the intermediate state, Matt. 7:22, 23; 10:32, 33; 25:34-46; Luke 12:47, 48; II Cor. 5:9, 10; Gal. 6:7, 8; II Thess. 1:8; Heb. 9:27.

Questions for Review:

What is the modern idea of *sheol* and *hades?* What objections are there to this theory? What is the Scriptural meaning of these terms? What is the difference between the doctrine of annihilationism and the doctrine of conditional immortality? What is the supposed Scripture basis for these doctrines? What objections are there to them? What is the Roman Catholic doctrine of purgatory? Is there any Scriptural basis for it? What is meant by the Limbus Patrum and the Limbus Infantum? What is the doctrine of the sleep of the soul? On what Scriptural data does it rest? What objections are there to it? What is the doctrine of a second probation? Is there any Scripture ground for it? What objections are there to this view?

References for Further Study:

Berkhof, *Reformed Dogmatics*, II, pp. 291-308; Hodge, *Outlines of Theology*, pp. 548-558; Mackintosh, *Immortality and the Future*, pp. 152-163; Shedd, *Doctrine of Endless Punishment*, pp. 12-74; Morris, *Is There Salvation After Death?;* Hovey, *Eschatology*, pp. 79-145.

GENERAL ESCHATOLOGY

The Second Coming of Christ

The New Testament clearly teaches that the first coming of the Lord will be followed by a second. Jesus Himself referred to His return more than once, Matt. 24:30; 25:19, 31; 26:64; John 14:3; angels called attention to it at the time of the ascension, Acts 1:11; and the apostles speak of it in numerous passages of their epistles, Acts 3:20, 21; Phil. 3:20; I Thess. 4:15, 16; II Thess. 1:7, 10; Tit. 2:13; Heb. 9:28.

A. **Great Events Preceding the Second Coming.** Several important events must transpire before the return of the Lord.

1. The Calling of the Gentiles. Several passages of the New Testament point to the fact that the gospel of the kingdom must be preached to all nations before the return of the Lord, Matt. 24:14; Mark 13:10; Rom. 11:25. This does not merely mean that at least one missionary must be sent to each one of the nations. But neither does it mean that the gospel must be preached to every individual of all the nations of the world. The passages referred to simply require that the nations as nations be thoroughly evangelized, so that the gospel becomes a power in the life of the people, a sign that calls for decision.

2. The Conversion of Israel. Both the Old and the New Testament speak of a future conversion of

Israel, Zech. 12:10; 13:1; II Cor. 3:15, 16; Rom. 11:25-29. The passage in Romans 11 seems to connect this with the end of time. Some infer from these passages that Israel as a whole, Israel as a nation, will finally turn to the Lord. But this interpretation is rather dubious. It is a very striking fact that Jesus did speak of the children of the kingdom as being cast out, Matt. 8:11, 12, and of the kingdom as being taken away from them, Matt. 21:43, but never speaks of their being restored to their former position. This is not even necessarily implied in Matt. 19:28 and Luke 21:24. It may be thought that Rom. 11:11-32 certainly teaches the conversion of the nation. In view of the connection it is more likely, however, that the expression "all Israel" in verse 26 simply means the full number of the elect out of the ancient covenant people. The whole passage does seem to teach that in the end large numbers of Israel will turn to the Lord.

3. THE COMING OF ANTICHRIST. The Bible predicts the revelation of antichrist, the man of sin, who sets himself up in opposition to Jesus Christ, but will be slain by the breath of the Lord at the time of His return, II Thess. 2:3-10. Scripture speaks of antichrists in the plural, I John 2:18 ("false Christs," Matt. 24:24), of the spirit of antichrist, I John 4:3, and of antichrist in the singular, I John 2:22; II John 7, also called the man of sin, II Thess. 2:3. The explanation for this lies in the fact that the spirit of antichrist, of opposition to Jesus Christ, was already apparent in the days of the apostles in the efforts of those who were bent on destroying

the work of Christ, Apparently, however, this opposition will finally reach its climax in the appearance of a single individual, who will oppose and exalt himself "against all that is called God or that is worshipped; so that he sitteth in the temple of God, setting himself forth as God."

4. SIGNS AND WONDERS. Several signs are spoken of as harbingers of the end of the world and of the coming of Christ. Scripture speaks (*a*) of wars, famines, and earthquakes in divers places, which are called the beginning of travail, to be followed by the rebirth of the universe; (*b*) of the great tribulation during which some of the righteous will suffer persecution and martyrdom for the sake of Christ; (*c*) of the coming of false prophets and false Christs, who will lead many astray; and (*d*) of fearful portents in heaven, when the powers of the heavens will be shaken, Matt. 24:29, 30; Mark 13:24, 25; Luke 21:25, 26.

B. **The Second Coming Itself.** After the signs just mentioned the Son of Man will be seen coming on the clouds of heaven.

1. THE TIME OF THE SECOND COMING. Premillenarians believe that the coming of Christ is imminent, which means that it may now occur at any time. Scripture teaches us, however, that the things mentioned in the preceding must transpire before the Lord's return, Matt. 24:14; II Thess. 2:2, 3; II Pet. 3:9. This should be borne in mind in the reading of those passages which speak of the coming of Christ or of the last day as near, Matt. 16:28; 24:

34; Heb. 10:25; Jas. 5:9; I Pet. 4:5; I John 2:18. From God's point of view the coming of the Lord is always near. Moreover, the apostles considered it as near, because Pentecost marked the beginning of the last days, that is, of the last dispensation. Besides, when they speak of the Lord's coming as near, they do not always have in mind the final coming, but may refer to some preliminary coming, such as at the destruction of Jerusalem.

2. THE MANNER OF THE SECOND COMING. The coming of Christ will be:

a. *A Personal Coming.* Many Rationalists and liberal theologians of the present day deny the personal return of Jesus Christ. They give a figurative interpretation to the glowing descriptions of the second coming, and take them to mean that the religious principles of Christ will gradually permeate society. But this does not do justice to such passages as Acts 1:11; 3:20, 21; Matt. 24:44; I Cor. 15:23; Phil. 3:20; Col. 3:4; I Thess. 2:19; 3:13; 4:15-17; II Tim. 4:8; Tit. 2:13; Heb. 9:28.

b. *A Physical Coming.* Some maintain that the Lord has already returned. They identify the second coming of Christ with His return in the Holy Spirit on the day of Pentecost, John 14:18, 23. But this coming is clearly not the same as the predicted second coming of Christ, for this is still spoken of as future after the pentecostal coming. Moreover, the following passages prove that the second coming will be physical, Acts 1:11; 3:20, 21; Heb. 9:28; Rev. 1:7.

c. A Visible Coming. It may be said that, if the Lord's return will be physical, it will also be visible. And Scripture leaves no doubt on this point, Matt. 24:30; 26:64; Mark 13:26; Luke 21:27; Acts 1:11; Col. 3:4; Tit. 2:13 Heb. 9:28; Rev. 1:7. Russellites are mistaken when they claim that the Lord returned invisibly in 1914 and now dwells in the air.

d. A Sudden Coming. Though several signs will precede the second coming, yet it will be unexpected and take people by surprise, Matt. 24:37-44; 25:1-12; Mark 13:33-37; I Thess. 5:2, 3; Rev. 3:3; 16:15. This is not contradictory, for the predicted signs are not of such a kind as to designate the exact time.

e. A Glorious and Triumphant Coming. Christ will not return in the body of His humiliation but in glory, Heb. 9:28. The clouds of heaven will be His chariot, Matt. 24:30, the angels His bodyguard, II Thess. 1:7, the archangels His heralds, I Thess. 4:16, and the saints of God His glorious retinue, I Thess. 3:13; II Thess. 1:10. He will come as King of kings and Lord of lords, triumphant over all the forces of evil, Rev. 19:11-16.

3. THE PURPOSE OF THE SECOND COMING. Christ will return at the end of the world for the purpose of introducing the future age, the eternal state of things, and He will do this by inaugurating and completing two mighty events, namely, the resurrection of the dead and the final judgment, Matt. 13:49, 50; 16:27; 24:3; 25:14-30; Luke 9:26; 19:15, 26, 27; John 5:25-29; Acts 17:31; Rom.

2:3-16; I Cor. 4:5; 15:23; II Cor. 5:10; Phil. 3:20, 21; I Thess. 4:13-17; II Thess. 1:7-10; 2: 7, 8; II Tim. 4:1, 8; II Pet. 3:10-13; Jude 14, 15; Rev. 20:11-15; 22:12.

Questions for Review:

What great event will precede the second coming of Christ? What does it mean that the gospel must be preached to all nations first? How should we understand the predicted conversion of Israel? What can be said against the idea that Israel *as a nation* will be converted? What does the Bible mean when it speaks of Antichrist? In how far is it possible to speak of Antichrist as present? In what sense is he still future? What signs will precede the second coming of Christ? Is the Lord's return imminent? In how far can it be regarded as near? Who deny the personal coming of Christ and what can be said in favor of it? How do they conceive of the second coming who regard it as a past event? How can it be proved that the second coming will be physical and visible? How can it be sudden when it will be preceded by several signs? What will constitute the glory of the second coming? What is the purpose of the Lord's return?

References for Further Study:

Berkhof, *Reformed Dogmatics*, II, pp. 309-318; McPherson, *Christian Dogmatics*, pp. 446-449; Dahle, *Life After Death*, pp. 268-390; Snowden, *The Coming of the Lord*, pp. 123-155.

The Millennium and the Resurrection

A. **The Question of the Millennium.** On the basis of Rev. 20:1-6 some believe that there will be a millennial kingdom of Jesus Christ, either before or after His second coming. Others, however, deny that Scripture warrants the expectation of such a millennial kingdom in any sense of the word. Consequently, there are three theories with respect to this matter, namely, the *a-millennial,* the *post millennial,* and the *pre-millennial* theory. The first is purely negative and therefore does not call for any separate discussion. It is the view adopted in this work, and holds that the second coming of Christ, the general resurrection of the dead, and the final judgment all synchronize; and that therefore the present spiritual kingdom of God passes right over into the eternal kingdom of Jesus Christ. The other two views call for a brief discussion.

1. Post - Millennialism. Post-millennialism teaches that the second coming of Christ will follow the millennium. The millennium is expected during the gospel dispensation, in which we are now living, and at the close of which Christ will appear.

   a. *Two Kinds of Post-Millennialism.* Some conservative scholars, both past and present, are of the opinion that the gospel, which will gradually permeate the entire world, will in the end become much more effective than it is at present and will usher in a period of rich spiritual blessings, which will be followed by a brief apostasy, a terrible final conflict with the forces of evil, and thereafter by the simultaneous occurrence of the advent of Christ, the general resurrection, ,and the final judgment. A great deal of present-day post-millennialism, however, is of an entirely different type. It does not believe that the preaching of the gospel and the accompanying work of the Holy Spirit will bring the millennium, but that this will be the grand result of a perfectly natural process of evolution. Man himself will usher in the new era by education, improved legislation, and social reforms.

b. *Objections to Post-Millennialism.* The fundamental idea of this doctrine, namely, that the whole world will gradually be won for Christ and will in the main be Christian when Christ returns, is not in harmony with the Scriptural representation of the end of the ages, Matt. 24:6-14, 21, 22; Luke 18:8; 21:25-28; II Thess. 2:3-12; II Tim. 3:1-13; Rev. 13. Some Post-Millennialists feel this and therefore introduce the idea of an apostasy and a tribulation just previous to the return of Christ, but they minimize these and represent them as events which have little effect on the main course of religious life. Moreover, the related idea, rather common in post-millennial representations, that the present age will not end with a great and sudden change, but will pass almost imperceptibly into the coming age, is also contrary to Scripture, Matt. 24:29-31, 35-44; Heb. 12:26, 27; II Pet. 3:10-13. There will be a crisis so great that it can be called "the regeneration," Matt. 19:28. Finally, the modern idea that man, by education, legislation, and social reform, will bring in the perfect reign of Christ, is contrary to all that the Bible teaches on this point. The future kingdom cannot be established by natural, but only by supernatural means.

2. Pre-Millennialism. Pre-millennialism holds that Christ, at His return, will raise up all the righteous dead, will convert the Jews and bring them back to the Holy Land, will re-establish the national kingdom of the Jews in unprecedented glory and power, and will then rule this kingdom with His saints for a thousand years.

a. *The Pre-Millennial Scheme.* According to Premillenarians the Old Testament prophets predict the glorious re-establishment of the kingdom of David in the days of the Messiah. Christ intended to establish the kingdom when He was on earth, but because the Jews refused to repent, postponed it to the time of His return. Meanwhile He established His Church, which is gathered out of Jews and gentiles. The gospel will prove insufficient, however, to convert men on a large scale. Finally, Christ will appear in the air, raise up all the dead saints, and snatch them away with the living believers to celebrate the wedding of the Lamb. There will be a period of tribulation on the earth, during which Israel will be converted and brought back to the Holy Land. At the end of the period of tribulation Christ will come down to earth and judge the nations. The sheep and the goats are separated, Satan is bound for a thousand years, antichrist is destroyed, the tribulation saints are raised up, and the millennium is ushered in. The kingdom now established is a kingdom of the Jews with world-wide dominion. Christ and His saints rule at Jerusalem, and the temple and its sacrificial worship is restored. The world is now speedily converted. After the millennium follows the final battle with Satan and his hosts, after which Satan is cast into the bottomless pit. Then follows the resurrection of the unbelievers and the final judgment at the great white throne. The Church is transferred to heaven, and Israel remains forever on earth.

b. Objections to Pre-Millennialism. This theory is based on an unwarranted literalism in the interpretation of the prophets and fails to take account of the spiritual interpretation suggested by the New Testament. It makes the kingdom of God an earthly and national kingdom, while the New Testament clearly represents it as spiritual and universal. It goes contrary to those passages of Scripture which clearly represent the kingdom as a present reality, Matt. 11:12; 12:28; Luke 17:21; John 18:36, 37; Col. 1:13. While the Bible speaks of the resurrection of the just and the unjust in a single breath, Dan. 12:2; John 5:28, 29; Acts 24:15, and represents the resurrection of the righteous as occurring at *the last day,* John 6: 39, 40, 44, 54; 11:24, it separates the resurrection of the righteous from that of the wicked by a period of a thousand years. Contrary to Scripture, it speaks of three (four) resurrections and four judgments. It fails to explain how glorified saints and sinners in the flesh can live and associate together in a world in which sin and death are still rampant. Finally, it erroneously seeks its main support in a passage (Rev. 20:1-6) which represents a scene in heaven and makes no mention whatever of the Jews, of an earthly and national kingdom, nor of the land of Palestine.

B. **The Resurrection.** Scripture teaches us that at the return of Christ the dead will be raised up.

1. SCRIPTURE PROOF FOR THE RESURRECTION. It is sometimes said that the Old Testament contains no proof for the resurrection of the dead; but this is hardly correct. Christ finds proof for it in Ex. 3:6, cf. Matt. 22:31, 32. It is implied in the passages that speak of deliverance from *sheol,* Ps. 49:15; 73:24, 25; Prov. 23:14, and is expressly taught in Isa. 26:19, and in Dan. 12:2. The New Testament, however, contains clearer and more abundant proof. Jesus argues the resurrection of the dead over against the denial of the Sadducees, Matt. 22:23-33, and teaches it very clearly in John 5:25-29; 6:39, 40, 44; 11:24, 25; 14:3; 17:24. The classical passage of the New Testament is I Cor. 15. Other important passages are I Thess. 4:13-17; II Cor. 5:1-10; and Rev. 20:13.

2. THE CHARACTER OF THE RESURRECTION. The resurrection taught in Scripture is:

a. A Bodily Resurrection. There were some in the days of Paul, and there are many today, who believe only in a spiritual resurrection. But the Bible clearly teaches a resurrection of the body.

Christ is called "the firstfruits" of the resurrection, and "the firstborn" of the dead. This implies that the resurrection of His people will be like His, and this was a bodily resurrection. Moreover, the redemption in Christ is said to include the body, Rom. 8:23; I Cor. 6:13-20. Finally, the resurrection of the body is clearly taught in Rom. 8:11; and in I Cor. 15. In this chapter Paul argues that the body of the resurrection will be identical with the body that was deposited in the earth, though it will have undergone important changes.

b. *A Resurrection of Both the Just and the Unjust.* Some present-day sects deny the resurrection of the ungodly. The Adventists and the Russellites both believe in their total extinction. It is sometimes said that Scripture does not teach the resurrection of the wicked, but this is clearly erroneous, Dan. 12:2; John 5:28, 29; Acts 24:15, though it must be admitted that their resurrection does not stand out prominently in Scripture.

c. *A Resurrection of Unequal Import for the Just and the Unjust.* The resurrection of the just is an act of deliverance and of glorification. The body is raised from the grave and re-united with the soul, but the great point in their resurrection is that their bodies are now endowed with a life that is glorious and blessed. This transformation is wanting in the case of the wicked. In their case the re-union of body and soul issues in the extreme penalty of death.

3. THE TIME OF THE RESURRECTION.

a. *Scripture Indications as to the Time.* According to Scripture the resurrection coincides with the return of Christ, and with the end of the world, and immediately precedes the final judgment. Notice how it is connected with the second coming of Christ, I Cor. 15:23; Phil. 3:20, 21; I Thess. 4:16; with the last day, John 6:39, 40, 44, 54; 11:24, and with the final judgment, John 5:27-29; Rev. 20:11-15.

b. *The Theory of a Double Resurrection.* Pre-millenarians believe that the resurrection of the righteous and of the wicked are separated by a thousand years. They base their contention especially on I Cor. 15:23-28; I Thess. 4:13-18; and Rev. 20:4-6. But none of these passages prove the point. The first does not speak of the resurrection of the wicked at all. The second merely says that the dead in Christ shall be raised up before the living saints are caught up in the clouds. And the third does not even refer to a bodily resurrection. Whenever the Bible mentions the resurrection of the just and the unjust together it does not give the slightest hint that the two are to be separated by a long period of time. It clearly teaches that the resurrection of the righteous, too, will be at the last day, John 6: 39, 40, 44, 54; 11:24.

Questions for Review:

What is the difference between a-millennialism, post-millennialism, and pre-millennialism? What is the view of post-millennialism? What two kinds of post-millennialism should we distinguish? What objections are there to this theory? What is in general the pre-millenarian view? How do Pre-millenarians conceive of the course of events? What are the objections to pre-millennialism? How can the resurrection be proved from the Old Testament? What proof does the New Testament contain? How can the resurrection of the *body* be proved from the New Testament? Who deny the resurrection of the wicked? What Bible proof is there for their resurrection? How does the resurrection of the just differ from that of the unjust? What does Scripture tell us respecting the time of the resurrection? On what passages do pre-millenarians base their doctrine of a double resurrection? What can be said against this theory?

References for Further Study:

Berkhof, *Reformed Dogmatics,* II, pp. 319-337; Hodge, *Outlines of Theology*, pp. 559-573; McPherson, *Christian Dogmatics,* pp. 446-454; Hovey, *Biblical Eschatology*, pp. 23-78; Milligan, *The Resurrection of the Dead.*

The Last Judgment and the Final State

A. **The Last Judgment.** The doctrine of the resurrection leads right on to that of the last judgment. It is one of the deepest convictions of the human heart and one that is not limited to Christianity, that all men will be judged in the future. The Bible teaches the coming of a final judgment in no uncertain terms. The Old Testament already speaks of it, Ps. 96:13; Eccl. 3:17; 12:14, and the New Testament makes it even more prominent, Matt. 11:22; 16:27; 25:31-46; Acts 17:31; Rom. 2:5-10, 16; 14:12; I Cor. 4:5; II Cor. 5:10; II Tim. 4:1; Heb. 9:27; I Pet. 4:5; Rev. 20:11-14.

1. The Judge and His Assistants. Christ, as the Mediator, will be the Judge, Matt. 25:31, 32; John 5:27; Acts 10:42; 17:31; Phil. 21:0; II Tim. 4:1. This honor was conferred on Christ as a reward for His atoning work, and constitutes a part of His exaltation. The angels will assist Him in this great work. Matt, 13:41, 42; 24:31; 25:31. Evidently the saints will also in some sense share in the judicial work of Christ, Ps. 149:5-9; I Cor. 6: 2, 3; Rev. 20:4, though it is not possible to determine precisely what part they will take.
2. The Parties That Will Be Judged. Scripture contains clear indications of at least two parties that will be judged. It is perfectly evident that every individual of the human race will have to appear before the judgment-seat, Eccl. 12:14; Ps. 50:4-6; Matt. 12:36, 37; 25:32; Rom. 14:10; II Cor. 5:10; Rev. 20:12. Some maintain that the righteous will be excepted, since their sins are already pardoned,

but this is contrary to such passages as Matt. 13:30, 40-43, 49; 25:31-46. It is also clear that Satan and his demons will be judged,, Matt. 8:29; I Cor. 6:3; II Pet. 2:4; Jude 6. Whether the good angels will also be subject to the final judgment is not so easy to determine, though some would infer this from I Cor. 6:4. They are represented only as ministers of God in connection with the work of judgment, Matt. 13:30, 41; 25:31; II Thess. 1:7, 8.

3. THE TIME OF THE JUDGMENT. Since the last judgment will be a judgment passed on the whole life of every man, it will naturally be at the end of the world, and will follow immediately after the resurrection of the dead, John 5:28, 29; Rev. 20:12, 13. The duration of the judgment cannot be determined precisely. Scripture speaks of "the day of judgment," Matt. 11:22; 12:36, and "the day of wrath," Rom. 2:5. It is necessary to infer from these and other similar passages that it will be a day of exactly twenty-four hours. At the same time there is no warrant to conceive of the day of judgment as a day of a thousand years, as the Premillenarians do.

4. THE STANDARD OF JUDGMENT. The standard by which saints and sinners will be judged will evidently be the revealed will of God. Gentiles will be judged by the law of nature, Jews by the Old Testament revelation, and New Testament believers by this revelation plus the requirements of the gospel. God will give to every man his due. There will be degrees in the punishments of the wicked as well as in the rewards of the righteous, Matt. 11:22, 24; Luke 12:47, 48; 20:47; Dan. 12:3; II Cor. 9:6.

B. The Final State.

1. THE FINAL STATE OF THE WICKED. Three points call for consideration here:

a. The Place to Which They are Consigned. The place of punishment is usually called "hell." Some deny that hell is a place and regard it merely as a subjective condition, in which man may find himself even now, and which may become permanent in the future. But the Bible certainly uses local terms right along. It speaks of a "furnace of fire," Matt. 13:42, of "a lake of fire," Rev. 20: 14, 15 of a "prison, and "abyss," and "tartarus," I Pet. 3:19; Luke 8:31; II Pet. 2:4, all of which are local terms.

b. The State in Which They Will Exist. It is impossible to say precisely what will constitute the punishment of the wicked. Positively, it may be said that they will be totally deprived of the divine favor, will experience an endless disturbance of life, will suffer positive pains in body and soul, and will be subject to pangs of conscience, anguish, despair, and weeping and gnashing of teeth, Matt. 8:12; 13:50; Mark 9:47, 48; Luke 16: 23, 28; Rev. 14:10; 21:8. There will be degrees in their punishment, Matt. 11:22, 24; Luke 12: 47, 48; 20:47. It will be commensurate with their sinning against the light which they had received.

c. The Duration of Their Punishment. Some deny the eternity of the future punishment. They maintain that the Scriptural words for "everlasting" and "eternal" may simply denote a long period of time. It is true that these words do have a limited meaning in some instances, but in such cases this is generally quite evident from the context. Moreover, there are positive reasons to think that these words do not have such a limited meaning, when they serve to designate the duration of future punishment. In Matt. 25:46 the same word describes the duration of the bliss of the saints and the penalty of the wicked. If the latter is not unending, neither is the former, and yet the everlasting blessedness of the saints is not doubted. Finally, other expressions are used, which do not admit of a limited interpretation. The fire of hell is an "unquenchable fire," Mark 9:43, the worm of the wicked "dieth not," Mark 9:48; and the gulf that separates saints and sinners is fixed and impassable, Luke 16:26.

2. The Final State of the Righteous.

a. *The New Creation.* The final state of believers will be preceded by the passing of the present world and the establishment of a new creation, Matt. 19:28 speaks of "the regeneration," and Acts 3:21 of the "restoration of all things." Heaven and earth will pass away, Heb. 12:27; II Pet. 3:13, and a new creation will take its place, Rev. 21:1. The future creation will not be an entirely new creation, but rather a renewal of the present creation, Ps. 102:26, 27; Heb. 12:26-28.

b. *The Eternal Abode of the Righteous.* Many conceive of heaven also as a condition which men may enjoy in the present and which will become permanent in the future. But the Bible teaches us to think of heaven as a place. It is the house of our Father with many mansions, John 14:2. Believers will be within, while unbelievers are without, Matt. 22:12, 13; 25:10-12. The righteous will not only inherit heaven, but the entire new creation, Matt. 5:5; Rev. 21:1-3.

c. *The Nature of Their Reward.* The reward of the righteous is described as eternal life, that is, not merely an endless life, but life in all its fulness, without any of the imperfections and disturbances of the present, Matt. 25:46; Rom. 2:7. The fulness of this life is enjoyed in communion with God, which is really the essence of eternal life, Rev. 21:3. While all will enjoy perfect bliss, yet there will be degrees also in the blessedness of heaven, Dan. 12:3; II Cor. 9:6.

Questions for Review:

What Scripture proof is there for the last judgment? Who will be the Judge? Who will assist Him in the work? What parties will be judged? When will the last judgment be? How long will it last? By what standard will men be judged? How can we prove that hell is a place? In what will the punishment of the wicked consist? How can we prove that their punishment will be unending? Will the new creation be an entirely new creation? What proof is there that heaven is a place? What is the reward of the righteous?

References for Further Study:

Berkhof, *Reformed Dogmatics*, II, pp. 338-348; Hodge, *Outlines of Theology*, pp. 573-587; McPherson, *Christian Dogmatics*, pp. 454-460; Hovey, *Biblical Eschatology*, pp. 144-176.

INDEX

INDEX

A

B

C

E

F

G

H

K

L

M

N

O

P

R

S